Chelem Papers

Stories and Ruminations

GRANT SPRADLING

ALSO BY GRANT SPRADLING

From High in the Mulberry Tree
Maya Sacrifice
Palenque Murder
David Goes Home
Imaging the Word (co-author, volumes II and III)

Publishing services by Hamaca Press
www.hamacapress.com

Design: Lee Steele

ISBN: 978-0-9911444-6-4

hamaca
press

Praise for Chelem Papers

In *Chelem Papers,* Grant Spradling steps out of his quiet writing retreat on the Yucatán peninsula and invites us into graceful face-off with the inevitable. Not simply an old man's reverie, the stories in *Chelem Papers* are an exploration of the issues we all face: the need for intimacy, the search for purpose, the call to love, the frailty of the body, the dazzling possibilities of the divine in us. Spradling grabs us happily by the hand and pulls us into his extensive travels as a young man, his years as a pastor, his stint in New York as a professional singer and more. He dares to ask what the meaning of a life might be. Working often at the intersections of religion, art, and sexuality, Spradling's stories have a clear message for readers of any age: In the end, it's about love.

Chris Strickland, PhD.

Grant writes from the heart and soul. His stories bring you right to the table. . . . And to see life through the point of view of a dog, gives one another look at one's life and how fragile and absurd it can be.

Kenneth French

Moving, funny, and intelligent! Reading his collection of short stories is like chatting with an old and trusted friend on a rainy afternoon.

Chloe Pacheco

I spend a lot of time in Chelem. I can't say everything that Grant writes about Chelem is gospel truth. But amazing things happen on that beach. Read the *Chelem Papers* and experience the miracles in your own life!

William Auth

For Clifford

So here I sit in the early candle-light of old age

—I and my book—casting backward glances

over our traveled road.

The strongest and sweetest songs yet remain to be sung.

Walt Whitman: *November Boughs* (1888)
"A Backward Glance O'er Travel'd Roads"

Contents

Introduction
Lorna Gail Dallin

I NEVER EXPECTED TO BE ASKED TO WRITE AN INTRODUCTION to a book. Never crossed my mind until my Writing Buddy asked me to do one for him—an introduction that is.

My reaction was to look for information on whether there are some parameters for writing one. A Google search turned up information for an author writing an intro for their own book or thesis, but nothing pertinent to writing for another author. I wanted some instruction: Does it have to be a certain length? Does it have to be solely about the author? what about levity? Not much help in telling exactly How To. So, I guess I am on my own and I can just let her rip!

There is much which is admirable about my writing buddy, Grant Spradling, not the least of which is his age . . . 88 years. Getting to this advanced age shows a certain tenacity which I find inspiring. He will tell you he is surprised to be the age he is and is full of speculation about how that happened. Even through his stories of youthful travels, he seeks to know more about himself as an octogenarian. Grant will give you glimpses of his creative soul in these stories of memories and insights, so I will leave his "life" details to him to tell.

As Writing Buddies, we sit across a table from each other by a pool, 11 a.m. on many a Mérida Monday morning. When we started as buddies, each week I would write something. Grant would write something. Never one to shirk the big themes, Grant digs into the Universal Questions of "who am I," what am I supposed to be doing, and who will do this with me? We would critique the work and talk about lots of other things, too. Then he began writing his magical mystery books and Grant got serious or he took the next steps and worked to have his words in print. And I just fooled around—with writing, that is.

Here is what I know about this writer. Or what I don't know. I have never heard Grant sing. I have never heard him preach (well, not exactly Sunday Sermon Preach). But I have been privy to his writing endeavors as a reader and commentator, as a writing buddy. Many a Monday morning we have sat and talked about the literary life, about writing, about remembering about what moves us to write. Grant's enduring support of the arts and artists has been part of those conversations.

Here in Mérida he supports and encourages his fellow writers in thought and deed, whether through the Mérida English Library, or the Writers' Group or by personal interactions. Many emerging writers have found inspiration in Grant's progress from dyslexic scribbler (the computer has freed him from the tedium of writing upside down and backwards) to published author of five books. No small feat. "Finish what you start" was practically scripture in his family and it has been bred into his bones. This too I admire.

When we get together, my friend Grant will show me a stretch that he has found helpful for a sore back—a writer's chronic complaint. He makes sure I have a plate of Black-eyed Peas and Greens on New Year's Day, to ensure luck for the coming year. He prods me to write. That is why (no doubt) he asked me to write this introduction. He is ever hopeful I will find my writing jones again. Grant wants us all to revel in the art of writing as he does. We who dabble are grateful for writers like Grant Spradling who care wholeheartedly for the art.

I love to read his stories and comment on them for correction or encouragement and I appreciate his prodding me. That is what a Writing Buddy is for. By the way, Grant says you should feel free to read these stories in whatever order feels good for you. They were not necessarily meant to be read in sequence.

And that's all she wrote—by way of an Introduction, that is.

Why

WHY DOES A DYSLEXIC CHOOSE TO BECOME A WRITER? BEATS me. Perhaps it is because, early on, I understood I needed help, and I have been blessed with mentors and kindness ever since.

And why *Chelem Papers*? My mate Clifford and I live in Mérida, Mexico. Several years ago, we bought a little sugar cube of a house a kilometer down the Gulf of Mexico beach from Chelem, a small fishing village and vacation spot. Solitary times I spend at our beach place are like Saturday matinees at the Bulldog Theater in my hometown, where as a kid I escaped to Neverland.

The hush of the surf lapping the beach's edge, the skittering sandpipers, squawking seagulls, and the fishermen's boats out on the horizon, open a floodgate to memory and spin my imagination into overdrive. With the generous editorial assistance of friends, I have pulled together some of the stories and ruminations that have visited me by the warm sea.

Two years ago I lay with tubes running out of an incision in my chest, wondering if I would finish the book I had been working on for a number of years. "Finish what you start" was nearly scripture in my family. Perhaps that and the excellent medical care, along with family and friends, and my publisher pulling for me, accounts for my speedy recovery. I sent that book, *David Goes Home*, off to my publisher, and couldn't wait to get back to put into words all the thoughts that were waiting for me to write.

Now I'm 88, gay, in the forty-eighth year of our love affair, and feel like I am just hitting my stride. Maybe they set my pacemaker too fast, because I am more eager than ever to tell you what I imagine and what I know.

I am ever that little guy on the edge of the group, enthralled by our school's handsome football hero. Somehow, no matter how mundane, whatever he says draws rapt attention, and his jokes, no matter how corny, ignite gales of knee-slapping laughter. I long for folks to pay attention to me as they do to him.

My sister once said, "Buddy never lets facts get in the way of his stories." She knows me; although many of my stories are close to what took place, all are as faithful as they can be to my imagination's children.

Seven More Years

I PUSH BACK THE WINDOW-WALL LETTING THE OUTSIDE IN AND take my coffee down to the water's edge, where at the tip of the wooden breakwater an ancient pelican meditates. The lime-shaded crystal clear water gently laps the sand as a workboat, miles out, glides along the horizon where the white chips are fishermen waiting for their day's catch. The morning is prayer.

I have come to the beach to await my muse. A fickle lover, she plays hide-and-seek. Am I not to channel some great wisdom—some transporting eloquence? Time is running out. Does pride blind me to enlightenment? Why have I been left to live so long and to stumble through palaces and slums? If not my muse, then might not the ancient pelican show me the way? Perhaps there is no *way*, no purpose. Did the evangelist mislead us when he shouted, "God has a purpose for you!" Is there no more for us to do than to eat, drink, taste, smell—to love and embrace—*to be* and then let go of our being. Is there no *way*, no calling, no battles to win, or goals to attain? Am I merely to partake of life's banquet, and, after I can savor no more, graciously depart? Is that all there is? My God, isn't that enough?

No, it is not!

After the cardiologist reported that I had had a heart attack and I awaited bypass surgery, I lived in a kind of limbo. Limbo extended into the drugged state before and after my heart stopped. It stopped only thirty seconds, and yet, I brag that I have dipped my toe in the hereafter.

As to a prisoner on death row, my cardiologist strode into my hospital room and reported that my life had been extended six years. If I were forty or fifty, that news might not have been particularly good news, but at eighty-six, I should be overjoyed.

"If I should die before I wake, I pray the Lord my soul to take!" As soon as I could speak, kneeling at the side of my bed I became aware of death. Soon I buried our beloved cats, dogs, and squirrels. Place a turtle in a red ant den, and soon there will be nothing but shell and bones. Still, since my colicky childhood I have enjoyed robust health, and thoughts of the *endgame* I have pushed to some future time when one wishes to believe he will be better prepared to let go. Hah! And yet we flirt with death. We even call brave those who risk death for fun, race-car drivers, and tightrope walkers. And our heroes are the brave knights, our soldiers. We admire and enshrine those who die, more than those who live and serve. Death gives *meaning* to lives.

Even the timid speed down the interstate at eighty miles an hour: press the accelerator, ease into the left lane, needle hits ninety; I misjudged the speed of the oncoming truck, but manages to squeeze back, not a bumper length to spare, and as the eighteen-wheeler rockets past, the adrenalin rush gives a thrill; I've cheated death. Yea! I'm a freaking bungee-jumper! As I slow to seventy, the tingle diminishes. Miles later the specter of nonexistence rides the car's hood.

And death hovers. I have worked late on a final report. The streets are dark. No taxis and the subway is nearly deserted. It is bitterly cold. The block before home, the streetlights are out. A hooded figure rounds the corner and heads in my direction. I pick up my pace and grope in my pocket for my house keys—a weapon or to quickly shove into the lock. Turning into the little garden in front of the brownstone, I look back, but cannot find him. Still, nearly stumbling I rush down the few basement steps. My hand is shaking. I have difficulty inserting the key into the lock. Finally, the lock clicks. I wrench open the door, step through, and slam it behind me. I lean back against the door. Only then, I exhaled the breath I had been holding since I first saw my supposed attacker.

Death was the farthest thing from my mind when I took off to spend a month secluded in a cabin in the woods. The cabin was situated on the side of a hill, out of reach to the internet or cell phone. What I had in mind when I leased the place was to finish the novel I had been pecking at for over a year. "Don't bother me," I told friends. "I've laid in enough supplies to last more than a month."

While putting my toiletries in the bathroom, I noticed the sliver of soap lying near the drain in the shower. I picked it up, put it in the soap dish, and thought no further of it until that night. I laid awake all night, seeing myself slipping in the shower, and lying there, helpless until I die.

At first light, I climb to the hill where I connect by cell phone.

"Come out for the weekend," I invite two friends.

"But I thought?" a friend says.

"Just for the weekend," I beg.

Once again, I've cheated death.

. . . And the dreams—falling, falling. We assure the grieving that their lost loved one is in a better place. We want to believe. We try to believe, construct steepled sanctuaries and flock to mega churches, and still doubt.

What my cardiologist must have thought to be good news, to me was like my teacher's warning me she was granting me two extra days to hand in my overdue assignment. I had thought I had until the end of the semester. She plays bridge with my mother. Surely she would give me 'til the end of the school year, but no, no more dillydallying! The good doctors have granted me six more years before I shuffle off to nonexistence, to find out and fulfill whatever my reason for existence might be. Hum! For many, the promise of life after death is a tepid analgesic at best.

Philosopher Paul Tillich reminds us that, whether we recognize it or not, we cannot escape the anxiety of not existing. The human capacity for self-awareness, the knowledge that as an individual we exist awakens the consciousness that one day we will not exist, *not be,* to use Tillich's words. We cannot escape our nonexistence, he tells us. We invent soul. No that is too crass—we are persuaded to a belief that creation has provided an escape from nonexistence through the imperishable soul. And yet, despite a gentle admonition that we let go of earthly treasures, we remain indelibly attached to our physical presence. Despite the growing evidence that soon we shall not be—the loosening of once firm flesh, the vanishing of our youthful beauty, shriveling skin and cartilage, and failing hearing and eyesight, we postpone morbid thoughts of the *end zone,* as Doris Grumbach dubbed those final days in her memoir, *Coming Into the End Zone.* We cling, even as we sing *Come Sweet Death* and listen to Dylan Thomas's tremulous recorded voice, "Do not go gentle into that good night, Old age should burn and rave at close of day. Rage, rage against the dying of the light."

I believe that I have a responsibility to the *Christ within,* and fail my *Inner Light. . .* Still lisping, I sang, hand cupped over an imaginary candle—the wall between imagination and adult reality scarcely formed. . . ."Hide it under a bushel? No!" I jerked my cupped hand away. "I'm going to let it shine, let it shine, let it shine. This little light of mine." Teach children to pray? How dare we?!

After Doctor Ray, my cardiologist from Bombay, India, gave me six more years, Doctor Abdulla, from Alexandria, Egypt, placed in my chest an expensive battery, setting my heart beating at seventy beats a minute.

～～～～～～

The heart business is only the latest of many existential moments, as pivotal as falling in love at the state fair, leaving Oklahoma to study in Boston, falling in love with the man sitting next to me at the organ concert in Boston, not returning to Oklahoma, as I was supposed to do and leaving the organist, the next lover leaving me.

～～～～～～

I am in Cambridge, Massachusetts, at the conservatory rehearsing Shubert's song, *Ir Bildt*. Madam Olga Averino is at the piano. In the song, the singer comes across a picture of a loved one. The last line goes, "But oh, I cannot believe I have lost you."

Madam Averino taught the Stanislavski method of acting. "To project the feeling," she told me, "you must feel the emotion. Search yourself for sadness like that of the song."

I imagined I had in my hand a photograph of my brother, whose bomber disappeared over North Korea. At the time I got the telegram that he was missing, I was in a work camp near the Rhine River. I was helping clear the rubble and rebuilding homes destroyed during the patchwork bombing by American bombers in WWII.

My brother's body was never found. In a drizzling rain, I walked out on a bridge to the middle of the river. The rain mixed with tears as I tried to fathom the irony. My brother, three years older, toweringly brilliant and talented, graduate of Annapolis at the top of his class, we had the kind of love-hate relationship that develops when a cute younger sibling comes into the household and steals the older child's spotlight.

As I sang *Ir Bildt*, I was once again alone, rain-soaked, on the bridge over the Rhine, blinded by tears.

"Darling," Olga stopped playing. She always called me darling. "The emotion is for the audience, not for you. You must be like a bird up in the balcony watching yourself having the emotion." Olga Averino, who Rachmaninoff helped escape the Bolsheviks, cautioned me. "It is not enough to make a lovely sound."

And so I became two, or perhaps there are three of me—the me you see and hear—who pops open a can of beer, grabs a paper towel to soak up the sweat as he pecks at the computer, swearing when the cursor jumps to where it is not supposed to be—the me who reads the lines he just wrote expecting his reader to find them brilliant. And still a third me—the me, I fondly believe—I want to believe—I *must believe*, who hides in that dark cave within and snuggles against my soul, unsuited for the harsh, vulgar struggle for a place in the sun.

Perhaps I have always been drifting off this way. If you understand what I am talking about, you sometimes drift off as well. Maybe it is the human condition. A friend waves a hand in front of your face and says, "Hello! Is anybody home?"

"I was in another time and another place," you say, as you return from laying with your lover in front of a fire, or wading along the surf's edge at sunset.

Sunset, I pour a drink and head down to the water's edge. I am among the seabirds again. I soar so high, I look back more than sixty years. My father in a new Model A Ford heads home on Route 66, west of Oklahoma City. Following a slow cattle truck up the long climb, he downshifts. At the crest, he pulls over to let the radiator cool. The highway is cut through a red sandstone ridge leaving sentinel-like peaks at each side of the road. From the escarpment, he looks out over the mile-wide Canadian River bed, where cotton-wood and willow saplings have grown since the last flood scoured its banks. It hasn't rained, it seems, for years. A town's grain eleva-tor—prairie skyscrapers—poke out of the Plains, which roll like swells on the primordial sea that once covered the land. Further on is Ghost Mound Mesa, and forty or fifty miles beyond the Mesa, the square-mile town laid out on the side of a hill, Deer Creek at its foot. The town was once as far as the Santa Fe railroad had pushed. Cattle from beyond the Red River were driven to the town's stock-yards to await shipment back East to slaughterhouses in Kansas City and Chicago. Those days, cowboys quenched their thirst at a dozen saloons and their needs in an equal number of bordellos. By the time I issued from my mother's womb, the Women's Christian Temperance Union had driven pleasure out of sight to roadhouses far from town.

My sight blurs. The Great Depression is ending. I'm in college.

It is Sunday morning after church. Our maroon Ford V8 is parked in front of a rambling Victorian affair, once the finest home in town, now a hospital. Mother runs out onto the porch screaming, "Daddy is dying!" Neither amyl nitrite nor prayers restart my father's heart.

~~~~~~~~~~

I look back to those pivotal, starburst-like, moments from which so many courses might have been followed. I see a hapless little boy growing up during the times that sand drifted across burnt wheat fields, and men, having lost their fortunes, jumped to their death. No cotton to pick, sharecroppers packed washtubs, and mat-tresses on tops of rattletraps, and kids, aunts, uncles, old folks and chamber pots in the back, headed for dreams on the other side of

Death Valley.

I am a child of Roosevelt's New Deal, which with its W.P.A., C.C.C., F.H.A., S.E.C., F.D.I.C., dammed the rivers, electrified the countryside, planted shelterbelts, rows of trees along fence lines to harness the sand-laden wind—built post offices, and bridges, and parks, provided health insurance, worker's compensation, and social security, pulled the nation out of the Great Depression, some say, began the slide to socialism. It was a time of Hopalong Cassidy, Tom Mix, and Roy Acuff, Gene Autry, Will Rogers, who never met a man he didn't like, Woody Guthrie, glittering Fred Astaire, Ginger Rogers and Gene Kelly dancing in the rain, Al Capone, Pretty Boy Floyd, Machine Gun Kelly and Bonnie and Clyde; and, there were Picasso's *Guernica*, Norman Rockwell nostalgia, Rothko Chapel and Barnett Newman's *Broken Obelisk*, Mickey Mouse and Bolero's fat women, Jack Kerouac, Allen Ginsburg, *Portnoy's Complaint*, and *Peyton Place*, the slaughter of millions of Jews, Chiang Kai-shek, then Mao Zedong, atomic fission and obliteration of Nagasaki and Hiroshima, Boris Pasternak, Marie Curie, Joe McCarthy, Palestinians' land confiscated, Gandhi, Martin Luther King, and Stalin, Khrushchev, Nixon, and Camelot—too brief. And there was Kennedy's assassination, and brutal murder of gay and gifted Matthew Shepard, left hanging on a barbwire fence, and the powerful NRA. "Either I live the rest of my life as a lonely man who wishes he were a woman or I live my life as a lonelier woman who hates herself," wrote Leelah Alcorn, a transgender teenager, in her suicide note. "There is no way out." And a black man is two times president and the U.S. Supreme Court assures gays the right to (finally) speak the name of the one they love.

I see myself bumbling like a ball in a pinball machine from one to the next existential moment. Not brave, simply trusting what may befall beyond this or that choice. Gone are my father and older brother, who might have warned against irresponsible wanders down dark corridors, and my grieving mother, bewildered by my zigzag course. Dyslexic from the start, I wrote upside down and backward. When prudence might have led to the well-trodden road, I took the one less traveled by. Has it made any difference after all is said and done?

And there I am now, pecking away at my computer. I'm half-naked; no one is around to notice. Internet and phone signals are weak. To call home, I go down the road to the shade of a sea grape tree. As I await Clifford's pick up, a black dog comes by and kisses my hand.

A family of crows has taken it into their head to bathe in the swimming pool just outside the sliding doors. I had a mind to push back the screen and let them in. I have such thoughts when I spend time alone. The squabbling chatter of the crows and the whir of the ceiling fan blend with the hush of surf lapping at the beach on the far side of the honeybush. Somewhere someone burns trash. I don't mind; it reminds me of my childhood as most things do lately.

As we humans were exiled from Eden, we took with us a longing for timelessness. It was a cruel deal that we exited into a dynamic universe in which time is ever changing.

~~~~~~~~~

And Doctor Ray from Bombay said something else. I'm sure he meant it to be more good news. He stood at the foot of my bed, proud of himself I suppose, and announced, "Every day for the next year you are going to feel better and better." Good Lord! I wasn't feeling particularly unwell before they cut me open, ripped the vein out of my leg and wrapped it around my heart.

I wanted to shout at him. How dare someone one scarcely knows play with one's destiny? What are you doing to me! What am I supposed to do with all this life you are giving me? We want it so much. We want to hold onto it, but for what? Am I supposed to join the Peace Corps? Or merely while away my time delighting in the cavorting pair of bandit-masked orioles challenging their reflection in the kitchen window, or sit, martini in hand, and envy the rich man's yacht skimming across the horizon. Shall I join the clouds-high raptors gawking down and cackling at my small beachside comedy?

Astonished

MY COFFEE GROWS COLD AS THE SUN SLIPS FREE OF DARK THUN-derheads, promising a spectacular ending to the day.

It seems a desecration to go inside during the hallelujah. I'm torn between the ravishing moments and wanting to tell of it. I'm six or eight years old again—astonished. I look up from my sand-pile construction project. Clouds have transformed into Jesus and the wise men, or maybe it is His disciples. I run inside and announce the *coming*.

"Mama, come look."

"Not now darling. Let me finish, then I'll be out."

"But Mama, they'll be gone."

"They'll be back."

I return outside. Jesus has already gone. A hawk sails through the whiskers of an old man, not Jesus at all. Mama has missed another miracle.

I'm unhinged from time these days; my mind leaps from my sand pile eighty years to an ICU. Smiley faces, ranging from a big grin to a deep frown, hang on the wall opposite the foot of my bed. From time to time a nurse comes in and asks me to choose a face that represents how I feel.

"We've added six or seven years to your life." The smiley face is my cardiologist. He doesn't say when the clock starts ticking. Perhaps it has to do with the drugged state I was in when he told me, but *added six or seven years* keeps repeating itself like a broken record. Not just the added years to my life, I hadn't been counting, but as healthy as I felt and taking care of myself—exercising a little, avoiding too many eggs and trying to keep alcohol consumption within reason. I figured four or five more good years until I started to get tired and maybe not have so much fun living, leaving the party wouldn't seem so bad.

I've tried to believe, beyond that final door, I'll meet up with family and friends, and I'd really be glad if I got licked in the face by our dogs, cats, goat, and prairie dogs—prairie dogs don't actually lick you in the face; they just sit in the palm of your hand and chirp when you feed them. Still, I have little enthusiasm for the life, if there is one, after this one. Life here and now has me as enthralled as when I was six in the sand pile. Is this a second childhood? If so, don't knock it!

I've changed. It's as if, while the doctors and nurses had me open, working on my heart, they took a side excursion and implanted fresh perceptions. Everything is more vibrant, colors, sounds—the dragonfly dipping in the pool, the ringlets it leaves, the thrum of the fishing boat skimming along the horizon, beetles and ants and hummingbirds, fragrance from the honeybush, and of rotting seaweed—the sunlight slicing across the wall igniting greens in the deep greens of the sea cedar, voices of children digging at the surf's edge and a scolding gull—the crinkle around my beloved's eyes, it all seems akin. I no longer can kill a roach or a hardworking ant without regret. Mosquitoes are an exception.

These days, lines from Thornton Wilder's *Our Town* come to mind. Emily asked, "Does anyone live every moment of every day?" To which the stage manager replies, "No. Poets and saints, they do some."

You See

YOU SEE—NO, OF COURSE, YOU DON'T SEE. HOW COULD YOU SEE as I haven't shown you or even attempted to describe my flying to you—assuming I had the skill to *put you in the picture,* as the saying goes. *You see* is an expression Professor Ehrensperger, looking across the frosted edge of his martini, used. I didn't interrupt him, as one shouldn't, when a professor looks at him or her right in the eyes—martini notwithstanding.

"If you are to continue living the type of life you are apparently intent on living, you must use discretion," he said, still holding his martini between us. He had rabbit-like front teeth, which occluded on the top edge of his lower teeth, causing the word to come out as dis-cre- (snake-like hiss) tzion the final syllable, he pronounced, "tzion," the way Germans pronounce "z," while most enunciate discretion with a "sh," as in, "shut the door." I explain so that you may understand that Harold had my full attention, and I remember every detail as though it were yesterday. As a matter-of-fact, the conversation in question took place in Boston's venerable Locke-Ober Restaurant some sixty-five years ago. So much for long-term memory, or is it short-term we are supposed to lose with age?

I called Harold, Harold, because, though he was my professor and deserved the respect his august position requires, at the outset of our conversation, he assured me that he wanted me to think of him as a friend and that I should feel free to address him as Harold, which was his given name, don't you see (no, we're not going there again).

In the precincts of the university, I continued to address Harold as "Professor," though sometimes with a wink-like knowing smile at my rabbit-toothed and hairless friend. Perhaps, *bald as a billiard ball* better puts you in the picture.

Continue living as I *chose*! Those days some benighted clergy believed that I opted to be the way I was born. About the time most of my friends graduated from experimenting in the barn loft to necking with girls, an older boy explained to me that, as a little hair grew on my legs and under my arm, I would want to neck and French-kiss with girls, as well. What a relief that would be! I waited and waited, until *one night at the state fair*—I've already described that big surprise in the same book I tell about Locke-Ober, but don't go looking for a lot of prurient stuff. That'll be in the next book.

Fortunately, those days I did the best I could to keep my desires secret. If I hadn't, I would have disgraced my family and would have been sent to a psychiatrist, who really would have screwed me up. But I didn't come to the beach to write about my *perversion* as my desires were labeled—it was the *"you see"* business that got me on to Harold and dinner at Locke-Ober.

~~~~~~~~~

Where was I? Oh, yes! I want you to see me at my computer again at Chelem Beach with electricity restored. Yep, stopped off at Costa Azul, and Brown Eyes was my waiter. I had two Sol beers, excellent *botanas* of ceviche and avocado and a *filete a la plancha con mojo de ajo*—grilled fish filet smothered in butter and roasted garlic.

Perhaps it was the beer or maybe the brown eyes that sent me flying off. I now promise myself to write at least two more pages before I grab a beer or mix myself a martini, and at the water's edge imagine myself among the homing birds specking the evening sky.

Flying Again

A HUGE WHITE BIRD PERCHED AT THE END OF A JETTY FOUR properties down from the narrow swath of sand for which we pay taxes to the Mexican government. The June morning I first saw the bird, I had taken my morning coffee to the jetty in front of our house where I tell friends I come to write my memoir.

The albatross—for that is what the big white bird turns out to be when I looked it up in my tropical bird book—had moved a jetty closer to ours that evening as I carried my martini to my favorite rock, where I commune as the sun gathers paints and brushes for her nightly extravaganza. Since morning I had written and then deleted a dozen times the opening paragraph of the memoir.

For the next four weeks, this goes on; morning coffee, evening martinis, the albatross hops closer, until one martini-ed evening the bird perched at the end of my jetty. I sensed something going on of which I had been totally oblivious. One might think it was the martinis, but I don't think so. The writer must be *observant*, God is in the details, you know. Observing is what makes writers write, and makes us a cut above the rest of the human race. Most humans, after they reach three years old, stop observing and start simply asking why, but we writers keep observing and sniffing. Even so, I was as oblivious as the next person to what was going on.

You will find what I am about to tell you difficult to believe. I'd find it *impossible* if it hadn't happened to me! A few days after the albatross arrives at the end of my jetty, he offers me a ride. How could I decline such an offer? At first, we did a low glide down the beach. Then gradually higher out over the water. We got on famously, and I started calling the bird "Al." He'd just cackle.

Why am I writing about all this? It's because I am leading up to telling you that the most amazing discovery of my whole life occurred during those flights. My discovery, maybe realization is a better word, could not have happened if I hadn't taken off flying on Al's back. Mind you, I'm no Samuel Taylor Coleridge, and my story isn't *The Rime of the Ancient Mariner*, nor is the story all about *me*, though my life is something to write home about.

Evenings, I'd take a break from my memoir, carry my martini down to the jetty and we'd be off. Try to picture me on the back of an albatross, balancing a very dry martini. Al would tease with sharp turns or go into a steep dive, but I never spilled a drop.

The big—a writer might write epiphany or existential—moment happened about a month after Al and I took up flying together. I'll never forget that afternoon. The thermals were fantastic. We were just out for our usual sunset flight, gliding through one cumulus cloud after another, far out over the Gulf waters, when an updraft lifted us higher into strata of imagination. We kept ascending higher into the stratosphere until we passed through time's walls. Gone were separation between time present, time past and time future. We had passed beyond the singularity into the zone before time existed.

My perspective on everything important changed. It was like after a heart attack, I died and then returned moments later with clear lenses, like the removal of cataracts. One sees more light than dark, more kindness than hatred—not just the eyes, the heart, or soul, if that is what you want to call the newness near the solar plexus.

Gliding on Al's back I saw eighty years before, my hometown in the middle of the dust bowl. Oh, my God, it came through as clear as a bell! I had known even then the truth for which I would search most of my life. Before I ran off to faraway countries, the secret I would seek in exotic places was already in my squirmy lap in the heart of the dust bowl.

From my Sunday school room, my imagination leaped like a circus acrobat, back millennia to a cave where my hairy ancestors are huddling, cowering from a thunderstorm. The young cling to their mother for comfort. She is my great, great, *a thousand greats removed*, grandmother. I detect a slight resemblance in our chins. The club-wielding chief of the clan, my great granddad, looks on helplessly. He can kill for them, but not the club or even the drawings etched on the cave wall give comfort. I write, *club* and *drawings*, but I may be off a millennium or so; my kin may not have yet developed that far. At this distance, it's hard to distinguish Paleolithic from Neolithic. Perhaps I see into a time when we are not yet quite human, whatever that means. But long before we begin to develop short fat thumbs, we are already curious as a cat. The young drive the adults to distraction—poking fingers into dangerous crevasses, climbing out on weak branches, or tweaking dinosaurs' tails. From the moment we slithered from the primordial sea, we have wanted to *know.*

About the time we learned to crack shells with a rock, we started inventing words to tell stories already shaping in our minds. And, to this day, stories remain humankind's most valuable invention, for through story we discover and tell who we are and why.

Because we *need to know,* we have tried all sorts of ways to figure things out—through a telescope, microscope, and particle accelerator. It seems that before the Big Bang, all was chaos. The Creator or Creators didn't quite get the job done, for there remains much chaos. We're in the middle of creation, not the end product! I think I've just jumped in over my head. I had best leave the subject to Einstein and Heidegger. Suffice to say, for some reason, the universe seems set on *gradual change.* From our human prospect we think of the universe as evolving and ourselves as having *evolved* from our hairy ancestors—they might disagree. Ask an ape or chimpanzee.

Before there were trees or animals—before there were stars or earth—all that existed was only one gleaming pinprick of substance dancing in a midnight of nothingness, a singularity; then, after an eternity the singularity, as tiny as the point of a pin, burst into the universe.

Physicists and philosophers have almost given up trying to figure out who or what set the tiny singularity off, coming up with answers such as, you can't know the unknowable, or since time starts with the Big Bang, you can't get before time. All the while poets and priests declared God or gods did it.

My albatross sees into the beginning of eternity, but my view only reaches as far back as a thousand years or so to before we started inventing stories.

Whoever the creator was before the Big Bang, he, she, or it, like a fan dancer, exposes a little here and a little there, but never the whole schemata! Maybe we can't stand knowing everything. In spite of our arrogance, we may have more *evolving* to do.

Our collective stories are the best tool we've got for understanding ourselves and our universe, spaceship explorations of Mars and Pluto notwithstanding. Science gives facts, but art took us beyond the stars well before the rockets.

The ancient Hebrews called the female aspect of God, Wisdom. Perhaps it is She who has been dribbling into our stories about as much knowledge as we can handle. Maybe She is the same as one of the Greek goddess, Erato—the spirit who whispers poems and stories we could never have made up on our own. Through story-telling mythmakers, we glimpse Lao-Tse on the back of a buffalo, the enlightened Buddha sitting under a banyan tree for forty-nine days.

The poet tells that *Ezekiel saw the wheels;*
Way up in the middle of the air.
And the big wheel run by Faith, good Lord;
And the little wheel run by the Grace of God;
A wheel within a wheel a rolling;
Way up in the middle of the air.

And writers Matthew, Mark, Luke, and John tell the wondrous story of a prophet who ascends to heaven.

Scientists take us to the edge of the universe, while artists and mystics fly beyond. Storytellers, mythmakers pass down the best and most enlightening wisdom, and thus we become civilized.

Al batted his wings a couple of times, executed an exquisite pirouette, which brought us out onto a plain, from which I glimpsed of Homer composing the *Iliad* and *The Odyssey.*

Just imagine, without the poets' verses, we would have little knowledge of the origins of our civilization, Agamemnon, or Achilles, or what to call the tendons that hold on our heels. The Greeks must have loved hearing all those stories.

Our myths, our sacred traditions, evolved over generations, have helped make us human. Sadly, these same scriptures are twisted to justify society's most inhuman crimes, causing many to reject the good in our heritage and search for guidance in exotic sources.

From Al's back, I see myself as a young man, kneeling in cathedrals and temples, or sitting intoning *ohm, ohm* with fellow seekers. I expected that through study and travel, I would learn some great exotic truths superior to those I learned in my own town.

After my long journey, I came home to the realization that I swim in the river of myths flowing from the confluent streams of Hebrew, Greek and Roman searchings for truth and before them, Egyptians and Babylonians. The precepts exploding out of the Middle East about two thousand years ago, filtered through imperial councils, reformations, and priests, were carried across half the American continent into the Oklahoma Sunday school room in a dusty church basement where I sat.

After my long quest for the exotic truth, it finally dawned on me that I had learned the most transformative truth yet to be fathomed by Homo sapiens, while I sat on brightly painted, spindly Sunday school chairs, studying my opposing thumb. The tattered yellowing pages, with pictures of bearded men and folks in long robes, were attempting to let us in on the greatest story ever told. The greatest mythic truth to which humans have evolved enough to begin to understand is a story so simple even a child can understand it. The myth? The fantastic story is about a fatherly Creator, who took human form to teach people to love one another as much as they love themselves. How to love everyone? I am pretty sure people need to start by learning to love themselves.

Along with loving each other goes love of our Creator. How do we love our Creator? Go outside and be astonished by the sparrows flitting in an elm tree, blackbirds on the telephone poles, squawking blue jays, parrots preening high up in palm branches, the rolling plains, cornfields, storms and mountains, oceans, coral reefs and porpoises. Be delighted by rivers and elephants, giraffes, prairie dogs, collies and mutts, and cats and wildebeests and aardvarks.

(You know the creator has a sense of humor.) Be transported by the caress of a breeze. Be lost in the stars, in the night and awakened amazed each morning. Love the universe and all that is in it—the single idea that may save all that exists. After all, we are all of the same substance. We all derive from the primal moment before the clock began to tick. I began to understand all this when I was eleven or twelve and when I turned the worn page and first saw *The Peaceable Kingdom.* I should have understood before I went off to faraway countries. From our cumulus puff, Al and I look down, and we see all kinds of different folks—Africans, Eskimos, New Yorkers, Asians and farmers and coal-miners and traveling-salesmen—all colors and sexes, and sexual preferences holding hands and declaring their love for each other, and the mystery beyond the planets. I think, yeah, we have some evolving yet to do, but, just maybe, we will evolve in a good direction before we destroy ourselves.

Toward the end of summer, Al faithfully awaited me as I arrived with my martini. It was low tide, so I waded out to the end of my jetty and sat next to him. He had become restless of late. Something caught in his gullet when he squawked. I had learned that the Gulf of Mexico was north of his usual habitat. It had been my luck that he had veered off course as adolescents will do. He had been resting, preparing to head back to Costa Rica the evening he first noticed me sitting on my jetty. Curiosity and something he had never felt before, a strange sense that we were somehow meant for each other, had kept him Gulf side. But September would soon bring *nortes* sweeping in across the Gulf. His instincts told him that he must fly south.

I sat my martini on a rock, reached up and ruffled his breast feathers. He lay a great wing across my shoulder, and we sat like that, quietly gazing at the evening show. I held back tears, knowing what was to come. Finally, as the golden orb sizzled below the western horizon, he sprung from his rock perch, and leaving a silver trail in the water, Al soared into a golden sky. Gaining altitude, he twice circled; then, long neck stretched southward disappeared into the night.

I didn't return to my coffee and martini routine for a month, but now, every evening you will find my body perched on our rock at the water's edge in front of the house where I tell friends I come to write. About sunset, my imagination takes off, as Al taught it, and it soars into cumulus clouds that build far out where water and sky are the same and time, past and present and future, are all one, and I understand that Al and I and the universe are of one substance.

I am a Trinity

~~~~~~~~~~~

THE SEA IS FLAT, SCARCELY A RIPPLE LAPS THE BEACH'S EDGE. I count three boats in nearshore and further out, at least a dozen white ships slip along the horizon. It must be a good day for fishing or catching *pulpo* (octopus) so prized around here. I am flying again out among the pestering gulls. I watch myself as the white-haired old fellow standing at the water's edge.

The me that observes me never grows up. Whether watching myself sail down the Malabar Coast, dining in a maharaja's palace, walking home after the last call at a bar haunted by lonely people, or waiting to run on stage as Ethel Merman belts out *There's No Business Like Show Business,* my flying self sees everything from the perspective of the boy living in a small town, situated in the bow of Little Deer Creek, west of Oklahoma City, where steam locomotives, great black wheezing behemoths, take on water and then speed on to Amarillo, Albuquerque and the desert beyond. The diesel "Santa Fe Zephers," that later replaced the steam engine not needing water, scarcely slowed to throw off the town's bag of mail and hook the outgoing letters.

I am a trinity, three selves. There is an inner self, an outer self, and the one who observes and flies quite a lot. Then there is one you see in the flesh, the white-haired, bespectacled old fellow telling his stories. My other two selves, people don't see, but dogs, cats, goats, horses, and donkeys can see the lovable me, while humans may see only the sometimes cantankerous old fellow.

The inner me is lodged, I suspect, near my solar plexus, if it exists, and is not a figment of my imagination. It is a soulful being hiding deep in the back of a cave. It is through the inner me that muses whisper stories I could never make up on my own.

I am eleven or twelve, heartbroken for some reason, a scolding by my mother or a fight with my brother. I don't recall the reason, but I still feel the heartbrokenness I felt that day, my arms hugging Prince, our collie dog. That is when I discovered my inner me. Prince saw beyond my runny nose and impetigo-infected scratches, the beautiful, lovable self, my inner self, buried deep inside me. I so desperately wanted folks to see that beauty, to be loved, especially by the brown-eyed sharecropper's son, who had just joined my fifth-grade class. The inner me was so clearly seen by every dog and cat I ever met, Cleo our goat, my uncle's black stallion, and even, perhaps, folks who see beyond my pretensions. Quaker friends have taught me that everyone has an inner light.

I look out a train window at sleeping Kansas. I am traveling East for the first time. I race above trees and rooftops, watching the boy in the train speed past telegraph poles. Light from the window flashes against the poles and bounces back to light the face of a boy in the train racing into the unknown. A small box next to the cold fried chicken his mother insisted he bring nestles next to him. His inner self huddles like his pet prairie dog.

Perhaps it was then I became aware of my out-of-body self, which sometimes hovers like a hawk about to land on a telephone pole, and other times glides like a vulture, catching thermals raising off Ghost Mound Mesa. That self saw me as a boy driving a tractor and sees me now pecking at a keyboard. And that flying self sees the tender self-cuddling near my heart. I mean no disrespect, but I kind of understand how God must feel—I mean being three in one. After all, we are created in God's image.

~~~~~~~~~~

I leave the water's edge, climb the honeybush-shrouded embankment, where, blown away by a hurricane, a house once stood. From out among diving pelicans, I watch myself reluctantly go to the house. The old guy pours a cold cup of coffee, sits down at the keyboard and with child-like trust starts pecking, believing that, if he keeps at it, almost without noticing, his shy mouse-like self will show its face and whisper to him an amazing story.

Myth

Returning home after having strayed long and far.

~~~~~~~~~~

AS I SIT ON MY PORCH BY THE SEA AND MARVEL AT THE INFINITE shaping and reshaping of the heavens out over a quiet gulf, I now understand that I view the universe through lenses bequeathed to me some eighty years ago, in a Methodist Church basement Sunday school room, in a small town out on the rolling Plains of West Oklahoma.

I have traveled far and expected that when I found what I sought, it would be wisdom inaccessible to those who stayed home and tilled the fields. I thought that through my travels and university I would become wise and admired. As I stood by Route 66, thumb out seeking a ride east to erudition, I thought "the truth" would be exotic—I would discover truths that others didn't know.

I wish I knew a better word than myth for the vessel which, I believe, carries our culture's most precious truths. Many take "myth" to mean untrue or fantasy. What I mean by "myths" are stories that tell truths accessible to poets, mystics, and stargazers. Myths existed long before humans learned the usefulness of reason. Through myth and story, we passed from generation to generation knowledge which lies beyond the grasp of pure reason. Reason brings us only to the edge of the material world, but from there we must leap if we are to know life's most profound secrets. Reason tells us the *what,* but cannot say the *why.*

Myth, I imagine being like the rivers along which civilizations evolved. The rivers of thought and stories flow out of our soggy prehistoric cradles. In the river, of which I write, myths float like small vessels bearing ancient cries of "who am I; where do I belong within the vastness of existence?" Questions that still nag me as I watch a flotilla of homeward bound pelicans.

The wellspring of wonderment existed before words. Maybe humans first formed words to find something that would assuage this primal longing—not so much to know what rocks and stars are made of, as to understand our relationship to them.

Civilizations sprung up along the Nile, Tigris, Euphrates, Ganges, Irrawaddy, Yangtze, and Usumacinta. And rivers of thought developed alongside their watery sisters. As the waters gathered alluvium, myths formed, revelations. The rivers of ideas birthed Leutze, Confucius, Zoroaster, Muhammad, and Buddha. Legends gathered around them so that what we now know is an amalgam of fact and imagination, similar to the way alluvium carried by waters deposited into the Bay of Bengal, the Yellow Sea, the Mediterranean and Bay of Campeche. Rich as these traditions are, none of those exotic rivers spilled onto the prairies of Oklahoma. The priceless myth, taught to me as a child, finds its source not in the shadows of the Himalayas, but rather in its wellspring flowing from near the Sea of Galilee.

My Sunday school myth flowed through Abraham and Sarah's dynasty. It evolved from Egypt and the wilderness-inspired Psalms and was shaped by Jeremiah, Isaiah, Amos. Hosea gave the first inkling of a loving God. The mythic river picks up the creation story and Gilgamesh stories in Babylon, and through Paul absorbs Greek philosophies. The myth amalgamated, and church councils macerated, Augustine, Aquinas, Calvin, and Luther interpreted. The thoughts spread through Europe, crossed the Atlantic, filtered through the Massachusetts Bay colonies, and crossed the Hudson and Allegany rivers. The Methodist version that found its way into my Sunday school was carried in the satchel of Methodist circuit riders from the hollows of Kentucky and made its way to the Indian Territory—land returned to the Native Americans and then snatched back.

Like a valued heirloom brought over from the old country by some long forgotten relative, myth, though it doesn't look like much, is priceless because it somehow connects us.

The myth I inherited has been misused, twisted, spat upon, and used as a pretext for the humanity's most heinous atrocities and bigotry, and yet, the most transformative idea seeped into my Sunday school. The truth, so humbly taught, is so simple it is missed by those of us who sought wisdom in far countries and mountaintops.

The Christ myth bears the simple truth that we are to love *one another as ourselves.* I nearly abandoned that simple truth in a search for a "truth" more profound, which I might learn from a guru on a mountaintop. I came close to squandering that shining jewel. *Why are we here? To love one another.* Life is simply for living and loving. Of course, to love others, we must learn to love ourselves. Even a child can understand that! All my time searching, I could have been learning how to love more fully!

Like the prodigal, I have traveled afar, visited the banks of the Ganges and Irrawaddy, slept in Krishna's temple and knelt before many images of Gautama Buddha, yet I would be bereft, were I not to come home to wisdom offered to me in the Christ myth.

The clouds have climbed into the stratosphere, flattened, spread and evaporated. An iguana suns on the wall out near the honeybushes. I can see my Sunday school teacher, Mrs. Quenlin, her glasses pushed down her nose, reading words I have already learned by heart, "Suffer little children to come unto me."

Traveling

THEIR FARM WAS ONLY FIVE OR MAYBE EIGHT MILES OUT OF town. It may have been closer. Nights I gazed out the upstairs window of the room where I slept. It seems as I look back, the landscape is always lit by blue moonlight, the trees and the outline of the barn and windmill are etched black against a slate-blue sky. The farm was too far away from town for me to hear the semitrailers barreling along 66 or the night trains rocketing toward California. It was the summer after I turned twelve, my first farm job was with Methodist folks who attended our church. I started at fifty cents a day, and by the end of summer, after I learned to drive a tractor, and even though I mowed down a fence, I advanced to a dollar a day. I can still feel the anguish of away-from-home-ness.

And yet even way back then, life seemed to lay somewhere other than where I was. Sharecropper classmates were always leaving school in the middle of the term, their folks pulling out after school cotton-picking-vacation and heading for California. Model A Fords, loaded down with kids, relatives, bedding, and washtubs drove down our Main Street, Route 66. I'd ask, "why can't we go to California too?"

The Wizard of Oz infected my dreams. Years later that a bartender in a gay bar on New York's Upper Eastside yells "Last call, last chance" and a guy standing by the piano, sings in a wobbly voice, "Somewhere

Over the Rainbow," *the gay men's lullaby.* That guy could have been me.

Is it part of being human, part of our DNA, this need to travel? Wouldn't it be wonderful to just stay where you were born, in a comfortable, familiar home, enough to eat and among people who accept and love you? For what are we looking? Oh, I understand for guys like me who had something to hide... is it to find a place where we can be ourselves or are we searching for ourselves?

I have liked being almost everywhere I have ever been; then why did I leave? Am I simply part of that western push? Our father and the state of Oklahoma were one-year-old when the Spradlings arrived in Muskogee, capital of the Indian nation. They hoped to lay claim to some land the government was giving. Our grandad was part Mississippi Choctaw.

My mother and dad moved two hundred miles farther west onto the hot, dry, dusty High Plains, part of the Louisiana Purchase that surveyors named the Great American Desert, not fit for development, so the government gave it to the Indians, displaced from the more fertile eastern part of the county.

The farmer I worked for quit work Saturday afternoons and gave me a ride into town. I'd say hello to my family, change clothes, and then head on down to Main Street, where I'd meet up with my gang, at Wicof's drugstore soda fountain. We would sit around drinking cherry phosphates until time for the Saturday night show at the Bulldog Theater. I would return to the farm Sunday night to be out in the field at daybreak. That summer I lost my baby fat. That fall, I took fourteen dollars of my earnings to C.R. Anthony and purchased a pair of leather-inlay cowboy boots. It was summer farm work until I went off to college.

~~~~~~~~~

When I returned home for mother's funeral, the farmer and his wife came up to me. "I'll bet you don't remember us," they said. I did remember, and those summers flooded back, and it felt home-like. By the time my mother died, I had left Oklahoma to study in Boston. I had traveled to Rio de Janeiro, and had spent a summer in a work camp helping rebuild German homes destroyed by Allied bombers, the same summer my brother's plane crashed somewhere in North Korea. I didn't yet know I would become a vagabond.

Billy Goes To Rio

~~~~~~~~~~~~~~

BILLY HAD CALLED THE PROFESSOR'S SUITE TO LET HIM KNOW that his ride was waiting and then wandered about the plush-carpeted hotel lobby. The air carried the caramel fragrance of cigars like the ones Billy's grandfather treated himself to once a month. The spittoons and the dark oak paneling gleamed. Billy had been in the grand old Skirvin Hotel once before. He had come down to the city for a church youth conference. After the meeting, their minister had brought four of them to lunch in the Skirvin dining room. Billy reddened at the memory of peas rolling off his fork, bouncing off his plate and leaving a buttery trail across the white tablecloth. He had never before eaten shelled peas without mashed potatoes.

Billy mostly took after his father, five-foot-six feet tall with dark complexion, but he had his mother's dark hazel eyes, wide and round, giving him a look of innocence.

Oklahoma Christian College's president had asked Billy to drive down and meet Professor Randolph, the author of "Designed by God," a repudiation of Darwinism. He was to chauffer the famous author to the college.

Each time the elevator doors opened Billy expected a professorial-looking gentleman to emerge. This time when he checked, it was a smoothly tanned younger man bearing no resemblance to the description of the person Billy was to meet.

The man checked his watch, went to the newspaper rack, selected a paper and crossed the lobby to a leather sofa opposite Billy.

"Hello," Billy said.

In Oklahoma, it would be rude not to greet a person with whom you made eye contact or who sits near you.

"Uh, hello," the man acknowledged Billy's greeting. He unfolded his paper and started to read, but after a moment he looked up and cocked his head quizzically. He then stood and extended his hand to Billy. "Excuse me. For a moment the thought passed through my mind that I knew you. Mind if I sit here?"

"Heck no," Billy said.

The stranger withdrew a silver case from his pocket, flipped it open, and offered Billy a slender cigarillo.

"No thanks." Billy shook his head.

"Do you mind?" The stranger asked and, not waiting, lit his cigarillo with a silver lighter matching the case. He drew in a long, satisfying breath, then slowly blew the smoke aside.

"My name's Billy. Well, actually it's William. I wish folks would just call me Bill, but about everybody has known me since I was a little kid. If I asked them to call me Bill, they'd think I was stuck-up. I guess I'm always going to be Billy unless I go somewhere else."

The stranger extended a manicured hand. "Well, you will be Bill to me. I am Aurelio. My mother calls me *Aurelioito*, but to everyone else I am Aurelio."

"It is mighty nice to meet you, Mr. Aurelio."

"No *Mister*, please, just Aurelio."

"You're not from around here, are you?"

"What makes you think that?" Mischief danced in the darkest eyes Billy had ever seen.

"Your clothes fit you nicer than men's from around here, and excuse me saying so, but you talk a little foreign."

"Oh, you crush me!" Striking his chest, Aurelio feigned grief.

"No, no! I think the way you talk is a lot nicer than us folks. We mostly sound like we're callin' hogs."

"You are a funny man, Bill. What brings you to this hotel? Surely not to entertain the guests?"

"I'm supposed to drive Professor Randolph up to my college." Billy looked at his watch. "And if the professor doesn't get down here pretty soon, he's going to miss his own lecture."

"Then you are a student?"

"Studying engineering."

"And you will build skyscrapers, here on the prairie?"

Billy laughed. "Well, kind of—oil rigs mostly. After I graduate, I may get to go to some foreign country. 'Til now, I've gotten as far as Kansas City."

"What foreign country?"

"Where there's oil, I reckon. Maybe Libya, Saudi Arabia, or even Nigeria. I don't much care. I just want to travel. Travelin' has been my dream since I was a kid."

Aurelio leaned his head back against the sofa. He slowly drew in smoke then jetted its stream toward the ceiling, "But Bill, my friend, those are ugly places. You must go to Paris, Rome, Rio de Janeiro or Buenos Aires, beautiful cities with culture." Aurelio turned, a stern look on his face, he said, "I can tell, my friend, you are a good person. You will not be happy in Libya, Saudi Arabia or Nigeria." Aurelio checked his watch and stood. "I would enjoy more visit," he extended his hand, "but my car will be ready now. I must reach New York the day after tomorrow." He held Billy's hand firmly in both his hands. "*Hasta luego amigo!*" he turned and headed for the exit.

At that same moment, the elevator door slid open and out

stepped a red-faced, rumpled gentleman, the brim of his fedora flopped down on one side. Billy had started for the professor when a tap on his shoulder turned him back. Aurelio handed him a card.

"Call me at this number in New York City next week. Call me collect. I may have a surprise for you that will make you very happy," he said and hurried for the door.

Billy stood puzzling, then remembered his mission and rushed for the professor.

As Billy guided the car through traffic, Professor Randolph explained that he had picked up a flu bug the past evening. The car was redolent of Listerine tinctured with something less medicinal. *Also picked up a bottle*, Billy thought.

~~~~~~~~~

With the gravity of one burdened with great wisdom and wearing an academic robe, sleeves slashed with crimson velvet, the professor strode in front of the student body, which had been waiting almost an hour. As Randolph scanned his audience, his chest swelled.

"Today, I stand before you young Christians to declare to you that you are not the decedents of an ape! Nay, you were formed as human by the Lord God Himself." A smattering of amens rose from the faculty. The professor's voice soared evangelistically, as he hit his stride. "I stand before the scientific world that would challenge the word of God, as David stood before Goliath. . . ."

In conclusion, he lifted a book. "This book," the professor's voice shook. "My book, *Designed by God*, is faith's answer to evolution. In these pages, I answer every assertion of the Evolution Conspiracy. If you want facts, they are here," he thundered, "and the fact is that this book," he slammed the book on the lectern, "has sold over five thousand copies. There's your proof!!"

Following an awkward silence, the president stood applauding, while the students joined in politely. Several shouted amen, amen, but Billy's biology and physics teachers just sat looking at the floor. He wondered how they dared not join in the applause.

~~~~~~~~~~

Aurelio's card, lying under Billy's desk lamp, sent Billy's mind drifting from his studies. He put the card in the desk drawer, but still couldn't keep from wondering what the stranger could possibly have meant.

"Probably wants to sell you a subscription to the Encyclopedia Britannica," a friend suggested.

"You shouldn't trust strangers, especially some citified guy you meet in a hotel," L.D, his roommate and closest friend said. "I'd tear the card up. Save yourself a peck of trouble."

But Billy did trust folks and nothing in his twenty-one years of experience had given him reason not to. Treat folks the way you want to be treated, and they will treat you the same way back.

He waited almost a week before he talked to his mother. "I don't really know what you should do. Your father would have," she said. "If you are like me, you'll just worry over it until you find out what the man has in mind. But honey, if he is selling something, just remember that we can't afford it."

"That's so exciting!" his girlfriend, Verna May, screamed. "Maybe it's a quiz show. He'll pay your way to New York! Maybe he'll want me too. Call him, Billy! Call him and be sure to ask him about me too!"

~~~~~~~~~~

"Who did you say is calling?" Asked a female voice on the other end of the line. "A Bill Schroder, you say? One moment please."

Aurelio probably had forgotten all about him, Billy thought as he waited. Secretary and all! Aurelio is too important to take my call.

The voice came on the line again. "Yes, we will accept the charges. Mr. Schroder, Mr. de Costa is on another line; please hold."

Billy bounced from one foot to the other growing increasingly embarrassed. The phone call was costing a fortune.

"Bill Schroeder!" Aurelio's voice came on the line. "Sorry to keep you waiting. I was about to give you up. Things go alright with your professor?"

"I'll bet this phone call must be costing you a bundle."

"Don't you worry about that, but I do have only a minute to talk. Let me explain. You say that you want to travel. How would you like to go to Rio de Janeiro?"

"Who wouldn't?"

"Do you have a passport?"

"I never needed one."

"Get one right away."

"But. . ."

"Now just listen. Get a passport and then a visa for Brazil."

"I guess I can do that, but why?"

"I want you to take a car down there for me. I can't get away from here right now. I'll pay all your expenses. Travel, hotel everything."

"Wow! I didn't know the highway went all the way down there, but sure, I guess."

Aurelio laughed. "Not drive. You'll be on a ship. It is sailing from New York in three weeks."

"You're joking. Now, why really did you want me to call you?"

"No joke, Billy. Get your passport and visa and arrange with your school to be gone for two to three weeks. Can you do that?"

"Yeah, I guess but. . . ."

"I've got another call coming in," Aurelio cut Billy off. "Don't worry. I'm going to pay all your expenses. Call me after you get your passport and visa. I've got to go kid." The line went dead.

Billy replaced the phone to its cradle, leaned his back against the wall and slid to the floor.

~~~~~~~~~~

"I want you in New York in two weeks," Aurelio said after Billy reported that he had obtained his passport and visa. "That will give us about four days to take care of a little business and for you to take in the city."

"Golly, Aurelio!"

"You just get yourself here, my friend. I'll reimburse you and give you enough to take care of you while you are here and in Rio."

"OK, I believe you. I've met you, and I trust you and all, Aurelio, but Mother, well she's awfully worried."

"Of course, Billy, I should have thought of that. Have her talk with Arthur Patterson. He's an attorney there in Oklahoma City. He has worked with us."

Billy breathed a sigh. "I hope he can reassure her."

"Here it is; Arthur Patterson, Attorney at Law, number 10 Classing Avenue."

Billy laughed embarrassed. "She still thinks I'm a baby."

"No need to be embarrassed."

As it turned out Patterson was a member of the Rotary Club Billy's father had belonged to. Patterson told Billy's mother he had greatly admired her husband. That cinched Patterson's credibility and, in turn, Aurelio's. She loaned Billy money for the train ticket to New York and a little extra for expenses.

~~~~~~~~~~

"Billy, you'd trust the devil himself," his girlfriend screamed.

"You were all for it," Billy said, "when you thought Aurelio would take us both to New York to be on a quiz show."

"That was one thing. You weren't sailing off," she cried, "with a total stranger. Maybe I'll see you when you get back but don't count on it. If you make it back!" She slammed the door.

Dean Wilder said, "Son, just how well do you know this, ah-hum, Aurelio, you say his name is?"

"I guess we talked maybe a half hour. He was staying at the Skirvin, sir."

"Half an hour!" The dean shook his head.

"And then I called him collect in New York, so you might say more than a week."

"Swarthy, with a strange name and a foreign accent?"

"His English was real good, and I didn't say swarthy. It was more like he has a nice tan."

"Now Billy, you know that I am no bigot." The dean peered over the rim of his half-glasses. His chins waddled as he spoke. "But you appear to be dealing with someone from one of those Latin countries down there."

"I appreciate your concern, Dean Wilder, but this is a once in a lifetime opportunity. I can't let it slip by. So, can I have permission for a two-week leave from school?"

"You don't understand, Billy. They are mostly Catholics down there. They simply don't share our morals."

"Aurelio's a good person. That's all I need to know."

"Very well." The dean shook his head. "Your grades are good. You are a good Christian boy. You may have two weeks' leave. I pray things turn out as you hope."

Billy felt queasy, as the reality of what he was about to do struck.

"Guy sounds like a pervert," L.D. said, watching Billy pack his suitcase.

"Oh, I wish your father were here," his mother sniffed. "I don't know what he'd say."

"I wish he were too." Billy and his father had been as close as any father and son could be. But Billy knew that if his father were alive, he wouldn't be going on this trip.

~~~~~~~~~~~~~~~~

Billy climbed on board the *Santa Fe Super Chief* bound for Chicago and on to New York City. Passport, visa and twenty-five dollars left from the hundred dollars his mother had taken from his father's insurance settlement.

"Mom, they have food on the train." He didn't want to look like a hick, but not wanting to hurt her feelings, he took the lunch box.

As the train slipped through the outskirts of the city, the clickety-clack of the wheels accelerated to a hypnotic tick, tick, tick.

Light from the train's windows flickered against telegraph poles, and, while Billy stared into the darkness, another Billy flew high above farmhouses, barnyards, and open fields and watched the lone figure pressed against the window of the speeding train. As far back as he could remember he'd lain awake long after his parents had told him to stop reading and turn his light off and he'd listen to the night train's mournful calls awakening dreams of far-off-places. Now that he traveled away from all that was familiar his other self, the self he always knew was there, came out of hiding.

At the second call for dinner, he roused himself, pulled on his jacket and made his way to the dining car, where an elegant black maître d showed him to a table set with heavy silver upon an immaculate tablecloth. He felt guilty for leaving his mother's cold fried chicken on his seat, he searched for the cheapest item on the menu, chicken á la king. He envied the nonchalance of the other passengers and was overcome with a feeling of insurmountable distance from the comfort of his family and friends and his dog.

"Grand Central Station! Last stop!"

Billy lugged his mother's gray Samsonite down a long dark platform into the great maw swarming with people, intent on wherever they were going.

Aurelio had instructed Billy, upon arrival, to go to the information island with a big clock in the middle of the station where he would be met by his secretary.

"How will I recognize her?"

"Easy," Aurelio said. "She is blond, medium height. She will be wearing a green coat with a gray fox collar. You cannot miss her. Your train is due in at 2:30 p.m. She will be there not later than 3 p.m."

"What if she is not there?"

"She will be, but if there is a problem, call her. Here is her name and address in Brooklyn. Her name is Valery Nimuncheck." He spelled the name. "I have to be out of the office."

"Where is Brooklyn?"

"It is part of New York City, a borough! Now stop worrying."

Billy had no idea what a borough was but didn't want to sound stupid.

He found the information island fifteen minutes before 3 p.m. He searched the crowd for blonds in green coats as the gold hands of the clock dial approached three, then three-thirty, four, four-thirty. At five he searched for a phone. To his dismay, there was not one New York phone book, but a bank of phone books. He found a phone information kiosk where a kind operator assisted him. There was no answer at the number listed for Valery Nimuncheck in the Brooklyn phone book.

He decided maybe he would feel less confused if he went outside the station and got his bearings. But the moment he stepped out into the madness of blaring horns, buses slamming to a stops, people crowding in one end and pouring out the back, everybody in a hurry—skyscrapers walled off any possibility of finding downtown; *every place he looked was downtown.* He retreated inside the station.

His feet began to ache from lugging the heavy luggage.

Every half hour he called the Brooklyn number with no results. His roommate had been right. The whole thing was a hoax. He was too ashamed to call home. He would spend the night in the station, and the next day somehow finds his way to the edge of the city from where he would hitchhike back. He made one last try to Valery's phone number.

"Oh, thank God!" the woman said. "I am terribly sorry. We'll explain everything later. Go now to the Hotel Diplomat. Aurelio is there. He is frantic. Ask for him at the desk, and he will take care of everything."

"How do I get there? Where is the hotel? Can I walk to it?"

"Just take a taxi. The driver will know the Hotel Diplomat."

Never in his life had it occurred to Billy to take a *taxi*.

~~~~~~~~~~

Aurelio rushed into the lobby, threw his arms around Billy and kissed him on both ears. Billy had never been hugged by a man other than his father and uncles, and none of them had kissed him.

Aurelio hurried him to the hotel desk, signed him in, and then took him to a room set up as an office, where three other men waited. Billy couldn't understand a word except when Aurelio interpreted. They took his passport and had him sign a bunch of papers. Aurelio handed Billy a hundred dollars to reimburse him for his expenses up to that point and another hundred dollars to cover his expenses during his stay in New York.

"I don't think I need all that much," Billy said.

Aurelio chuckled. "This is New York, kid. Spend it. You'll get another hundred for your shipboard expenses and when you get to Rio, money for your stay there and your flight back to Oklahoma City via Lima, Peru. The next four days you are free to do whatever you want to do. Just be sure to be here in the hotel Friday morning at eight. And by the way," Aurelio placed his arm across Billy's shoulder as he led him from the room, "you are sailing on the SS Brazil. The largest ship in the Moor McCormick Line."

"Uh, I . . . I don't know what to say."

"You said you wanted to travel," the other men laughed with Aurelio. "Well, you're traveling in style."

"Will I see you?" Billy asked. "I don't know anybody."

"If you like," Aurelio said. "I will take you to dinner tomorrow night. Nine o'clock OK?"

"OK!"

"Glad we found you." Aurelio ruffled Billy's hair and sent the bewildered boy reeling down the hall to his room.

～～～～～～～

Billy's history teacher advised seeing the Metropolitan Museum of Art, and his science teacher the planetarium. His choral director said, "If you possibly can, be sure to go to the opera." All of them cautioned against strangers, pickpockets and Central Park at night. How they would know these things, Billy couldn't imagine, as they had all seen the great city on tours surrounded by fellow Oklahomans.

The hotel concierge gave Billy directions to the Metropolitan Opera. "As it is Saturday," he said, "there's a matinee. It is about a twenty-minute walk, down Broadway, beyond Time Square, past Macy's."

The opera was *Salome* featuring Rita Gore. Gold leaf flaked from the box office, where he bought a standing room ticket. The venerable old opera house was past its prime. He showed his ticket to an usher who directed him to the back of the orchestra section crowded with well-dressed men. The area was so full people bumped into him as he sought a place to stand near the rail dividing standing room from the last row of the orchestra. Everyone smelled good, but not of Old Spice which he and his dad used.

Miss Gore stepped on stage to thunderous applause. She was huge. Not beautiful like any lady he had ever seen, not even in movies, yet she was more compelling even than Rita Hayworth. Her wing-like eyebrows arched into a mass of black ringlets falling across her plump shoulders and down to her waist. Moons of blue and long brushes of lashes shadowed her eyes. Her fat lips were painted shiny red. She wore a blue satin shift which shimmered against her flesh as she strode toward a couch piled with tasseled pillows. Ropes of jewels, plunging between her full breasts, swung across her belly. As she reclined, sensually massaging her big thighs, her crimson talon-like fingernails dimpled into her soft flesh. Her voice was like dark chocolate.

At intermission, the lights went up. The man who had stood next to Billy turned and smiled. "Gore is marvelous, isn't she?"

"Wow," Billy said. "I've never heard or seen anything like her."

"You're not a regular?"

"Heck, no. This is my first time. This is my first opera, my first time in New York!"

The man pushed back freeing his arm and extended his hand. "Harold Thurman."

"Billy." He cleared his throat. "I mean Bill Schroeder," he said as he maneuvered to gain enough room to take the offered hand.

Someone bumped Billy sending him against Harold. "Excuse me!" Billy said. "This place sure is crowded, isn't it?"

"Rita Gore is one of our favorites," Harold said. "Let's move into the lobby. I'll buy us a drink."

Following the final curtain, they strolled down Seventh Avenue to a small diner. Harold insisted on paying for the coffee.

"You don't need to do that. I've got money."

"You are a guest in my town."

"This sure is nice of you. I heard that New Yorkers weren't friendly, but everyone has been real nice to me."

"How did you happen to be standing at the Met?" Harold asked.

"That was the only ticket left, and my chorus director back at O.C.C. told me to be sure to see an opera if I had a chance."

"Didn't anyone explain . . . don't you know why men buy standing room?"

"Because the tickets are cheap, I guess, but most of you guys looked like you've got enough to buy a seat. Funny, now that you mention it, I didn't see any women."

~~~~~~~~~

"*Salome* is your first opera?" Harold asked as he stirred sugar into his coffee.

"Not really. *Porgy and Bess* came to Oklahoma City, and I once heard an opera singer named Mona Polly, but nothing like this!"

Conversation wandered. Billy told about his girlfriend and her being mad at him, about his ambition, and his dog. Harold listened, fixing Billy with smiling eyes, warm brown with flecks of gold and green, not dark like Aurelio. Billy kept talking to keep Harold smiling. He acted as if he couldn't learn enough about Billy, and Billy kept pouring out.

"Boy, I sure am talky. I've just about told you my whole life. What about you?"

"I'm not interesting. I'm in finance and grew up across the river in New Jersey."

"Got a girl?"

Harold shook his head.

"Good looking guy like you?"

Harold looked out the window as if searching for an answer. Finally, he looked back holding his gaze on Billy.

"Guess it is none of my business, huh?"

~~~~~~~~~~

They stood at the curb as a river of yellow cabs, horns blaring, sped by. "Let me hail you a cab," Harold offered.

"No, I'll just walk. I want to see all I can.

Billy had never seen so many people in such a hurry. When he turned to shake Harold's hand, Harold threw his arms around him, crushed him in an embrace, and then pushed Billy away, as if he were contagious.

"The light is green," Harold said. "You had better go." He pointed to the traffic light.

As Billy reached the far curb, Harold called, "Oh, Billy, be careful,"

Billy imagined himself sitting up next to the blinking red lights of the tallest building. From there, he watched himself enter the mêlée of the yellow, honking, screeching, glittering, maddening stampede below. His imagination carried him far out to sea, where a ship, awaited him. He heard tango music, and he could see into the future, yet he couldn't see the way he had come, and he was afraid.

Work Camp

~~~~~~~~~~

COLD BEER IN HAND, I FOLLOW THE DEEP GROOVE LEFT BY AN iguana in the sand stretching from our Gulf-side porch. Star-like footprints bracket the big lizard's path to the honey and cedar bush-shrouded embankment which spills to the water's edge. School back in session, the beach is bereft of human habitation. I position myself on a smooth rock in the breakwater near shore and await the oncoming sunset. Unperturbed by my intrusion, a pelican nonchalantly airs his wings, and out in the Gulf, the bird's relatives execute ungainly nosedives into schools of fish. The lowering sun washes pink a cruise ship out from Galveston, which creeps over the horizon, making its way to Progresso. Another ship comes to mind:

~~~~~~~~~~

LE HAVRE, FRANCE: JUNE 1954

I am leaning over the railing as the *SS Italia* slips into La Havre harbor. It is the spring of 1954, the end of my first year at Boston University School of Theology. The *Italia* has survived the war as elegant transport for Italian military brass. The refurbished ship is much like the liners that sailed across the movie screen at my hometown Bull Dog picture show.

I make the Atlantic crossing quartered in a small compartment below water level. I am carrying twenty-five dollars to last me the summer. Credit cards are not yet invented, and I have no traveler's checks. Still, I feel like a movie star. To escape the dank lower decks, I spend much of the crossing wrapped in a blanket on C deck huddled in a chair and imagined the movie star, Myrna Loy, in the chair next to me. Had a Hollywood star been on the *Italia*, she would have been on A deck. Later that summer, a friend, Tate Bran, will wire me sixty-five dollars.

~~~~~~~~~~~

The *Italia* sails into La Havre harbor. I shoulder my rucksack and at the foot of the gangplank join fellow workcampers. As we await our guide at a nearby café, I taste my first glass of licorice-flavored Pernod. Funny, the things one remembers.

I am with a group sponsored by the American Friends Service Committee. We are on our way to work camps in a still-divided Germany, where we will join German and youth from other nations helping rebuild homes destroyed by Allied bombers. Friends, Quakers, believe we each have an *inner light*. By meeting violence with nonviolence, we help build peace; we bring forth one another's *inner light*. Some call this light the Christ within.

I don't remember when or how I came under the sway of Mahatma Gandhi's *passivism* and Albert Schweitzer's *reverence for life*. Adolescents often rebel against the norm. Nonviolence suited my temperament and the piety of my upbringing. Oh, I fought when I was called a sissy. I had to or be branded.

The Friends Service Committee put us up in a student hostel located in Place Pigalle, a neighborhood whose raunchy reputation led Allied soldiers to nickname the area, "Pig Ally." The Folies Bergere and Moulin Rouge were near our hostel.

That summer I would become lost in northern Germany,

hitchhike to Amsterdam, hike in the Alps, and receive word of my brother's death.

~~~~~~~~~~~

A pair of frigatebirds, knife-like wings scarcely beating, glide across the blazing western sky, and the cruise ship docks at the end of Progreso pier aglow in the setting sun.

How in the hell did I get where I am now? "Follow your bliss." Is that what I have been doing all my life? A lot of it sure didn't feel very blissful!

The evening before I came out to the beach I started telling my partner, Clifford, about my work camp summer. After forty-seven years together I still haven't run out of stories about my life before we met. I repeat myself, and Clif merely indulges me, as people sometimes do folks my age.

Clif, from a small town in the Texas Panhandle, has traveled as well. First with a wheat harvest crew all the way into Canada, then two times to Vietnam.

He was mustering out when he met a Metropolitan Opera director, said goodbye to the Navy, and took off for Italy with the director. They tooled around Italy in a Fiat convertible.

Who wouldn't have fallen for Clif, as I did (and save him from the opera director)—tall, slim, wide-shouldered, eyes a cloudscape of colors, a mop of auburn-streaked chestnut brown hair, an utterly beguiling gap-toothed grin, and an accent reminiscent of the accent I thought I had left behind in Oklahoma. We met, all tuxedoed up, at an opera party. He was with the director, and I was at the time an aspiring tenor. But I've gotten ahead of my story.

~~~~~~~~~~~

Our first night we made a beeline the Moulin Rouge cabaret, once loved by artists, of whom the most iconic was Toulouse-Lautrec.

I remember as much the hostel's minuscule drip of water, which passed as a shower, and the hole in the floor toilet, as I do the high-kicking can-can girls.

One evening, I strolled up Montmartre with a teacher from Indiana. While passing a bar, a very drunk and very effeminate young man backed through the door onto the sidewalk, nearly colliding with the teacher and me. As the obviously gay drunk staggered on down the street, the teacher said, "Good Lord that is Tommy Jackson; he teaches in our school. Still, in the closet myself, I recall the chill I felt. Even this far from home it wasn't safe to be one's self.

The Paris office assigned where in Germany we were to serve. The work camp at which I was to spend most of the summer was not yet ready, so I needed to serve two weeks in Krefeld, just below Colon on the Rhine River, and then proceed to Oberwesel in northern Germany. The secretary chuckles, "they are not a very well-organized program. Once even we sent someone to one of their camps and the camp wasn't there."

"What if that happens to me?" I ask.

The secretary shook his head, "Oh, that couldn't happen again."

~~~~~~~~~~

With a map and instructions in English as to how to reach Krefeld, and then, two weeks later, Oberwesel, I say goodbye to the friends I have been with since leaving the States. We hug each other and promise to stay in touch; then I strike off for Krefeld on my own. It seems it has been my destiny that most of my traveling life has to be alone.

Even though I flunked German, I used what little of the language I remember. However, almost always I found a German who spoke much better English. I arrive in Krefeld with little difficulty, and, rucksack hoisted on my back, hiked to the assigned youth hostel a short distance from the banks of the Rhine River.

In Krefeld, I worked alongside a Dane and two German young men, Swiss, and Jewish-American young women, and an English woman old enough to be our mother, who had hitchhiked across Holland. When asked if she spoke German, she replied, "I have learned if you speak English loudly and clearly enough, they can understand English." For the next two weeks, I dug ditches and cast concrete blocks.

Meals at the hostel cost about twenty-five cents a day. I most remember large quantities of blood sausage. It took nearly a week of near starvation before this Oklahoman managed to stomach the sausage. Most of my life I had battled to keep my weight down to a hundred and thirty-five pounds. At five-six, there isn't much room for fat. By the end of that summer, I managed to be well below my goal.

Too exhausted to go into town at the end of the day, we usually just sat around, chatted and played checkers or chess. But years later, when I saw the movie, *Cabaret*, memories flooded back of a Saturday night a group of us work-campers went to the Kit-Cat Club. The place was in a cellar in the middle of a mostly bombed-out neighborhood. We would never have found the place without a Krefeldeder to guide us along a cleared path to the cellar door, down some steps, and into a crowded, dimly-lit room, walls covered with wooden wine crates.

We were treated to free beers, while in a cone of light at the rear of the room, a chanteuse gave a poor imitation of Marlene Dietrich's *See what the boys in the backroom will have*. Toward the end of the evening, forgetting tired muscles, we locked arms with the other patrons and rocking back and forth we sang:

"Du, du liegst mir im Herzen, du, du liegst mir im Sinn."
You, you are in my heart.
You, you are in my mind.

You, you cause me much pain.
You don't know how good I am for you.
Yes, yes, yes, yes you don't know how good I am for you.

~~~~~~~~~~~~

The sun sinks into the Gulf of Mexico, leaving a sliver of pink strata suspended in the pale gray sky. Tears run down my face; I sing, *Du, du, liegst mir im Herzen . . ."* recalling the profound feeling of oneness of that night sixty-two years ago.

~~~~~~~~~~~~

With directions and a pamphlet describing the next work camp where I was to spend the balance of my summer, I board a train for northern Germany. Late that afternoon, the train pulls into Oberwesel. The station house is out of a child's picture book. The station master shakes his head when I ask, in practiced German, directions to the *arbit's lager*, work camp. I show the station master the brochure clearly bearing the name of the town. Still, the man shakes his head, then tells me to wait, someone will help me.

Half an hour later, a young man, who speaks about as much English as I do German, takes me into the center of the village. Picture book buildings surround the square centered on the village well. Wood timbers crisscross the houses' sand-colored walls, and straw thatch covers their sharply sloping gabled roofs.

My guide calls through a window of a large building opened onto the street. An arm reaches out signaling that we should enter. Inside, my guide introduces me to a large red-faced man sitting behind a cluttered desk, the *burgermeister* of Oberwesel. Again I show the brochure but am greeted with a shake of the head. The burgermeister, indicating for me to stay, dismisses my guide. He then calls out the window to someone else. It seems he carries on half the town's affairs through the open window behind his desk.

Presently a blond youth about my age arrives. His name is, of course, Hans. He speaks perfect English and explains that the work-camp never got organized. The burgermeister in the meantime phoned the Paris office. They tell me, I am to return to Krefeld for the remainder of my time in Germany. However, the burgermeister opens his arms expansively. Hans translates. "You must stay here for some days as a guest of the city."

"You will stay in my home," Hans continues, smiling broadly.

Stunned, I gladly accept.

Hans' home, like the rest of the town, could be a set for Richard Wagner's *Die Meistersinger von Nürnberg*. Built of clay and reinforced with oak beams, the barn is in the middle of the house. I sleep between voluminous goose down comforters. Cows are taken out to pasture in the morning and brought into the house in the evening. Water is carried from the town well.

During those idyllic days, Hans and another student, Erick, and I hike in the surrounding hills. In a pasture on the side of one of the hills, we lay on our backs. Looking up into a cloudless sky, and chewing on straws, we marveled that only a few years before our people were killing each other. *Du, du liegst mir im Herzen ...*

The night before I leave for Krefeld Hans takes me to a gathering of the men's chorus. They pump me for information about American jazz, about which I know very little. Stumbling on the words, I sing *Edelweiss* along with the chorus.

The following morning I stop by to thank the burgermeister and am again shocked when he hands me a hundred marks.

I tell him, "I can't accept the money."

Hans tells me, I must. His people are grateful the Americans spared their village. A lump in my throat, I board the train and that evening I am greeted with open arms as I trudge, rucksack-laden, into the Krefeld *yugungevonhime.*

~~~~~~~~~~~~~

A gibbous moon weaves through palm fronds as I climb the honey and cedar bushes covered embankment, to the cottage, where I say I come to write, but more than write, I relive my long existence, at least the times I choose to tell about, and some I wish that had never happened.

~~~~~~~~~~~~~

The week after I returned to Krefeld, when I came in from work, a telegram awaited me. The message, gone first to Paris and then forwarded to Krefeld, reached me a month after my brother's plane disappeared through the clouds over North Korea. I didn't tell my friends what was in the telegram, but they understood it was bad news and left me to my thoughts.

The telegram said there were no further sightings of the plane or my brother. Perhaps not in the ordinary sense, yet I felt my brother watching as, hurting and confused, I walked out over the Rhine River Bridge. Did I even have a right to be hurt, considering what my mother and sister are suffering, my dad gone? And the cloud of suffering hanging over the bloody rubble left by my country's patch-work-bombing. Even in my grief, the irony does not escape me that my brother was on a bombing run at the same time I was rebuilding what my nation had destroyed. I welcomed the cold drizzling rain soaking clothes and hair and mingling with my tears.

A coal-laden barge ghosts through the inky Rhine below. I watch the stern's red light suspended in darkness glimmer until night swallows the craft. Lights were out when I returned to the hostel.

The next morning I bid tearful goodbyes to my work-camp friends. I needed to wander, yet I had little idea of where I was going.

~~~~~~

I make another drink and drag a chair out onto the porch. Lights from fishermen's boats blink in darkness.

~~~~~~

After Krefeld, the rest of my time in Europe is a blur. I recall squeezing my rucksack and myself into the back of a Volkswagen Beetle, two jolly men weighing well over two hundred pounds squished in the front seats. A Swiss girl I met in the work camp, and I hike in the Alps for a week then I hitchhike to Holland where I was scheduled for passage back to the States on a troop carrier converted to a student ship. Almost in a daze, I visited the Rijks museum with its rich collections of Rembrandt and Vermeer paintings. Yet it was Van Gogh's paintings at the Stedelijk Museum, that most moved me.

Walking along a canal, I met Gerhard, tall, a head of blond ringlets. His small room looks out over a moonlight-glittered canal. We would met again years later in Greenwich Village. Neither of us was the same person who met on a starry night beside an Amsterdam canal.

Shortly before boarding my ship, I drifted into a bookstore and buy an English translation of Dostoevsky's *The Brothers Karamazov*.

~~~~~~

A high-school-aged group, wearing T-shirts ablaze with, "Wander with Windsey," boarded ahead of me. Their leader, potbellied, whistle on the end of a lanyard, jolly Windsey, brought up the rear. I overheard one of the Windseys reply to a fellow passenger who enquired where they had visited, "Oh I don't know, but if it is famous, we've seen it."

"Did you visit the Louvre?" the questioner asks.

"The big museum? Yeah, boring!" Callow as when a month before they set out on their expensive tour of Europe's great cultural shrines.

Another youth complains, "If these are the happiest days of my life, I want to die!"

My compartment was again below water level. There were no deck chairs, no Myrna Loy. I spent most of the passage up on deck in a sleeping bag leaning against a bulkhead, reading Dostoevsky.

The ship's captain tried to navigate around a storm, but the ship still rolled as if it had a round bottom. To avoid being swept overboard, I wedged myself between an exhaust vent and stairs, where there is enough light to continue reading into the night.

Near the end of the voyage, I came to a story in Dostoyevsky's book where Jesus returns to earth. The Grand Inquisitor visits Jesus in prison where the church has sent Him, and asked Jesus, why had he returned to upset the order the church has established in His name during His absence. I feel dark inside and wonder if it is right for me to go back to the study of theology.

I finish the thick book as the ship sails under the Verrazano Bridge into New York Harbor. The Windseys, tired of wearing their traveling clothes, throw them overboard.

~~~~~~~~~

CHELEM, 2016

Clif has caught a ride out from the city. We sit sipping our drinks on the porch, our chairs drawn close together. Lights of far-out boats gleam like jade beads strung across the inky darkness.

I rinse our glasses and turn out the lights. The soft hush of waves lapping the sand down below the honey and cedar bushes lulls us to sleep. I dream of my brother at the control of a Piper Cub. He learned to fly at a grassy field near our farm. Sometimes he'd dip the plane's wing as he flew over our barn. *Du, du liegst mir im herzen.*

Stranger in a Foreign Land

~~~~~~~~

I HAVE CLEANED THE WINDOWS, DUSTED THE FURNITURE AND now, a folded towel under my knees, I attack the wax buildup along the baseboard. Alvin Labatt, Harvard Professor of French Literature, needs help readying his apartment for a party this evening. Sitting back on my haunches, I admire my work. How satisfying and uncomplicated.

Job finished, I jump on my scooter and head to my maid's quarters room. I must hurry to get dressed in time to return to the party as a guest. Labatt has hired someone else to tend bar and serve hors d'oeuvres.

I'm broke, getting around on a rickety motor scooter, living in servant's quarters, a gardener, and happily scrubbing floors.

How quickly my life has changed. A year before I was a minister at First Church Congregational, tooling around in a convertible, sharing with my handsome lover a great apartment on Beacon Hill, and gobbling up my salad days. Then my lover took off with a young friend. I began taking uppers, amphetamines, to lose weight and lift my spirits, and downers, barbiturates, when I came down off the uppers and felt like killing myself—nights I'd gulp Butisol as well as slugs of bourbon. I was killing my sweet lover with my possessiveness and moods, along with myself, and questioning what the hell I was doing in the church. I was thirty-two and needed to find out where to go with the rest of my life. Why I thought I'd find more answers traveling than cruising bars or praying beats me.

Letter of credit in my pocket on a snowy morning, the man I met during my last semester in theology school, and with whom I had shared the following eight years, drove me to the airport. I was flying to St. Thomas, Virgin Islands, and my first stop on what will turn out to be a year and a half vagabonding around the world.

A friend who owns the Foc'sle Bar needed a vacation, so on arrival on the island, I took over—wiping the bar, flipping beer caps, and mixing Cuba Libres. It is a sleazy, last-chance bar.

~~~~~~~~~~

The island's streets were jammed with tramping mobs; Carnival had reached a fevered pitch, climaxing a week of growing madness. The air, redolent of sweat, vomit, and beer rang with the bing-bang-bong of steel bands, clapping hands, tromping feet, and beer cans beating syncopated rhythms.

Miss Louise, a beautiful island lady with ten children and no husband, sat at the bar with a film producer. She said, "Mama says I am like a bird sittin' in a tree, laughin' and singin' and talkin'. I need to be free. Guess I am a bird. Why worry about your problems? I say do something about them and have a good time." Louise gave away her last two children and had herself fixed so she couldn't have anymore. Later, she and the producer sped by in an MG, scarves flying behind them. They screamed and laughed as they hit a bump and were lost into the night.

The crowd, still tramping, eating and drinking, moved to the waterfront. Midnight: Only the barmaid, a Puerto Rican couple lost in an embrace, and a man sleeping at the end of the bar and I remained in the Foc'sle. I turned to the little book I had brought with me, *The Courage To Be*, by Paul Tillich, a philosopher/theologian, who had escaped the Nazis.

I had gone to hear his Museum of Modern Art lecture on Art and Reality, which opened a new way of thinking about art.

"Art breaks up the surface of reality, and through the cracks, one may glimpse ultimate reality," Tillich had said.

Ultimate Reality! So I'm not alone! Others sense that there is something more. Tillich expressed thoughts I had never been able to put into words, sensing that a transcendent reality underlies the surface of things.

Following the lecture, I sat almost all afternoon gazing at Picasso's huge *Guernica* painting. The heartbreaking image of the terrified horse still burns in my mind. Late that same afternoon I moved on to Henri Matisse's *The Dance*, and from then on I have confused art—art which speaks from the soul—with religion—not only painting but literature and music.

Because Paul Tillich was nominally a member of our church, though he never attended, I was chosen to ask him to give a lecture at a meeting of church educators I was helping organize. I'd already heard that the famous professor, whose picture had been on the cover of Time magazine, liked his cocktails.

His office in Harvard Yard was across the Cambridge Common from the church I served. My appointment was his last of that day, so, after he had agreed to speak at our meeting, we continued our conversation at a bar near the Yard.

"Do you know bourbon, our American whiskey?" I asked Tillich.

"No," he said. "Be my teacher."

"Very well," I laughed. "You stick to philosophy, and I'll stick to whiskey." That sort of broke the ice. In fact, drinking sort of glued our brief friendship.

I confessed that I had not read his famous three-volume *Systematic Theology*—still haven't.

"Don't bother," he said. "Read *The Courage to Be*."

And reading his little book, I have become aware of my anxiety about meaninglessness. I was, and am still, haunted by the evangelist seeming to single me out, shouting, *"God has a purpose for you!"*

I came to a passage in the book I had underlined when I first read it. "This is the message; a new reality has appeared in which you are reconciled. To enter the *new being,* we do not have to do anything. We must only be open to be grasped by it."

Some years later, when I learned that he was ill in the hospital, I sent him a bottle of Jack Daniel's with a note "Spirits from your pastor."

~~~~~~~~~~~~

A large sweaty man, pallid from fear, rushes into the bar screaming, "Call the police! A girl has been stabbed down by the waterfront. She is bleeding."

I called the police. The maid ran out with the man, and I returned to my reading.

I wasn't a particularly gifted student. The scholarship I received almost by accident, whisked me out of conservative Oklahoma to Boston and liberal theology. Escaping the Bible Belt, I felt as if I had stumbled from the desert into an oasis after a long journey. In place of moral rectitude and believing the unbelievable, I was initiated into the struggle for social and economic justice. Martin Luther King, working on his doctorate, was a classmate.

Lonely nights, I looked out across the glittering Charles River from my dormitory window. Downriver, on the Cambridge side, beneath the somber dome of MIT, geniuses poured over the inscrutable, while upriver the bright and privileged studied beneath the lighted cupola of Harvard's Dunster House. I had no idea then that one of those students was John Updike. I would one day find his writings to be deeply satisfying and inspiring, mainly his chronicle of the life of the middle-class everyman, Harry "Rabbit" Angstrom, a car salesman, was much like my father, a traveling auto-supply salesman.

"Nothing is more distinctive of the Old Being than the separation of man from man." And thus I read between the opening of beer bottles and mixing rum and Coca-Cola into the morning hours.

Four a.m., the Puerto Rican couple leave. I turn off the jukebox. The drunk sleeping at the end of the bar slips off the stool. I lift him to his feet and help him out the door, pull down the shutters and lock the door behind me. As I climb the moonlit hill, I see only the eyes and teeth of the few stragglers I pass.

"One is afraid of having lost or of losing the meaning of one's existence," I read that night, before closing Tillich's book.

~~~~~~~~

Morning, I take my coffee out onto the porch overlooking the harbor. The elegant yachts have sailed away, and Puerto Ricans returned to their island, leaving St. Thomas exhausted. Beer cans and wine bottles will clutter the gutters for weeks. The bar owner is due back soon. Tickets bought, I will soon be off to London, Rome, Accra, Ghana, and Cape Town. From there, I don't know.

I toss the bitter coffee into the bushes and head down the hill to the bar.

~~~~~~~~

Eleven a.m., the island still sleeps. I carry buckets of water out and wash down the open sewer running along the side of the bar. Swarms of flies chase stale urine down to the front of the still-shuttered building next door. The white-hot sunlight streams through the door opened to the empty street and cuts a long rectangle across the splintered floor. I grab a can of insecticide to kill gnats dancing in the light. "Nah, let them live." I return the spray can to the bar.

A shadow fills the rectangle as someone steps into the bar. "Hi," a well-formed young man says, approaching the bar. "Shirley sent me."

Shirley owns a sign shop a few doors down. She's from Oklahoma City. She and the bar's owner sort of took me under their wings when I first made it from my little town into the big city. They could tell I hadn't a clue about what was going on.

The newcomer takes a stool across from where I am standing behind the bar. Like fine dust, light from the outside seems to cling to him. The gnats have become a garland around his head.

"I'm Martin. He extends his hand. "Shirley said for me to tell you I'm a gift." He smiles sheepishly. About six feet, solid yet gracefully built, curly auburn hair, he had an air of innocence about him, as if he were freshly minted.

There it happens again! The light in the bar brightens each time he smiles.

"How about a beer or something?" I ask.

"Thanks, but I don't drink, but you go on ahead. You live alone?" Martin asks.

"For now."

"When do you get off?"

"Carnival is over, if we don't have any customers, I'll close at ten. You're from the States?" I ask.

"Yes, but I'm living in San Juan for now." Martin stands to leave. "Got to go back and help, Shirley." He reaches into his pocket.

"Nah, it's on the house."

"Well, nice meeting you." "See you around," he calls as he passes into the blinding sunlight, taking some of the bar's light with him.

Precisely at ten, Martin shows up.

I close the bar, and we climbed the hill toward where I was staying, Martin's arm across my shoulder.

He stays with me, helping clean around the place until it was time for the bar owner to return.

I didn't quite get it when he told me he gave Shirley back her money. What money was he talking about?

Martin packed his few things. He was taking the noon ferry back to San Juan. He urged me to stop off to see him in San Juan before I head on. He practically begged me. I told him I would stop on my way through to New York, where I was scheduled to head on to Europe and then Africa. He threw his bag over his shoulder. He seemed forlorn as he headed down the hill to catch his boat.

I stood on my porch watching him trudge down the hill toward the pier. Out in Charlotte Amalie Harbor, a small sloop sails past its protective headlands, making for the open sea. I wanted to call out, "Turn back little boat." Martin and I and anchorless folks like us are on that boat. We are like the bird in an old Greek poem:

Little bird of mine, who has wandered far,
A foreign country greets you. I too know your sorrow.
What shall I send you, stranger? What can I offer you?
If I send apples, they will rot; roses fade,
Grapes dry out, and quinces wither.
I'll send you my tears in a golden scarf.
What else can I send you, stranger, in a foreign land?

The owner returned. I flew across to San Juan. Martin met me at the airport.

A week later, when I started to pack, he came into the room, sat on the bed, and flipped my bag shut. "You don't need to do all that traveling you're planning to do. Stay with me. I'll take care of our expenses. You can do all the writing or whatever you wanted to do right here."

"But how," I asked, "would we live?"

"Oh, easy. What the old fellows I meet give me is plenty for both of us." Then I understood what he meant when he said he had returned Shirley's money.

I extended my stay another week before I caught my flight.

Eighteen months later, the day was cloudy as the freighter I have taken out of Yokohama, Japan, sailed into the port of Oakland. As the ship pulled against the pier, the clouds broke, and a shaft of light fell onto Martin, leaning against a packing crate.

~~~~~~

Most of the guests have gathered at Professor Labatt's by the time I skid in front of the house I had just finished cleaning an hour and a half before.

~~~~~~

I still open *The Courage To Be* and find new depth each time I do. The meaning of *being* changes as my hair turns white and wrinkles form. This octogenarian now understands the purpose of life is *living*—living each moment, each day and night, as full and kindly as possible.

~~~~~~

Martin volunteers as a head usher for the San Francisco Opera. He has adopted a Puerto Rican boy and sent him through Stanford. When one of my books appears on Amazon, it receives effusive reviews from a Martin Diaz.

Elephant

~~~~~~~~~~

I ARRIVE IN CAPE TOWN, ONE OF THE MOST BEAUTIFUL CITIES in the world, squeezed as it is between the Cape of Good Hope and the sheer bluff of three-thousand foot high Table Mountain with its clouds like spilled sugar cascading down its face.

I had only a vague idea as to where to go next —Johannesburg, Nairobi, Addis Ababa, Luxor, Timbuktu? You name it. I was feeling like the bird in the Greek folk song: *Little bird of mine who has wandered far, a foreign. . .* The love affair I had thought would last all my life had ended after six years. Yeah, I was bleeding my way around the world. Well, sort of. I was reading John-Paul Sartre and bouncing, you might say, from existential moment to existential moment.

I stayed in Cape Town a couple of weeks. A guy I met gave me an introduction to his friends in Durban, a port city on the Indian Ocean I had never heard of. The Durban fellow handed me on to Walter Boxer in Johannesburg, and thus I was vagabonding my way around the planet.

When I showed up at his door, Walter was still dressed for the office, in a finely tailored dark suit, maroon cravat tied in a Windsor knot. I noticed the gold cufflinks and on his ring finger a star ruby the size of a Cadillac bumper, not on his pinky, thank God. His black hair flecked with white strands was parted and slicked back.

Walter was Warner Brothers' South Africa representative. He bore the suavity I had imagined for a Hollywood executive, but didn't act like it.

"Make yourself at home while I get out of uniform and into something comfortable." He handed me a beer and took one himself.

The beer was cold. The living room looked out through floor-to-ceiling windows on a cityscape that resembled almost any big Midwestern city in the States.

Walter reappeared smelling of French cologne. His idea of comfortable was still elegant He was a medium-sized man of about forty-five with only a slight paunch.

"I've got plenty of room. You're welcome to stay here," he said. "Use the guest bedroom as long as you like."

I got the feeling that I wasn't the first guy headed up the east coast of Africa to receive Walter's hospitality.

The following evening, Walter invited a couple of friends over for cocktails, and at some point, the conversation got around to the Kruger Park, Africa's second-largest game reserve.

"Let's all go!" It was Terry Cowling, the younger of the two guests. I judged that he was about my age, thirty-two, his partner closer to Walter's age.

Walter had friends with a compound near the park. "The guy owns a diamond mine, never uses the place. He has invited me to use it whenever I want to. Why don't I give him a call?"

Terry's partner couldn't leave his work, but urged Terry to go on. Like his partner, Terry's accent was British, but unlike his partner's long English face, Terry's was Irish Mick, puckish and ruddy. He had reddish blond hair and impish blue eyes. Tightly built, one imagined him on a soccer field.

Me, I'm built sort of like Terry except my build comes from summers working on farms and swimming, and I've got dark hair and gray eyes, not China blue.

~~~~~~~~~~~~~~~~~

That afternoon I soared like a hawk and watched our Austin-Cambridge weave through Johannesburg's suburbs and out onto the High Veldt, a great expanse of land like America's High Plains.

The slow rise of the land, viewed through the crystalline air, seemed limitless and, from the hawk's eye view, our car appeared no more than a beetle crawling across vastness. Flat-topped thorn trees appeared to be mere flicks of paint on a blank canvas. Ahead the highway shrunk into a ribbon, disappeared, reappeared as a thread and then vanished altogether into the far distance.

We sped through Bantustans where the natives were confined, the white Afrikaners having reserved the arable land for themselves. As if to push back the surrounding desolation, the Bantu kraals, wattle huts enclosed within whitewashed mud walls, were lavishly decorated in orange, blue and yellow designs. A young man wearing a beautiful beaded belt stood near the gate of one of the kraals. In exchange for a candy bar, he allowed us to take his picture. Soon we were confronted with a dozen small outstretched hands. An elaborately adorned young woman appeared. Her photo cost us a roll of candy mints.

After about three hours, we dropped into a green valley, where a slender steeple rose from a cluster of houses nestled in the curve of a river. The scene was reminiscent of a New England village. The residents were Afrikaners, mainly folks of Dutch ancestry who enforced apartheid, a rigid separation between white and black South African citizens, the people whose land the Afrikaners confiscated, much like Native Americans were treated.

Plateaus rose high above meandering streams irrigating the fertile bottom land, and the air grew redolent of orange blossoms.

Finally, we arrived at the turnoff for Matalian, population 74. As directed, we crossed railroad tracks and came to the entrance to Glendora Farm. A quarter of a mile down a lane lined with jacaranda trees, their lavender blossoms hanging like bunches of grapes, we arrived at a cluster of thatched adobe-walled buildings on the bank of a river, our host's compound. He had wired ahead to his houseman, "Big One," an enormous black man who greeted us as we stepped from the car.

The place was opened and ready for our arrival. Four thatched-roofed buildings stood on a smoothly polished red concrete platform. The buildings consisted of two-bedroom buildings, a central living and dining room and a cookhouse/bathroom building. All the buildings opened to a view of the Crocodile River and jungle beyond. The ground around the platform was bare, hard packed dirt, almost as smooth as the platform and the same terra-cotta red. About a hundred and fifty feet from the platform a high wire fence separated civilization from Kruger Park. A startling British note was a rose bed in the middle of a curbed island of lawn. All the rest of the area was hard packed red dirt.

Big One filled a huge tub with steaming water. I won the draw, and without hesitating, plunged in. Up to my chin in suds through the bathroom's opened doors, I gazed across the Crocodile River, to shadows gathered in Kruger Park. Walter brought me a dry martini and smoked oysters on toast. I savored the mingled fragrances of Beefeater's gin, bubbling soap, and jungle, and concluded then and there that I was meant for luxury, which is wasted on those accustomed to it.

Growing tipsy, as we in turn bathed and drank, someone put on an Elaine May and Mike Nichols recording in which May plays the dumb blonde and Nichols plays the part of the talk-show host, Jack Parr. In the recording Nichols, impersonating Parr, asks what May thinks about Albert Schweitzer. She replies that they are close, but not yet intimate. Nichols says, "You know Schweitzer is in Africa." May responds, "So Al's in Africa!" We thought the line was hilarious and throughout the rest of the trip we kept repeating the line, "So Al's in Africa." We laughed so much my sides ached. (You had to have been there.)

We finished baths and cocktails and, giggling like teenagers, a bottle of wine in hand, we drove in search of dinner at the only place of business in Matalain. A rough wood table and a few chairs sat amidst pots and pans, kegs of nails and coils of ropes.

Over our two bottles of red wine, the garrulous owner, The Baron friends called him, recounted his odyssey. He had fled Lithuania ahead of the Bolsheviks, settled in Vienna and then fled the Nazis. Too old to escape, he lamented South Africa's choking apartheid.

Despite his woes, The Baron cheerfully prepared a savory meal of veal and garden vegetables and a dessert of mulberries over ice cream he had made himself. After dinner, he showed us the venom splattered glass cage containing spitting adders, which he had recently caught. The snakes are particularly lethal, as they spit as far as eight feet to blind their victims. The earth around dwellings is kept clear and smooth and the platform polished so that the vipers cannot slither into the rooms.

~~~~~~~~~~

The next morning, before the sun had cleared the treetops, Big One opened a gate for us to enter Kruger the back way. Right away, we encountered huge red-beaked blackbirds bigger than large turkeys, and, moments later, a family of wild boars. The toothy male threatened while his sow preened.

We followed the road along a river bank where hippopotamuses imitated boulders and crocodiles imitated logs. Heading further into the forest, we came upon a family of giraffes. Apparently as interested in us as we were in her, one of the giraffes leaned down and, fluttering her vampish long eyelashes, peered in our rented Austen-Cambridge window. Walter blew her kisses.

We passed through scrub onto a broad savannah stretching miles to the blue outline of mountains rising from neighboring Mozambique—shoals of zebra, wildebeests, and gazelles grazing peacefully in the sea of grass. None of us spoke. We didn't ooh and ah; we had been given a glimpse of Heaven—the way life on earth should be. Then a gazelle lifted its head, spotted us and, on signal, an antlered corps de ballet sprang into elegantly choreographed leaps, followed by rivers of wildebeests and zebras, black and white and gray, swirling through the tall grass.

Walter shifted and quietly backed away. In the denser forest, we passed corridors of smashed undergrowth and came to a washtub-sized deposit shimmering with insects. We were upwind; still, stockyard fumes filled the car, but no elephants were in sight.

Terry announced, "I'll kiss the first one who spots an elephant."

I crawled out the car window and, sitting on the windowsill, called, as I would a puppy, "Here elephant, here elephant, elephant, elephant!"

In that instant—I'm not embroidering the facts as I am wont to do—in that very instant about fifty yards in front of us, an elephant broke through the trees; first one, then two, finally a majestic bull stomped into view. The bull turned facing us. His enormous ears flapping and his trunk upturned, he was picture perfect. Terry handed me my camera. "Closer, closer," I yelled.

The bull trumpeted and stomped. Magnificent! I snapped away, thrilled by a photo that could get me on the cover of *National Geographic*!

"Not yet," I screamed when Terry grabbed my legs dragging me back into the car. "Just one more shot!"

The car's gears clashed into reverse, and the car careened backward. I was still muttering about my lost photo when I saw the bull was charging, gaining! There was neither time nor space to turn, and, in reverse, the car wasn't able to outdistance the beast. We were crunched down in our seats, peering over the dashboard and expecting at any moment a hoof to stomp us into the axels. Then, inches from the car's hood, he reared back onto his haunches, raised his trunk like a Golden Glove champion, trumpeted triumphantly, and, rump swaying, sauntered back to his admiring herd.

"So Al's in Africa!" Terry quipped.

～～～～～～

"Christ almighty! You bloody fools!" The ranger at the park exit exploded when we reported what had happened. "Didn't you read the sign as you entered the park? That area is off-limits. It's calving time! We don't even let the big tour vans with experienced guides in there, much less puny cars like yours. You're God-damn lucky to be alive! Get out before I have you arrested."

～～～～～～

I kept up with Walter, sending him cards as I zigzagged on around the world —Nairobi, Beirut, New Delia, Bangkok, San Francisco and on to New York where I bunked in with a friend. I had been back about a year when I got a call from him inviting me to a party. He was in the city on some Warner Bros. business. Well, the party was a big glitzy affair where I was feeling out of place until Walter pulled me aside.

"I've got a surprise for you," he said and led me upstairs to a study where a guy was sitting in a swivel chair with his back to us.

"Look who's here," Walter said. The guy swiveled around and then just sat there staring as if he had seen a ghost. Finally, he jumped up, ran around the desk and grabbed me.

"I owe you one, elephant boy," Terry Cowling said, pulling me to him and planting a kiss hard on my mouth, thus fulfilling the promise he made back at Kruger Park.

The Blue Scarab

It was ten in the morning as I recall, maybe a little later, when the blue scarab first caught my eye—better I should say, its blue glint winked at me. I had allowed myself to sleep late. Why shouldn't I? I had no one to account to. I had been alone, more or less, since I said my Boston goodbyes six months before. *No, I'll take a cab to the airport. It's best we say goodbye here at the door.* Why is that? That is a long story I'd prefer not to go into at this point.

Why had I even set out on this journey? I'm not sure I can explain even if I were so inclined, and *why* I am in Luxor, the site of ancient Thebes, staying in the Winter Palace Hotel is not particularly germane to my finding the blue scarab; suffice to say, I had barely made it to the final breakfast call that morning.

Having finished breakfast, I stepped out onto the awning-shaded porch of the sprawling heavily-corniced Victorian structure, built in the heyday of Britain's longest reigning monarch, where red-faced Englishmen already sipped Pimm's-cups, and gravel-throated complained that the colonies are nothing as they used to be. There was not the slightest breeze. The Nile lay flat as a frying pan, feluccas leaned against the shore like prostrate whales, and their steersmen lay supine in the shade of limp lateen sails. Indeed, already the heat brought to mind Noel Coward's *Mad Dogs and Englishmen Go Out in the Midday Sun!* Intrepid Tilly-hatted Elderhostel, water-bottle-toting elders, were already returning from Tutankhamen's tomb, as pith-helmeted Germans staggered back from Karnak Temple, guarded by Ramses' giant-muscled statues.

I decided, before the heat became utterly unbearable, to take a stroll along the street beside the Nile, and found myself engulfed in a bucolic fragrance, reminiscent of life I thought I had managed to leave on the farm, the smell emanating from the hot pavement frying the droppings left by carriage horses.

Flies buzzed around the entrance of a shop I stepped in to escape for a moment the acetylene heat. As my eyes adjusted, I made out an Arab sitting in the shade just inside the shop's doorway. At least he looked Arab, dark complexion and dressed in a white robe. With the palmetto fan, he cooled himself and shooed the flies, waved me in and, in the same gesture, signaled to a scrawny man hovering over brass kettles on a heap of coals down by the river's edge. Between languorous beats of his palmetto, Hamed, I was to learn his name, gestured for me to take the stool across from him.

He asked if I were American.

"Why, yes," I said. "How did you guess?"

In reply, he simply chuckled. We were about the same age, I judged. He didn't appear to be much stouter than I am but with the robe, it was hard to tell. He seemed to have a suavity one associates with oriental merchants.

As we spoke, the scrawny man brought from the Nile bank two steaming brass cups. Hamed poured a half-cup of sugar into one and offered what I took to be tea. I'd have much-preferred lemon-ade, but in the Orient, one must accept, *always* with the *right* hand, and, if at all possible, consume whatever is offered. With a smile and slight bow I took the scalding syrup, as in the same moment, further back in the shop, like a firefly in a midnight forest, a sparkle flashed on and off. Perhaps, I thought, it might be my eyes not yet adjusted from the sunlight, yet it tweaked my curiosity as to what might lie in the shop's gloomy clutter.

Tea ceremony complete, Hamed invited me to look over his antiquities or so advertised. It was, of course, the only polite thing for me to do. Most of the objects, he told me, had been found in the sands, on the other side of the river, in the Valley of the Kings, near the Pharaohs' cave tombs.

Hamed told me that, centuries ago, in their haste to find gold and precious stones, grave robbers scattered thousands of amulets, scarabs, and the like. Although a trinket may have once laid near Pharaoh's mummy, it is of little or no archeological value. Thus it is legal to sell these small fragments from antiquity. As I write, fifty years after the events that took place on the banks of the Nile, I now understand that words, such as *legal,* which I once thought conveyed immutable facts, are imprecise at best. Pretending curiosity I didn't have, I feigned interest, as Hamed directed me toward piles of dusty curios which reminded me of the arrowheads and broken pottery displayed in roadside shops along the highways in New Mexico or Arizona.

There was no sparkle in the dull browns, yellows, and greens ceramic bugs. No wonder the grave robbers cast them aside. Yet, as dull as these scarabs seemed, their very abundance, if indeed they are authentic, suggested the power the ancient Egyptians believed these scarabs imparted. Hamed seemed to me to be an honest guy. I know, I have been accused of seeing the world through rose-tinted glasses, but my rule is to trust people until they show that you can't. That said, I didn't altogether dismiss the possibility that there could be a hot kiln, somewhere on the back streets of Luxor, filled with hundreds of unsacred, powerless curios. But if the pile of scarabs I sifted my hand through were fake, why hadn't the forgers made them a little prettier?

Hamed had been gracious. I should buy a trinket to show folks back home and brag that it came from a mummy's tomb, never mind if it were genuine or not. I didn't plan to spend a fortune, for I still had continents to cross.

I don't know why. Maybe it was the mummies' tombs, but lately, I began to think about my own destiny, my fate—the fate of these scarabs.

I had no intimation that three years after that day I sat on the banks of the Nile River toying with an ancient amulet dug from sand near Pharaohs' tombs, I'd be studying for an understudy part in the Broadway show *Kismet*, singing:

Princes come, Princes go,
An hour of pomp and show they know;
Princes come and over the sands,
And over the sands of time they go.
Wise men come,
Ever promising the riddle of life to know,
Wise men come, Ah,
But over the sands.
The silent sands of time they go
Lovers come,
Lovers go.
And all that there is to know
Lovers know;
Only lovers know.

I was looking to buy something by way of expressing my appreciation for Hamed's hospitality. He was the only person I had talked with since I arrived in Egypt — him and Tab Hunter, but Tab wasn't really a conversation. We were both cashing checks at the counter of the Nile Hilton at the same time. Hunter was searching for a pen, so I loaned him mine even before I had finished signing mine. The handsome movie star's smile was my reward. (One wants to get as much mileage out of such serendipities as one can.)

As scarabs are supposed to be sacred, I thought they'd make an interesting gift for my Catholic aunt. I set my price limit at five dollars. I'd pretty much forgotten the blue sparkle until, toward the bottom of the scarab pile, *there it came again*, the sparkle. I dug a little farther and touched a smooth surface cooler than the other objects. I worked out of the pile of ugly bugs a lovely cobalt blue porcelain scarab with a silvery underglaze.

"How much would this cost?" I asked.

"You don't want that," Hamad said. "I am sure it is a fake. It shouldn't have been in with the others."

"But I do want it." For some reason, I wanted it very much.

"Well, if you want, I have to have" . . . Whatever the amount in piasters, I calculated it to be about twenty-five American dollars—over budget. As I said, I had miles and miles ahead of me.

"Thanks, Hamed," I said. "And thanks for the tea. I'll think it over."

"This one," he held one of the dung scarabs, "I can let you have for half that price, and I'm sure it is genuine."

"You are very kind." I was getting a little suave myself. "I'll come back later."

He cut the price on the blue as I headed for the blinding light of the door. "You are too kind," I tell him, but. I felt a pull, a yearning to possess the little blue trinket.

I was inordinately disappointed to find the shop shuttered when I went back to it after lunch. It wasn't the scarab as much as it was someone to talk with. I returned to my room, turned the ceiling fan on high, and crawled into bed with Agatha Christie's, *Death on the Nile*. When I awakened, the Sun God Ra neared the sandy horizon. I splashed water on my face and reentered the world of the Pharaohs.

The shop was open, and Hamed greeted me like a long-lost friend. We repeated the hot-syrup ceremony. Hamad told me that the ugly scarab, which he urged me to buy, had once laid in Tutankhamen's tomb. In Cairo, he told me, I would pay a hundred dollars or more. I smiled, but didn't budge. I was hooked on the blue scarab, but, much as I wanted it, I would pay no more than five dollars. Why didn't he want me to have it? Though the scavenger claimed he had dug it from the sands near the tomb of Queen Hatshepsut who came to the throne of Egypt about 1478 BC, Hamad said, the curio was most likely a counterfeit, which was why he didn't want me to buy it; the dung-colored scarab was far more likely to be of ancient origin. He practically wept, as he came down to ten dollars for the blue scarab. I thanked him and, feeling more and more oriental, said I'd think a little more about the purchase. Bargaining had become a high point in my day. The blue scarab wasn't really that important, or was it?

I joined guests on the Winter Palace porch, where the English gentlemen returned to their porch positions, continue their sloe-gin-fizz induced decline into oblivion, as the Sun God Ra sizzled into the limestone bluffs on the far side of the Nile.

I awakened with a blinding headache, nevertheless determined to see King Tut's Tomb that morning. I took two aspirins, slipped into shorts and made it to first call for breakfast. With a notable exception, the British have done their colonies grave disservices. I have in mind their version of toilet paper, and in general their food. However, *English breakfast* almost makes up for it: smoked kippers, suet pudding, and beef-and-kidney pie. I stuffed myself with sausage and even some kidneys and then ran for the early boat.

As I made my way up the gully to the mouth of Tutankhamen's tomb, I again felt obeisance should be paid, and I resented the chatter of fellow gawkers. *If they would only be quiet, they might have felt a sense of awe, a sacredness.* I had felt the same the day before as I walked from the river up through an avenue of Sphinxes toward Ramses' towering statue.

By the time I returned to the east bank of the river, Hamed's shop was again shuttered closed.

The next morning, eager to avoid scalding tea syrup, I took two coffees heavily laced with milk and sugar to Hamad's shop. As we sat, he asked about my family. I told him my father died while I was in college. He told me his grandfather had founded the shop shortly after the Winter Palace was constructed, and his father carried on the tradition. One older brother had gone off to England and another to the oil fields in Libya and his sisters to arranged marriages. The brother in England was arranging for him to come there to study archeology when his father's long battle with malaria came to an end. Allah, it seemed, had decreed that Hamad should run the family business and look after his grieving mother.

It was my last day. I'd be on the train to Cairo the next morning. We hugged this time as I left with the blue scarab in my pocket. I'd paid the equivalent of eight dollars.

I was halfway up the Winter Palace steps when Hamad breathlessly caught up with me waving the money I had given him. "Please, it is a mistake! I cannot let you have the scarab." He was almost crying.

"You want more for it?"

"No, no. It should not be for sale! I like you too much."

"But why, Hamed don't you want me to have the scarab?" I had grown to like Hamed, felt we had become friends, but I was becoming annoyed.

"It is fake. It should not be in my shop."

"But it is beautiful. OK," I said, "thirty piasters more!"

"I don't want the money. If you will not return the scarab, at least take the money back." He shoved the wad of piasters into my hand and ran back toward his shop.

I hated leaving Hamad on that note. I returned to my hotel room, disturbed that I'd be leaving in the morning and wouldn't see Hamad again to repair the tear in our friendship. I placed his money in an envelope and handed it to the desk clerk with instructions that the money should be returned to Hamed. I had made a number of friendships along the way, and each time I moved on, I felt fraudulent. As brief as the acquaintances, they felt genuine, and yet, as I moved on, I knew we'd likely never meet again; maybe we'd exchange letters, but they would taper off and in a year or so we might not be able to remember the name of the nice person we met in a sidewalk café in Cape Town or Johannesburg.

Most of the wrinkles had fallen out of my white wash-and-wear pants and shirt. It was my dressiest outfit—all white, belt and shoes, completed with a red and green silk ascot at my neck. It occurred to me that the beautiful scarab I slipped into my pocket would make a handsome neck piece. I was a little early for dinner, the bar was filled with a tour group, and the chairs on the porch were all taken, so I crossed over to the riverside of the avenue and joined the promenade as I had done the first evening I arrived in the ancient city. Some of the guests were boarding one of the feluccas tied to the bank. Two other boats had already set sail, leaving one still waiting. The steersman waved to me, "American, come—moonlight sail." He gestured that I should come aboard. Ascot and all, I was disappointed he didn't take me for British. Not wanting to be snooty, I replied that I was waiting for dinner. He called back, "Then wait on my boat and I practice my English."

I succumbed. He reached over and helped me across the narrow gangplank. He was not the steersman I had noticed on the same boat my first night. "For English lesson, I give you free sail," he said, once I landed on board.

With a long pole, he pushed us off from the bank. The sail caught the wind, and we glided out into the middle of the river. It was one of those, *look at me now* moments, *far from home, sailing in a felucca, under lateen sail between the ancient city of Thebes and the Valley of the Kings.* The other boats, having headed in for the first call to dinner, we were alone in the middle of the Nile. I looked back at the lights coming on in the hotel just as the boat leaned. The bundle of rags stuffed under the stern, I had noticed while coming aboard, shifted, and a hand flopped out.

"American!" The boatman had caught me staring at the hand. Events shifted into slow-motion. As I tell the story now, I still see those teeth turn red by the setting sunlight. "You not such a good teacher," he pulled a knife, also glinting red. Maybe you give me your money." I had cashed two hundred-dollar traveler's checks just before I left Cairo. At that moment I'd gladly give him all I had, catch the next flight to America, and never leave home again. Hoping that was enough to save my neck, I reached into my pocket and found only the scarab! I had left all my money in my other pants. Pretty as it was, I didn't think a fake trinket gave me much negotiating room.

"My money is at the hotel," I said lamely.

"Then you give me something else!"

I don't know what he had in mind, but I'm sure I wouldn't like it. I hadn't been so afraid, nor had I felt this warm sensation growing in my pants, since the recess when all the other kids had already left the playground, and the biggest bully in school cornered me.

A gust caught in the sail, careening the boat, so the yardarm splashed into the water. It almost seemed part of his plan, as knife clenched in his teeth, hanging onto the gunnels, he worked his way toward me. As he neared, the wind whipped from the opposite direction, rocking the boat sickeningly. Still, he came. It was worse than the school-yard bully. Then it happened. His eyes grew as round as proverbial saucers—I ducked, he didn't. The yardarm smashed my saucer-eyed murderer into the Nile. Let him wet *his* pants. A siren's shriek split the air, and a police boat, searchlight sweeping, sped from the shore.

I arrived on the porch of the Winter Palace to a standing ovation. They congratulated me for my bravery and skill in apprehending the murderer. I accepted the applause as modestly as I could, knowing it was the doing of the warm blue scarab in my dry pants pocket.

Kismet, Blue Scarab, call it what you like—I bounced on unscathed from front streets, back streets, dark allies, spidery caves, and opium dens (not really *opium*, hashish, I think it was, but opium makes a better story) around the world to disembark at last from a freighter at an Oakland dock. There is a *there, there,* Miss Gertrude Stein!

The scarab?

A cobalt testing authenticated it. Yep, about 1500 BC.

India

MY LIFE HAS BEEN LIKE SPLASHING IN THE RAIN FROM ONE puddle to another. On a whim, I follow certain rivulets and ignore others. From puddle to puddle, I've skipped—from fear, from hope, from open arms to rejections, from school to playground, to bars and lovers, Cape Town, Addis Ababa, Damascus, New Delhi and the World Council of Churches Assembly.

1962, New Delhi World Council of Churches Assembly, was the one fixed date in my crazy around-the-world vagabond. There, I served as a steward, a flunky, mainly ushering, unpaid—except for a dormitory bed and lunch. Still, I felt the job was an honor in some ways. From my vantage point in the balcony, I watched Nehru greet the assembly, and an Anglican bishop arriving, robes flying, on a bicycle, and all sorts of clergy in plain suits, fancy robes, miters, crosiers, and hoods, shoving and angling to be seen, as they processed past the world's news cameras. Billy Graham, like a queen bee, was surrounded by sycophants. The scenes brought to mind Christians I had watched a month before, shoving and crowding into the Holy Sepulcher.

I got to know John Wesel, a Manchester Guardian India stringer, who covered the Assembly. He turned out to be a font of introductions. The Assembly was a friendly bunch.

A few days before the Assembly closed, over drinks with John and the president of a Presbyterian Seminary, John said to me, "Wherever else you go, don't miss Ceylon! But first, you've got to look up my friend Shanti Kumar Moragee in Bombay." I knew where Bombay was and how to get there, but I had only a vague notion as to the location of Ceylon.

As the Assembly drew to a close and I joined in singing the final hymn, I had a ticket to go the rest of the way around the world and yet not a clue as to where I was going or why.

~~~~~~

I was packing when John came by my dorm. "Look up my old colleague, Shaun Mandy who lives on Taprobane, one of the most beautiful places in the world." He handed me a note with Shaun's phone number. "It's a small island off Ceylon's southern shore. He's lonely as hell down there. The old goat'll be delighted if you go to see him. It is a paradise, too far-off the beaten track for many folks to go there." Then he handed me a telegram from Shanti Kumar Moragee. It read, "Tell your young friend to come stay a fortnight if he likes."

"Yeah, I took it upon myself to introduce you. You don't seem to have much of an idea of where you are headed. Shanti's a nut, but a kind nut! Not many guys get a chance to stay in a Krishnovite temple. He's even got Mahatma Gandhi's ashes enshrined there."

John was right. As we sang the last hymn and received the final benediction, I hadn't a clue as to what was to befall me.

~~~~~~

Shanti's chauffeur met me in a beat-up Ford at the Bombay train station, and drove me to Gandhigram, a stretch of Juhu Beach north of the city.

Dressed in loose white cotton pants and shirt, Shanti stood awaiting my arrival next to a shiny three-foot-tall bronze elephant, with trunk upturned, as if trumpeting me into Krishna's sanctuary. He is about my height, you might say *short*, about five-foot-six, and only beginning to spread in the middle. His smooth, coppery complexion suggested he was in his forties. However, his white hair and well-trimmed white beard put him older. Not particularly handsome, his earnest wide-set black eyes were what drew me to him.

The temple grounds are behind Shanti's wife's large villa, which overlooks Juhu Beach, while Shanti's temple and residence overlook his wife's cow pasture. The elephant and all the other bronze images along the path leading to the temple entrance had been freshly anointed with ghee (purified butter).

Shanti's family—the wealthiest family in India before the stock market crashed in the 1920s—still owned two steamship lines. Keeping the smaller line for himself, Shanti had bequeathed the larger line to his wife, perhaps, as a wedding gift, an arranged marriage, no doubt.

We passed Gandhi's ashes enshrined in a simple urn and set in an unadorned niche in the temple garden wall. A doll-size gold Krishna on a velvet cushion formed the focus of the temple room. The god held a gold ball in his outstretched hand representing butter, which Krishna was known to like. Krishna's gilded carriage pulled by white horses, which might have stepped off a merry-go-round, pranced along one wall, and an equally elegant boat, set in stocks, waited to take Krishna for a sail on the pool filling the center of the room.

Shanti explained Krishna is always on his mind, even in his dreams. When he is in the market, his mind is on finding things to please Krishna. What toy today? Hot days, perhaps something cool, such as silver, will please his God, or on warm days, something carved in ivory. Krishna's eye sockets are beeswax into which Shanti presses jewels — emeralds, amethysts, or topaz. It was a form of devotion. As he spoke of his god, he beamed like a grandparent talking about his grandchild. I envied his simple piety.

A guru who had been a friend of Gandhi lived in a small cell in the back of the temple building. He was as learned in Judeo-Christian theology as my professors in theology school, in addition to being a Hindu and Buddhist scholar. Not at all what I imaged an Eastern Holy Man to be, he reminded me of my kindly theology professors in Boston. I could have talked with him for days, and not grown tired. I wonder what would have become of me if I had stayed as I was welcome to do.

As Christmas grew near, Shanti sent me on his ship about halfway down the western Indian coast to visit a friend who I had met at the Assembly. He was associated with a Presbyterian Mission in Vengurla.

On board, I felt like royalty with my private cabin and dining with the captain, while fifty or sixty passengers camped out on steerage amidst bundles of belongs and gathered around their meals spread out on bright clothes. The truth is, the folks on the lower deck appeared to be having more fun than I.

The mission, as I found most Protestant missions, was operated by the most conservative and joyless representatives of their denominations. I suspect it comes from missionaries thinking they are called to save the heathen from their immoral beliefs and convert folks to a stern existence of sobriety and hard work in this life to inherit the kingdom in the next life. Life was hard for the people the mission served.

Christmas day, my friend took me to his home. His house was made of wattle, smeared with a slurry of cow dung. The dung, I was told, repels insects. We sat on an earth floor; the only furniture was a footlocker. My friend's mother huddled over coals in a depression behind the dwelling. Christmas dinner consisted of tortilla like chapati dripping with ghee, a luxury for them.

The mission sits on a bluff from which we gazed across a bay to Goa, a Portuguese protectorate, where it is believed two thousand years before, Saint Thomas brought Christianity. As I listened to the sounds of fireworks and jubilation of the people of Goa enjoying themselves, I wonder how the Presbyterians could win any converts to their grim version of the Gospel. The offering at the service I attended consisted of three tethered chickens and a few melons. It was a hard-scrabble existence.

<hr />

I returned on Shanti's ship as it made its way back up the coast to Bombay, Gandigram, and Krishna.

I shared with Shanti a thirty-foot by thirty-foot square room, above the temple room, where we slept and took our meals. Banquettes covered with richly-embroidered fabrics pressed against the walls. My bed was one of the banquettes, beneath a wide opening to the outside. In the middle of the room hung Shanti's bed, under a colorfully embroidered canopy, swung from four brass chains, each link the image of a god—monkeys, elephants, cows, and buffaloes. Silk mosquito net draperies were let down at night to engulfed the banquette which could sleep a dozen guests, but during the time I was there, I was the only guest. Mornings I rose early and ran on Juhu Beach before joining Shanti in the ritual of feeding and dressing Krishna, after which we had our breakfast, food that had first been presented to Krishna.

Taking another of the Manchester Guardian reporter's suggestions, I found a map and began making plans to head for Ceylon, which hangs like a teardrop off the southern tip of India. Shanti urged me to stay, but, as warm as his welcome had been, I felt it was time for me to go.

A flight south to Ceylon was not included in my plane ticket, so I decided the cheapest way would be to take a train to the southern tip of India and then find a boat crossing. I located on a map a train, which I thought would take me to a ferry across the narrow channel between the two nations. But then, kind Shanti arranged ship passage, which would carry me to Cochin. His own ship did not sail farther south than Vengurla, about halfway down the west coast, but his wife's sailed to Cochin, almost the southern tip. Her ship turned out to be a long, white ocean liner. There were no folks in steerage, and I didn't dine with the captain. Still, I paid nothing. How would I ever repay so many kindnesses?

~~~~~~~~~~

"Gray broom-like rain swept over the Arabian Sea as my ship slipped from Bombay harbor, bound for a place I had never before heard of. We sailed far out from the coast where occasionally a graceful lateen sail of a felucca skimmed along the horizon.

Cochin

~~~~~~~~

THREE DAYS AFTER WE SAILED FROM BOMBAY MY SHIP SLOWED, turned toward shore, and passed into a wide bayou where land and water struggle for dominance. The other passengers went to their cabins to gather belongs to be ready for debarkation, leaving me alone to endure the imperious scrutiny of a heron gazing from under the leafy shade of mangroves, raised above the water on spidery, barnacle-encrusted stems. There came an occasional splash, followed by a squawking frenzy, and then an eerie quiet fell over the steamy desolation. Thus, I watched for half an hour until we glided against the dock of Venice-like Cochin, sprawled on the banks of the Chalakudy River.

~~~~~~~~

The Malabar Hotel seemed to be the only place the taxi driver thought I would be comfortable. It had been an exclusive club during the days of the British Raj, and so reeked English, I felt my one-tenth English DNA rise to the surface. The weather was hot and steamy, as it had been my entire time in India.

As soon as I got to my room, I grabbed my bathing suit and headed for the pool where, in the shade of a poolside awning, a Buddha-like gentleman, drink in one hand and palmetto fan in the other, supervised his thirteen-year-old son swimming laps. I plunged in right after the kid and swam a couple of laps myself. When I stopped to rest, Buddha called, "I say, there!" Gesturing with his fan, he beckoned to me to come near. "You're the new guest?"

"Just arrived," I tell him.

"Staying a spell?"

"I have no schedule."

"Hah! Definitely not British or Australian," he said jokingly. "Don't tell me! Canadian? No American!" He clapped his hands. "From the middle of that country, I hazard. I pride myself on accents," he said. "One doesn't often find your type down here. The Taj Mahal is the only thing brings Americans to India these days—that and tigers. Come up, join me in a Pimm's Cup or whatever you like." He appeared already to have had more than one cup, or whatever it was he was drinking.

I climbed out of the pool and wrapped a towel around my waist lungi-style, as I had seen many of the men wearing.

"Sit, sit!" The large man extended his hand without getting out of his chair. "It's much too hot to stand around. What will you have?"

"I'll have the Pimm's. I've heard about the drink, but never tried one."

Shortly, a rattling pitcher arrived. Ice, fruit, cucumbers, and mint swirled in amber liquid giving off a fragrance of allspice and juniper berry, suggesting that a generous portion of gin fortified our punch.

The grandson of the Maharaja of Cochin poured us each a tall glass, as he introduced himself and toasted, "Here's to the colonies!" He chuckled. "You got out way ahead of us!"

Oxford-educated, my host, Shancranya Palot, would be the Maharaja had the succession been patrilineal, rather than matri-lineal. As it was, his uncle is the maharaja, and, the nephew, share a villa in the country with the Dowager Maharani.

"I'm headed for Ceylon," I told my host. "Cochin is farthest south the ship would bring me, so, in a day or two, I'll take a train to the ferry port and cross over to Ceylon. I plan as I go," I told him.

Plan? At that point in my life, to say, "I planned," is almost laughable.

His son had climbed out of the pool and impatiently stood wrapped in a towel. Grunting, Shancranya pulled himself from his chair. "You must see all of our beautiful city of islands. Perhaps I can obtain my uncle's launch to show you around." Turning to leave, he affectionately leaned on his son's shoulder. "I'll leave a message with the concierge. If I can make the arrangements, meet us at the hotel dock at ten," Shancranya called over his shoulder, as they headed off.

~~~~~~~~~

Ten-thirty the next morning, a white thirty-foot-long vessel awaited at the foot of the hotel's dock. The ship's brass boiler, gears, and piston drivers of its steam engine gleamed like gold. A fringed awning shaded the stern deck where Shancranya, sitting in a wicker chair waved me aboard. That afternoon we landed upon a garden-like island in the middle of which stood Bolgatty Palace, a big sprawling structure with wide verandas. It resembled a Victorian plantation house, more than what I imagined for the residence of an oriental potentate. It was built in the 1800s, as a bribe from the Dutch East India Company to allow its merchants to sail in ahead of the British, and buy spices in the good maharaja's domain along the rich Malabar Coast.

I learned that I could stay in Bolgatty Palace for less than I was paying at the Malabar, so for the next three days, I became the lone guest, with the palace, grounds, and servants to myself.

I dressed in my nice clothes—white wrinkle-free pants and

shirt, and an ascot at my throat, and strolled the grounds, as if I were a pukka sahib, strolling his vast royal palm-shaded estate. The grassy lawn sloped to the water's edge, where, out in the estuary, flat vessels, with bows upturned like Cleopatra's barge, scarcely made headway under tattered square sails and, like teasing children, feluccas crisscrossed the bay, the tips of their lateen sails rippling the turbid water. Two months before I had watched, from Luxor's Winter Palace's veranda lateen sails ripple the Nile.

And evenings, as I sat in the drawing room in a richly brocaded wingback chair, the back a half-foot higher than my head, I didn't have a clue to what lay ahead. I hadn't looked at the map carefully. If I had, I would have noted that Ceylon doesn't exactly *drip* off the tip of India; the island's northernmost land is slightly to the *east* of the southern end of the subcontinent. I didn't foresee that I would board the wrong train—that what should have taken a few hours, would take me a long, sweltering hot day, and when I finally got there, my Indian visa had expired. I would almost miss the last ferry of the day to Ceylon's Colombo.

Sublime in my ignorance, I would mark my place in the book I was reading, and content myself by wandering down to a dock where turbaned fishermen, their dark skin glistening in the failing light, stretched their nets like angel wings.

I was perfectly comfortable in my palace when Shancranya sent a boat over with an invitation to visit the villa he shares with the Dowager Maharani. A car awaited me at the dock, and I was driven inland about twenty miles. The car pulled through majestic gates, teetering on rusted hinges. We circled goats grazing in a dried-up fountain to the front of a shambling two-story affair, I judged, covered nearly a city block.

Shancranya was standing in the tall doorway. Ushering me into a darkened vestibule, he explained that before he extended my invitation, he had failed to check with the servants as to the condition of the upstairs rooms, where he had expected me to sleep. He hadn't climbed the stairs in years to rooms he learned were filled with bags of Malabar pepper, in which civet cats now nested. A cot was set up for me in the banquet hall-sized room he shared with his son. There were also a few bags of pepper in the corner of that room. It must have been a good year for the precious Malabar pepper.

There was no running water. The servants kept the WC supplied with buckets of water. Nor was there toilet paper. One is expected to use a pitcher-like affair with an upturned spout. Unable to find so much as an old newspaper, I resorted to gathering leaves. The most satisfactory sized leaf, when dried, is used by native craftsmen as sandpaper.

The maharani, who only once a month emerges from her darkened wing of the palace, sent me a gracious apology. She explained that she would not impose the crotchety presence of an old woman on the bright young guest. Shancranya explained that once a month, they got out the vintage Rolls Royce, and she makes a royal progress through the market.

A day later, on the steps of the "Country Palace," Shancranya engulfed me in his arms to say goodbye. I swallowed hard as the car circled the fountain, the goat still nibbling. I had been allowed a moment inside a waning magnificence. I knew I would never be back—never could come back. If I did, it would all be gone as if I had merely dreamed the whole time in Cochin.

~~~~~~~~~

I hate leaving, but something, a voice in the night calls my name: "Grant, it's time to go, time to go!" I had hated leaving Shanti in his temple at Gandigram, and I hated leaving Shancranya and his son.

I considered myself an old hand at India train travel. I had taken the train from New Delhi to Agra to view the Taj Mahal, and to Bombay, and hadn't I taken British-built trains up the east coast of Africa?

About midday the train pulled into where I expected to find a ferry to Colombo, Ceylon. But the place was swarming with throngs of worshippers crowding into an enormous temple, not a ferry. I've arrived in the place where legend has it, Vishnu hurled stones into the sea so that he could stalk across to Ceylon to rescue Lakshmi, who had been abducted by some other god. It was the southern-most tip, alright, but there were no boats bound for Ceylon! And Ceylon is indeed *near* the southern tip of India. However, the island drips off the *east* of the tip, not exactly *off* the tip of the subconti-nent!

I finally make it to the right place that afternoon as the last ferry of the day was boarding, but not so fast! My visa had expired a month ago! My explanations fall on deaf ears. I thought these guys spoke English! I apologize, and, after apologizing, practically on my knees, and writing an affidavit, dripping with more apologies, I was permitted to board, and left India for Ceylon.

Ceylon

~~~~~~

ALONG WITH FADED NOTES OF A JOURNEY AROUND THE WORLD made half a century ago, I take my coffee to the porch. Half of my mind watches fishing boats out on the Gulf, and the other half gazes out over the Indian Ocean from the veranda of the Mount Lavinia Hotel, formerly a British club. I am on the outskirts of Colombo, Ceylon. It is 1962; the Empire is over.

I have been writing in bits and pieces the memoir about that time in my life. As I write, the comment of my dear friend daunts me. We were at a typical six o'clock New York cocktail party. He pulls me aside, and though he has lived in New York for a number of years, he retains his Tennessee accent.

"Bud," he says. Back then, family and friends called me Bud. "No one is interested in where you have been. Talk about something other people are interested in—the latest Broadway show or Durrell's *Alexandria Quartet*. Everyone has read the *Quartet*.

I have long since read Durrel's masterpiece, and have seen many Broadway shows, but not at the time of the story I am about to tell. I am thirty-one when I sit on the Mount Lavinia Hotel veranda. My great love affair is over, and I have no job to return to—the curtain is fast drawing closed on my salad days, and I haven't a clue as what is to come.

A little more than a year before I arrived in Ceylon, my lover drove me out of Boston and out of his life. That morning, snow scuds ahead of the car as the man I have loved for eight delirious years drives me away from our Beacon Hill apartment into the maw of Sumner Tunnel under Boston Harbor to the airport. I've been a possessive, jealous fool. I have quit my position as associate minister in a big Cambridge church. It is time I gave my lover a break and figure out what to do with the rest of my life. My plane takes me to Charlotte Amalie, St. Thomas, the Virgin Islands, where I will run a friend's sleazy bar while he takes a month's vacation. Six months after that, I'll be a steward at the New Delhi World Council of Churches Assembly. Between those two dates—London, Rome, Accra, Ghana, Nigeria, Cape Town, Kenya, Addis Ababa, Khartoum, Luxor, Jerusalem. Why? Sometimes I have no idea—sometimes I meet someone who introduces me to someone who lives somewhere; someplace I've never heard of until the day before I board the next plane, train or a shared car.

By the time I reach Ceylon I have been gone from home a year. I have bumbled around Africa. I looked up an old classmate in Damascus, no longer "just old Yusuf." An uncle had died, and he had been elevated to pasha, something like sir, dating from the Ottoman Empire days. But he was still, "good old Yusuf." I steam bathed with praying Muslims in the Virgin Mary baths near the Mosque of the Rock, knelt in the Holy Sepulcher, drove to Baalbek, fooled around in Beirut, dwelled in a Hindu temple, and I turned a year older. New Delhi and the Virgin Islands bar are behind, and soon Ceylon would be.

My airline ticket ready to expire, I cash it in as soon as I reach Colombo. I'll figure out some other way to make my way back. Back to where?

They refund in U.S. dollars, and as my luck would have it,

Ceylon's banks are on strike. The only way to get local currency is on the black market, which pays triple the legal rate. I smile, imagining what the parishioners of the church I left a year before would think of their "Reverend" running a bar and dealing on the black market.

I move from the modest hotel where I have been staying to the elegant seaside Mount Lavinia. Up to this point in my journey, I have been penurious. Now I am flush with Ceylonese rupees.

I have forgotten much in the intervening years, but how can I forget, chubby Ray Langelou. Ray's thinning hair is a curious shade of auburn. We meet the first night in the hotel bar. Right off, he tells me that he owns a Paris art gallery next to Maxim's. He tells me, he owns a Rolls-Royce and sells art mostly to Americans.

"I never sell the Americans anything very bad," he says. "They were good to me during the war." He pauses a moment, then shrugs. "Of course, I never sell them anything very good." He buys me a drink.

The following morning I watch the nubile youth diving from rocks jutting out of the surf rolling in near the hotel. They are like bronze sculptures as they cling to the crevasse, poised for the next swell. I look over the shoulder of a guy sitting on the beach sketching. He invites me to join him. It turns out the Gauguin-like painting in the hotel lobby is his. In the picture, a dhoti-clad youth stands beside a leopard at the edge of a jungle thicket. Anyone of the divers I had watched that morning could model for one of Charles Baskerville's romanticized paintings.

~~~~~~~~~~~

Baskerville and I have drinks together that evening. He was heading off on an excursion around the island and offered to share the car he was renting. Our first destination was Sigiriya, where he wanted to do some sketches. Late afternoon, clearing a low hill, we confronted a scene right out of Kipling's *Jungle Book*. Rising out of dense jungle stood Sigiriya, an ancient citadel on top of a gigantic monolith. No wonder Baskerville wants to draw it.

The artist had gained notoriety when his portrait of Dwight Eisenhower appeared on the cover of Time magazine. He has painted Nehru's portrait and trekked into Nepal to paint a picture of the prime minister decked out in a huge turban with rubies dripping like a cluster of grapes.

I looked up Baskerville two years later. He was back in his New York studio, and I had become a Broadway gypsy, singing in *Kismet*. I'd drop by his place when I had a rehearsal near his 57th Street studio. His portrait of Helen Hayes as Victoria Regina reigned over his studio. A theater had just been named for the celebrated actress.

Baskerville was sort of a celebrity hound. One afternoon when I stopped by, he was hungover. The night before he had accompanied the Maharani of Jaipur to Truman Capote's famous Ritz party. Their pictures were splashed all over the society columns. Another time, the artist confided that "Jackie O" was taking lessons from him. He said, "When I told Bunny Williams, she said she couldn't wait to tell Mrs. William Randolph Hearst. I said don't you dare. She'll spread it all over town."

I found a muscle-man from the cast of *Kismet* to model for a painting he was working on.

I've been fortunate to meet people far more sophisticated than I. If I hadn't met Mabel Crenshaw, with whom I shared a taxi from the Jerusalem airport—so much like Margret Rutherford, I took to her immediately—I would never have seen Baalbek. I'd never even heard of Lebanon's greatest Roman treasure, until she suggested we rent a car together and drive around the Dead Sea to Damascus, stop off at Baalbek, and then on through the Cedars of Lebanon, and down to Beirut. If I hadn't met John Wesel, I wouldn't have made it to Ceylon or met Baskerville.

~~~~~~~~~~~~~~~~

The Temple of the Tooth, enshrining Buddha's tooth was a must-see for visitors to Ceylon. The artist had already traveled to Kandy and sketched the temple on the grounds of the royal palace complex of the former Kingdom of Kandy. Ancient tradition has it that whoever holds the relic governs the country. Baskerville didn't wish to make the trip again but urged me to go. He promised that the funicular train passes through some of the most magnificent scenes in the world. So, two days after we returned to the Mount Lavinia, I boarded the train bound for Kandy. He had not exaggerated. The old British funicular train crept through both natural beauties such as waterfalls, forested mountains, misty peaks, and precipices, as well as man-made tea estates, pine forests and engineering feats including bridges to one of the most sacred places of worship in the Buddha's world. Ceylon is like somebody made it up, ringed by sandy beaches and majestically rising over six thousand feet.

I wanted to be there for the morning procession. I had heard about the processions when worshippers pay homage to Buddha's enshrined tooth. I was on my own again, as I have traveled most of my life.

While I was folding my clothes in my backpack, I came across John Wesel's note with Shaun Mandy's Taprobane phone number. I made the call, and, as John predicted, Shaun enthusiastically invited me to visit him, but that story will have to wait.

Following paths alongside the train, swaying as gracefully as ballet dancers, sari-clad women and bare-chested, dhoti-clad men carried baskets of fruit, clusters of coconuts, or stalks of bananas on their heads. The Singhalese share the same racial ancestry as the Indians, and yet in manner, the way they walk, gesture and dress seem quite different. Some forms of Hinduism, I am told, are as restrictive as conservative Protestantism, while Buddha's philosophy lends itself to engaging and savoring life, more in harmony with the islands lavish tropical nature.

The old funicular wheezed into Kandy at about dusk. I found a small inn not far from the white-walled palace and temple nestled beside a lake turning golden in the fading light. My bath that night was in an ornate ceramic urn large enough to submerge my entire body. Now I know what a potted plant must feel like. The soap flooded the room with the fragrance of sandalwood.

Morning mist still clinging to trees' upper branches, I hurried toward a line already forming near the temple wall, turbaned men, and women in silk saris; the women's shiny hair pulled tight into long braids. They hold lotus blossoms, rose petals, mangos, bananas, and papaya. Many of the worshipers had anointed their bodies with coconut oil, its fragrance mingling with the smells of fruit and flower. The women's' silk saris were dyed in many soft colors. They wore hibiscus blossoms tucked in their hair. The woman in front of me carried an almond-eyed child. Her flawless cinnamon complexion, as well as the child's, glowed from within. Only I take notice of the elephant lumbering past, with Sabu, the Elephant boy, straddling the massive neck.

The warming sun breaking through the morning mist is welcomed. I came unprepared for the cool night. My small inn offered no blankets.

Suddenly drumming and a screeching whine split the air, gates to the temple grounds fling open, and the procession moves forward. As we shuffle toward the sound, I hold my thumbs in my ears and cover my eyes, then flip my hand back bird-like, playing the universal game of hide-and-seek with the giggling child glancing over her mother's bare shoulder. We round the corner into the temple forecourt and confront a fairy-tale palace, dazzling white, with an ornately carved red tile roof.

At the foot of red-lacquered stairs, worshipers remove their shoes. On each side, bare-chested young men, wearing blowsy turbans and pantaloons cinched to their slim waists, pound tall drums, and standing at the top of the stairs, similarly clad youth strangle adenoidal screams from clarinet-like instruments.

As I climbed the stairs and drew near the shrine housing Buddha's tooth, the exotic setting and music give way to a feeling that has returned often since I left the States. I have had the déjà vu-like sensations only a few times, and yet, though fleeting, they reach deeply. The excitement came when I visited Westminster Abbey. I was the only soul in the vast nave separated by the rood screen from the goings-on in the chancel and choir, and yet, I felt connected to cultures across centuries. I first recall this numinous feeling as I sat at sunset on a mountaintop in Arkansas. And the feeling came after I escaped the pushing and shoving along the Via Dolorosa in Jerusalem and sat quietly under an olive tree, gazing back at walled-in Jerusalem. I had this feeling once while I stood on Cedar Hill looking over the rooftops of my hometown and beyond to a patchwork of fields, a creek running through them. One time when I went to the pond on the far side of our pasture, I sat under a cottonwood tree skipping rocks when our calf came up and nuzzled the back of my neck. That night, I lay awake listening to the plangent bleat of the Santa Fe train rocketing through the dark, and I felt at one with all that existed!

~~~~~~~~~~~~

Unaware of a brewing revolution, I booked freighter passage from Ceylon to Burma. The freighter was to sail from Trincomalee, located on the far side of the island. It is another train ride up and over the crest of Ceylon to the slender northern tip. I leave behind the gilded Buddha, the great stone carved Buddha, the reclining Buddha, the mountain tea plantations, Taprobane, the temple enshrining Buddha's tooth, and the graceful Singhalese folk.

My mind takes flight; I look down at myself. I have watched myself drive a tractor pulling a plow around and around and around until, at the end of a long week, a field of wheat stubble turned rich chocolate. And I watched myself stand across from the Texaco station, at the intersection of the street where I grew up and Route 66, thumb out, begging a ride east. At this moment, I see myself alone in a swaying threadbare train compartment, a relic of the Raj. I stretch out across the musty seat and think back over the past month—has it been only a month in this most beautiful place? Unanchored, I lose my sense of time.

My past seemed to me to be like a wad of gum stuck under the edge of a school desk—the long struggle to make passing grades, schoolyard fights, the things boys do behind barns. the plowing and harvesting, dancing, and lying about who I am or who I seemed to be becoming.

Looking from the open train window across the island's verdant slopes, the thirty-two years since I squiggled from my mother's womb have vanished into the mists. The reclining Buddha and Buddha's tooth are more real than prairie windmills or Oklahoma church steeples.

~~~~~~~~~~~

Late afternoon, the train pulls into Trincomalee, a crescent of low buildings embracing the bay. A hundred yards from shore the black hulk of my freighter lay at anchor. I am as oblivious to brewing unrest among the Tamil people, Hindus who inhabit this northern part of Ceylon, or of their massacres to come, as I am of the coup d'état plotting in Rangoon.

～～～～～～～

The sun has sunk near the Gulf's waters as fishing boats, weighted low with the day's catch, make their way to their port. Where has the day gone? Daydreaming when I intended to write. Write! Is that what I think I am doing at this late date?

My mind, like a bouncing ball, bounces from time to time, wheat fields to Buddha temples. One moment I am plowing, and another I'm leaning on the bar at a New York cocktail party, or I'm lost in a forest.

"Where is the life that once I lived?" I hear Alfred Drake's rich baritone singing Cole Porter's song. "Where is it now? Totally dead." I stand in the wings waiting to go on stage. *Not dead to me.* One of the privileges of old age is to relive the ecstatic moments and leave behind the dross. Keep the *enchanted evenings* and leave out the rejections and betrayals—the times they never show up as they promised they would. But also tell of when he arrived with cold Champagne, and you never made it to supper. Make yourself glamorous, tell of palaces, fine drawing rooms, and restaurants, the famous people you have known, but leave out that you were never one of them, and leave out the dark alleys and heartache.

I'll write about Burma later, but first Taprobane.

.

Taprobane

A RECENT *NEW YORK TIMES* ARTICLE BROUGHT A RUSH OF MEMO-ries as does almost everything lately. I had visited Taprobane a few days before I left Ceylon. The article brought it all back:

On a bright morning, sometime in 1962 or maybe by then '63, I rode along rails heading south out of Colombo, Ceylon (now Sri Lanka). I was on my way to Taprobane, an island Paul Bowles once owned.

Two weeks before I had taken a ferry across from southern India to Ceylon, arriving the day after the government had closed the banks due to some crisis, or the employees had gone on strike; I don't remember which. Whatever the cause, it turned out to be my good fortune for the only way for me to change my money was from the black market at an amazingly good rate—as I recall, the equiva-lent of ten cents to the dollar that is ten cents would buy as much as a dollar had. As I had been traveling nearly a year, I also had to cash in the balance of my round-the-world plane ticket, for which I received US dollars. Again by exchanging that money on the black market, the next leg of my journey, passage on a freighter from Ceylon to Burma, cost me only fifty dollars. I had money to spare. Until I cashed in my dollars for Ceylonese rupees, I had been stay-ing in no-star hotels, but now affluent, I checked into the elegant beachfront Mount Lavinia Hotel, where I met the society painter Charles Baskerville, a friend of the Whitneys, the Vanderbilts, and Jackie O. But that is another story.

"I say, how good of you to ring up. A friend of John Wesel, are you?"

I had met John at the World Council of Churches Assembly in New Delhi, where he was covering the Assembly for the Manchester Guardian. He insisted that after it ended, I should visit his old friend, Shaun Mandy, a retired India correspondent for the Guardian, living in Ceylon. "You must not leave the East," John said, "before you visit that magic place." (Other kind advice I received came from the president of a Presbyterian seminary: "Before you leave Asia," he advised, "be sure to take in at least one *blue movie*." Up to that time, I had never viewed a porn film. I remedied that gap of education in Kowloon.

The phone line to Shaun Mandy crackled as if it were a transatlantic cable. "Well, my boy, you must come down. Stay a fortnight if you like—plenty of extra room—just a couple of old duffs rattling around. Take the train to Dandrahead, after you get off, cross over to the beach side of the tracks. You'll see my island."

"How do I get across to your island?"

"You walk. Oh, yes, quite, quite. Simply roll up your pant legs. Or take them off if that's your pleasure–ha, ha."

British made, the train was right out of the nineteenth century, no central corridor, and each compartment with a door opening to outside. The breezes of the Indian Ocean flowed in one side of my compartment and out the other side. We clickedy-clacked mile upon mile between coconut palm plantations and pristine beaches dotted with out-rigger canoes pulled up onto the sand. I don't recall how long it took I was so enthralled with the serene beauty.

At Dandrahead, the railroad occupied a narrow strip between a wide beach and the foot of a mountain. I stepped down from my compartment and, as instructed, I grabbed my backpack and headed down the beach in the direction of a forested outcropping rising a few hundred feet from the shore. Women in flowing saris and men, their lungis tightly wrapped around their hips, cast long shadows on the coral sand invoking Monet paintings.

Two pink-faced men, wearing blowsy knee-length shorts, strode in my direction. The taller, as they drew near, called out, "is it the young American we've been expecting. Shaun Mandy here." He reached out a hand.

"Ian Ersconscott," the other, introduced himself and extended his hand.

They led the way, wading through shallow water to the island. We then ascended along a zig-zag path. A Belgian count had bought the island in the nineteen twenties and planted every specimen that he could find that would grow in the tropics. The surviving plants had flourished. About sixty feet above the sea, we broke out of the jungle onto an expansive lawn covering the top of the island. In the center stood an octagonal neo-Palladian villa. Eight verandahs fronted by small gardens extended from each side, outward from a grand central hall rising thirty feet to a dome. From the central hall, a person looking through open doors is rewarded with a spectacular view of mountain, beach, or sea. The whole villa is designed as open as possible, to allow the flow of space and air. With verandahs spilling out to embrace the garden and stepped terraces hovering over the ocean, one has the sensation of living outdoors.

The Count, Shaun explained, painted his villa in lavish colors and gold leaf. Some flecks of the paint and gilding of the original decoration still peek through, but Bowles, from whom Shaun had bought the island, stripped away as much as possible of the ornate decoration and painted the whole affair white.

Members of the Mady Mac Mummers, sort of took the *country kid* under their wings, after I arrived to study at Oklahoma City University. They already were fashioning the lifestyle, they thought bohemian, which was sweeping the country. They introduced me to the writings of Truman Capote, Tennessee Williams, Gore Vidal, James Baldwin, Mary Renault and Christopher Isherwood, helping alleviate my humiliation, as I acknowledged my secret desires and the kind of person I was becoming. It must have been through the Mummers I caught my first titillating whiff of the scandalous lives of writers and artists who found their freedom abroad. Gertrude Stein's and Alice B. Toklas's Paris salon, where expatriate literary figures and artists gathered in their elegant apartment, became lodged in my naïve imagination. Ever since then, I have carried utopian visions of interloping in gatherings of thoughtful, free-thinking, open-minded folks.

Paul Bowles was a part of Stein's circle. She pushed him to go to Tangier with Aaron Copland in the summer of 1931 They took a house on the Mountain above Tangier Bay, and eventually, Bowles made Morocco his full-time home. Known best as a composer, Bowles became a prolific writer. I am haunted by his novel, *The Sheltering Sky*, and the film, inspired by his long sojourn in North Africa.

In 1950 Bowles traveled to Ceylon, where he first saw Taprobane. The forested outcropping captivated him, and two years later, with proceeds from the sale of his novel, *The Delicate Prey,* he bought the tiny island, jutting up only a few yards off Ceylon's shore. Two years later he returned to the Taprobane with his writer wife, Jane, and a group of Moroccan friends. Peggy Guggenheim followed a short time later.

Jane, unwell and unable to concentrate, returned to their Moroccan home. Two years later, Paul sold the island to Mandy and returned to Morocco, where for the rest of his life he graciously played host to a *who's who* of writers and artists who found their way to North Africa. Paul and Jane's lives anticipated the hippie generation's experimentation with free-love homosexuality and bisexuality and the use of recreational drugs. He was still very much alive at the time I visited his fabled island. I imagine him at that time smoking kief as the muezzins call the faithful to prayer.

He was still busy, recording music of different Moroccan ethnic groups, and translating Moroccan authors. Good lord, the guy started to read at the age of three. Ever since I read Bowles' *The Sheltering Sky,* I can't shake fantasies about North Africa. And I envy the many who made it to Tangier, whom he graciously received.

~~~~~~~~~~

"No need to close your doors unless you wish to shut out the light," Mandy explained. "You will have complete privacy. Only Hamed comes to this level. His family, cooking, laundry, and so on take place at a lower level."

Shaun pointed out a small structure resembling a sentry post, teetering where the lawn drops into the sea.

"I dare say," he said, "you'll find our best view from the privy. There's no need for a door. When you are sitting there, nothing between you and the South Pole. Sun's past the yardarm, my boy, time for a drink." He led the way through a small garden into the open end of the drawing room, one of the rooms, which radiates from the central hall.

We joined Ian, a cousin to the Queen Mother. He raised a tumbler in greeting. Ian spends his life floating around the former British Empire. The royal family apparently preferred it that way, and he seems perfectly happy to oblige. I soon learned that on Taprobane, almost any time of day, *somewhere in the Empire the sun had crossed the yardarm.* The expression, I learned, signifies that the sun has passed the tip of the topmost spare of a square-rigger, thus indicating it is past noon, and an acceptable time to have a drink. Hamed, lithe as a serpent, wearing a blue-green lungi, a perfect complement to his honeyed complexion, served the drinks.

~~~~~~~~~~

For the next three days, I climbed along trails pushed through the botanic jungle planted by Count de Mauny Talvande. Shortly after midday, I would join Shaun and Ian for drinks, and again, as the sun cast long silver shafts across the waters. One evening, after his third or fourth drink, Ian raised an unsteady glass in a toast: "Here is to one of our own added to the family. He was referring to Antony Armstrong-Jones, Princess Margaret's new husband, who had just been named, the First Earl of Snowdon.

Hamed decorously moved about the place, cleaning, straightening, bringing food up from the kitchen, and intuitively having drinks prepared before being asked. As if by magic, fresh blossoms replace the wilted lying about on tables and shelves. One afternoon while I watched catamarans skim past the island, I caught Hamed diving from a rock at least fifty feet above the water's surface. More sea animal than human, he entered the water without a splash and surfaced minutes later far out at sea.

Evenings, screened by vegetation in the small garden in front of my room, I bathed with dippers full of water from large urns placed under roof spouts. The soap lathered copiously in the fresh rainwater. The stars seemed near enough to touch. In bed caressed by the breeze off the southern sea, I lay under mosquito netting. The waves, pounding sixty feet below, beat a timpani accompaniment to the forest night sounds. My last morning on the island, I awakened to find an exquisite hibiscus blossom on the pillow next to my head.

I would like to have accepted Shaun's invitation to stay for another week, had I not already booked freighter passage set to sail in four days from Ceylon to Burma. Shaun and Ian walked me across to the beach, and there we bid a tearful farewell.

Halfway up the beach, I looked back. Shaun and Ian were already making their way up the path; the sun has *passed the yardarm.*

Breakers fountained at the base of the rock where Hamed stood waving shyly. Could last night have actually occurred, or was it only a dream? Dream or reality, it made no difference.

"Whereas the tourist generally hurries back home at the end of a few weeks or months, the traveler belonging no more to one place than to the next, moves slowly over periods of years, from one part on the earth to another. Indeed, he would have found it difficult to tell, among the many places he had lived, precisely where it was he had felt most at home." —Paul Bowles, The Sheltering Sky

Tim Street Porter has contributed to the *New York Times* a fascinating article about Taprobane. Go to search and type in: In Sri Lanka, an Island of Detachment and Desire.

Bay of Bengal–Burma

~~~~~~

I HAD HAD ENOUGH OF CHELEM BEACH, ENOUGH LONELINESS for a while. I was back in our home in Mérida; Clif was still in Amarillo, visiting family. Sometime in the early hours of the morning, I awakened to small sounds—quiet rustling, a rat or *zorro* (opossum) scrounging in the bodega; soft thumping, cats mating, perhaps; drip, drip, condensed dew, drips onto the porch roof. Our Chihuahua, Chico, curled beside me is too deaf to be disturbed, and Amiga, a rescue dog, at my feet, too indolent. I lay in sublime torpor, snuggled under a light blanket until towering palms etch the eastern sky. I then brew a pot of coffee and slip on a robe. A white cat leans over the pool lapping water from its reflection. Scarlet-throated gold and tangerine canna lilies cluster behind terra-cotta urns. The sun breaks through the eastern scrim of clouds, igniting a green fire in translucent bamboo and banana leaves.

~~~~~~

I have just finished reading *The Piano Tuner*, about a nineteenth-century excursion into Burma. I'm both admiring and envious. Daniel Mason wrote his *best seller* while still in his twenties, and a medical student! Well-written, the adventure unlocks another store of memories. The protagonist arrived by steamer out of

Calcutta, India. I, seventy years after the story takes place, arrived by freighter out of Trincomalee, Ceylon. Still not much seemed to have changed in the intervening years.

~~~~~~~~~~~~~~~~~~~~~

My freighter's small cabin boasts a single bed beneath a porthole. A small wood desk and a lamp affixed to the bulkhead. Hinting at the ship's vintage, layers of paint, thick as orange peel, have been painted over.... All the bathroom facilities are crammed under an encrusted shower head into a telephone-booth-sized cubical.

We, twenty-four passengers, play cards, drink and dine in a single lounge the size of a comfortable living room. One other passenger is traveling alone, a middle-aged Indian gentleman. The first day out, he plunks a wad of cheroots in the middle of a table, and explains that the stubby cigars have been aged in arrack liquor. Offering the cigars around, he lights up. Immediately the whole space stinks like scorched urine. I know the smell. The cheroot brings back a Boy Scout camping incident. When the time came to douse the fire, an older boy had the idea; the smell of our combined urine drove us out of the box canyon where we had camped, and we slept the remainder of the night in a hay field.

Keeping pretty much to myself, I spent much of the trip out on the deck watching for flying fish to erupt from the slate flat water. Six knots an hour, the old clinker takes a week to cross the Bay of Bengal. There were lots of flying fish.

We reached the Irrawaddy Delta and headed up a channel toward Rangoon. Folks gathered bundles and set them out on deck. All I had I'd carry over my shoulder when we got there. I was sitting at the bar when the cheroot smoker sat next to me. We'd hardly spoken the entire voyage.

"Where are you staying," he asks, "when we get to Rangoon?"

"I don't know," I said. "Some hotel, I guess."

He looked at me in disbelief. "Son, you don't just get off the boat and wander around. Rangoon isn't that sort of place. You must stay with my family and me."

My mouth drops. I don't know what to say, other than "OK."

It turns out he was a spice merchant. His home was a two-story stone building—offices, storage and living all in one. I was shown to a cot in the corner of an upstairs office with gunnysacks of Malabar pepper, I knew from the smell, and other spices taking up half the space. Down a hall, I was shown my latrine, a metal trough that drains into a hole in the floor over which I was to squat.

The next morning, I thanked my kind host profusely, took my things and left. I felt like a heel. I found a hotel that must have been grand in colonial days.

After settling my things in my room, I returned to the lobby. I ask at the desk where I might cash a traveler's check. His response was like I had asked directions to Timbuktu. A young man I had noticed loitering in the lobby when I came into the hotel approached and asked if I needed a guide. The glance from the desk clerk was not reassuring; however, I find by trusting folks, I usually receive in kind. How could I travel around the world alone without trusting? When I asked the young man, can he lead me to where I can change traveler's check, he pulled me away from the desk and, looking to be sure no one can hear us, said he knew where I could get the best rate.

It was getting dark when I climbed into a rickshaw with my new-found friend. We headed into a neighborhood that wasn't particularly reassuring. I begin to question my honesty theory as we traveled deeper down dark streets and alleys lined with tenements with laundry hanging out the windows. Finally, we stopped in front of a doorway; inside, light spilled from behind an iron grill-work at the far end of the room where a Buddha-like, bald-headed

Chinaman sat behind a grill. "Chinese want American money," my friend whispers. I slid my traveler's checks under the grating, and Buddha pushed a fair exchange back to me. I suspected the money was counterfeit, but that was neither the place nor time to question.

We were rickshawing back toward the hotel when my friend asked if I would like to see a blue movie. Finally, I had my opportunity to follow the advice of my friend, the president of a Presbyterian seminary, whom I had met at the New Delhi World Council of Churches Assembly; "Don't leave the Orient without seeing a *blue movie.*"

My guide told me that the movie was in the big tenement complex next to where we had stopped. I paid the rickshaw driver and sent him on. Then my friend told me that to see the movie, I must have a woman with me. I wasn't keen on that, but he insisted, and I figured, in for a penny, in for a pound. He took the equivalent of five dollars from me. Telling me to wait right there, he headed off into the dark. He was only a few paces ahead of me when I called, "Wait, I'll go with you."

He was already swallowed in darkness by the time I started running after him. Still calling "wait," I ran toward where he had disappeared into a dark corridor. I ran down one tenement hall, laundry slapping me in the face, and another, until, halfway down the third, it dawned on me that what I was doing was very dangerous.

~~~~~~~~~

The following morning, planning to visit a friend I had met in New Delhi, I bought a train ticket for Mandalay. I notice more uniformed military and vehicles around than I had seen the day before, but don't pay much attention. How was I to know a revolution had started while I was running around in a rickshaw, illegally changing money and trying, unsuccessfully, to get hooked up with a prostitute to take in my first blue movie?

As I checked out of my hotel, I mentioned that I was catching a train to Mandalay. The desk clerk's eyes widened in surprise. "Are the trains still running?" he asked.

"Why I guess so," I said. "I have a ticket."

I shouldered my bag and headed to the train station on the far side of the great gilded Shwedagon Pagoda, known as the Great Dragon or Great Golden Pagoda, which enshrines ten hairs from Gautama Buddha's head, as well as relics from four other Buddhas. The 325-foot-tall stupa reminded me of the toy tops we used to spin in our schoolyard. My top usually ended upside down with its point sticking up like the pagoda. Uniformed soldiers clustered at street corners. Near the train station, an armed tank stood guard. I smiled naively at the smooth-faced soldiers who looked like children and continued my way to catch my train. I am not particularly courageous. Sometimes I think that if I had any idea of what lay ahead, I'd never have stepped out of the house.

~~~~~~~~

A bald-headed monk swathed in a saffron robe curled in the corner of the opposite bench. We exchanged nods and smiles, though he didn't appear all that welcoming. I would later understand his need to distance himself from me. I was again *clickety-clacking* on a relic of the Raj. Out one side of our compartment, I looked over the wide Irrawaddy River on one side and the other a landscape scattered with stupas and lacy towers erected in homage to the Lord Buddha. We were never out of sight of reminders of the enlightened saint.

An Englishman I met on the freighter explained to me that the British were never able to properly incorporate Burma into the Empire. "The Burmese never learned to play a proper game of cricket," he declared.

By the time I arrived in Mandalay, the friend I was to visit had fled with his family, fearing that, as Christians, in the ensuing rebellion their lives were in danger. It then occurred to me that it might be a good idea for me to move on to more a peaceful climate, so I boarded the next train back to Rangoon. I had no fellow passengers; in fact, the train for Rangoon was practically deserted.

A day later, back in Rangoon, I learned that the train that had followed mine was blown up, and all passengers wearing Western-style clothing were shot.

I flew to Bangkok where I had an introduction to Jim Thompson who had made Thai silk famous all over the world.

Flight to Mexico

~~~~~~~~~~

THE DISHWASHER LOADED, AND REMEMBERING THE ORCHIDS in the gumbo-limbo tree need watering, I hook up the automatic sprinklers to go on twice a day. Then, I pour another cup of coffee I don't really want.

"Time to go," I call.

"So early?"

"I like to have plenty of leeway." He doesn't argue. I used to like rushing to the airport in the nick of time, but not any longer.

We embrace before he walks me to our front gate. Pressing against his belly is comforting. He drives along the Atlantic side of the island. The beach is crowded with nubile spring-breakers. At the terminal, as he lifts my heavy bag from the trunk, onlookers note the handsome younger man assisting his gray-haired lover. In Key West one assumes . . .

Half an hour later the plane lifts off the end of the runway, gains altitude over derelict boats careened on the flats between Key West and Stock Island, then banks over turquoise-veined backcountry dotted with hundreds of mangrove hummock. I am melancholy. I am an old man living on an island a hundred miles at sea.

The flight to Miami is a little over thirty minutes. I then have a two-hour wait for my Aeroméxico flight. I start to crack open a *who-done-it* novel I have brought along when I glimpse a bouffant, like a Louis XIV wig, floating above the crowd. The hair sits upon a sharp-featured, heavily made-up woman in a pants suit tapering to a pair of spiked heels. It is Honey Bush, a famous Key West transsexual entertainer.

As Honey Bush exits down a corridor, my attention shifts to a couple on the cusp of their youth. People watching is more interesting than finding out who holds the dagger over the pulchritudinous breast.

I again lay the book aside. The dagger can wait for the Mexico flight. The couple enters a pricey, glass-enclosed boutique across from where I am sitting. It had been her beauty, I imagine, that had attracted him to her. I picture her as a high school cheerleader. Gray hair now frames a face of open candor. A slight twist at the corner of her lip suggests a quick sense of humor. For some reason, I'm grateful that she has left the gray in her hair. From cheerleader, I suspect, she has grown into a woman content with herself. Children? They must be with the grandparents, letting the parents take a weekend in the Bahamas. Caught in the ebb tide of age, she's a swimmer. I imagine her rolling her eyes at her suave suntanned husband, nervously fingering the store's display of expensive fabrics. He was a knockout on the tennis court when they met, but isn't anymore. The blazer doesn't hide the paunch. He touches up his silvering hair. His shirt, probably silk, harmonizes smoothly with the soft peach color of his well-tailored slacks.

They are Unitarians. The pastor to whom they turned for counseling suggested the little vacation and referred them to Gail Sheehy's book, *Passages,* about the thirty-year change-of-life crisis most folks go through. For the kid's sakes, I hope they make it.

My flight is called. I start to put the *poised dagger* in my carry-on, but, on second thought, leave it on the seat. Let someone else wade through to the predictable outcome.

~~~~~~~~

It doesn't seem to me to of be my own doing. Maybe it was the chance that came during my senior year in college to go to Rio de Janeiro that influences me. Perhaps I thought traveling would make me *somebody*.

One thing seemed to lead to another—the trip to Rio, the summer in a German work camp to rebuild homes destroyed by my country's bombers, the diving in the Grenadines, the windjammers, and now Mexico.

~~~~~~~~

Fifteen minutes into the flight I look down from twenty-five thousand feet and search for our island. Often this time of day I'd be out on our back deck reading. I look up and see a vapor trail. I think of Clifford down there now, as this plane sketches a vapor trail above him. He is so vulnerable, at the tip of islands, strung like a scorpion's tail.

It came to me when I was on my hands and knees in our garden, or perhaps when I sat back on my haunches to admire the coral stone I had cemented together to make a fountain; if not then, when I was up hanging in our gumbo-limbo tree fastening bromeliads. More likely it came to me a warm afternoon out on the back deck after I had dozed, and the book I was reading had fallen open on my chest. I read so slowly as a youth. I still read slowly, but I now read all the time, I guess trying to make up for the lost pleasure. I still haven't even gotten to *Anna Karenina*.

To be honest, I don't remember just when it came to me; a year ago? Or five years ago? I lose track of time. Perhaps, at some deep subconscious level, I understood that New Year's Eve night over forty years ago when I asked him to come home with me. Whenever:

a week ago or forty years ago the existential realization broke through my foggy consciousness that *there is no Mr. Right;* never was, never will be. He is simply an inseparable part of me. There is no more leaving this lover and in a few months or years finding a new, more attractive one—not possible, because no matter what, for good and bad, like my arm, I can't cut it off because it hurts. My right arm is essential. If I lost him, it would be like losing an arm—not just one arm, both arms and legs. Arms are a poor metaphor—a light would snuff out and never turn on again. That's it; he's the light, the North Star of my life.

If I am to love him at all, I must take him as he is, ill temper, tantrums, no longer young and slim, not working at his art, not as I wanted him to be, not eating right, but as he is!

I wasn't looking for a mate when we met. I didn't want one. My previous affairs had left me bruised and feeling rejected. I lied about my age, as theater people do, thinking he would be gone before I needed to tell him I was fifteen years older than him. I expected our affair to last a week or two, no more than a month. After all, in New York, trim and handsome, fresh out of the Navy, and fifteen years younger than me.

───≈≈≈≈≈≈───

Nights, after Dad called, "Lights out," I hid Captain Marvel under the mattress, and lay awake listening to downshifting semitrailers out on the coast-to-coast Highway 66, or long after midnight, I'd awaken to the distant growl of the Santa Fe's big diesel pulling its mile-long burden. Like a Siren's song, the train's mournful horn called to me and I imagined myself aboard that night train, rumbling on to Texas, New Mexico, Arizona, and on to California. Other times I'd be hitching a ride on the semi, bound for Oklahoma City, Topeka, or Kansas City—traveling, traveling, always moving on to that *somewhere on the other side of the rainbow.* Perhaps it was one of those nights the seeds of wanderlust took root in me, and still drives me, timid as I am, to leave comfort for faraway places.

Writers migrate to Key West to write, but I am flying from Key West to Mérida, on the Yucatán Peninsula, to put together a memoir of a gay clergyman, ex-Broadway singer-dancer, and writer, turned eighty.

Squeezing between the tip of Cuba and the thumbnail of the Yucatán, water turns amazingly blue, like the second rinse water into which mother poured the same bluing with which she rinsed her hair. In a few days or weeks, the Gulfstream will carry these blue waters within a mile or so of my mate. My plane passes over congested Cancun and begins its descent through colonnades of clouds. Rains have turned the jungle lush. Near Mérida, small villages, once plantation-like haciendas, dot the landscape—I don't know yet that I will invent a murder in a fictitious pool on one of those haciendas. I have yet to meet the owners of one, Oklahomans like myself, living their fantasies, as I do mine. The haciendas now mostly lay in ruins or are pricey honeymoon hotels.

~~~~~~~~~

I am in Mexico now, near a small fishing village, school out, crowded with children. They buzz down the road on all-terrain bikes or zip past the beach on jet skis. I leave this computer stacked with the stories I have fantasized since I landed more than twenty years ago. My mate is in the city working on a huge canvas. I grab an ice-cold beer and head down to the beach. A white cruise ship is docked at the end of Progresso's five-mile long pier. Tourists flock from the ship into buses that will zoom them off in the roasting sun to have their picture taken in front of a Maya pyramid, or in the middle of a sacred ball court.

Pelicans dive, frigatebirds soar, and sandpipers scurry. Down the beach, children kick a soccer ball, and out in the surf, a boy and a girl make love. The white sail of a boat skimming the far horizon beckons, but I am content, at least for this moment, to stay where I am.

I've strayed a long way from the beginning of this story, if story it is, haven't I, as I have strayed a long way from home.

Singing Memoire

~~~~~~~~

CLIFFORD ADJUSTED THE CAMERA ON A TRIPOD, GESTURING FOR me to move nearer to the keyboard as my accompanist, Bill, hammered out the accompaniment. *"Una fortiva lagri ma,"* I began.

Antonio Formicini sang the aria nearly forty years ago in the Boston Opera production of *E'lese d'amore* (Elixir of Love), with Beverly Sills, his amor, sitting on a bench. The joke backstage was, Formacini had a terrible accident. He fell off his lifts.

I was an extra in that production. I had appeared once before in a Met touring company production of *Carmen* in Oklahoma City; Risa Stephens was Carmen. I stood outside her dressing-room door to catch a glimpse of her. When she came out all done up as the gypsy, she saw me standing there. She gazed at me batting her long fake eyelashes at me and winked. I nearly melted. I was smitten by opera. Those experiences and my brother dominating the living room every Saturday, his ear pressed against our Motorola, listening to the Met broadcast.

I don't know what became of Formicini, but Beverly, of course, became a star.

I stopped, coughed, and took a sip of water. I had stopped singing ten years before when I realized I had missed the brass ring.

I might have made it if, while I was under the influence of lysergic acid, the psychiatrist hadn't said to me, "Perhaps your art is with people." I might not have gone into the ministry and instead pursued a singing career. I had always sung, and if I had kept on, there might have been time for me to have succeeded.

<hr>

To reach the thrilling high notes, the tenor's money notes, as one of my teachers called the high B's and C's, requires continuing practice and exercise.

"Sing more forward," Bill said, "like Katharine Hepburn spoke—'Are the calla lilies in bloom?'" Hearing that I had once been a singer, Bill had coaxed me to see if I still could. Clifford restarted the camera. It was his idea, the recording. My throat felt scratchy. It was too late.

<hr>

Illya Darling, the musical based on Jules Dassin's movie *Never on Sunday,* was my fourth and last Broadway show. In the show, as the film, Melina Mercouri played the leading roles in both the film and the musical. I shared my dressing room with stunningly handsome Robert La Tourneaux, a pleasant enough guy. Saturday night after the final curtain a black limousine throbbed at the stage door, waiting for Bob, as the rest of us rushed, still rubbing off makeup, to Eighth Avenue where we jumped in a beat-up old stretch limousine that sped us out to Long Island to catch the last ferry to Fire Island's Cherry Grove. Bob having ridden out in solitary splendor, arrived moments behind us.

While we drove out of the city to Sayville, from where we caught the Fire Island ferry, fellow passengers, cast members of the Broadway play, *Cactus Flower,* regaled us with promises that a new play about to open was about to knock the socks off Broadway.

Shortly before *Illya* closed, La Tourneaux left our cast to play the cowboy in *Boys in the Band.* It did make Broadway history.

I had appeared with Nancy Walker, Alfred Drake, Georgio Tozzi and Ethel Merman, and had an affair with the Danish dancer who looked as if he had stepped off the pages of a Hans Christian Andersen story, yet, except for a few understudy and walk-on parts, I had gotten no further than gypsy singer-dancer.

One night, standing in the wings waiting for my cue to dance onto the stage, I suddenly had a vision of myself ten years older, still in the chorus, the dream of singing the great classical songs a faded memory.

A week after *Illya Darling* closed, I auditioned for the Metropolitan Opera Studio.

"OK," the studio manager said before I finished the second song. "That'll be enough." My heart sank. Then he said, "Pick up your music, and sign your contract in my office. Rehearsals start next week."

I stumbled off the stage in a daze. The pay was enough for me to maintain my fourth-floor, cold-water walk-up in Manhattan's Yorkville. We rehearsed in the same rooms under the opera house as the stars, sometimes catching glimpses of Tebaldi, Sutherland, or Corelli. I was covered in goose pimples the time I rode the elevator with Rudolf Nureyev.

The Studio was John Gutman's baby. He was one of a troika of managers who served under Rudolph Bing. Like Bing, Gutman was a Viennese Jew, not handsome but so elegant—always silk cravats, cuff-linked shirts, polished nails, and brilliantined silver hair—he was attractive, especially to the young prima donnas. The Studio was his responsibility. He frequently descended from the pantheon at the top of the Met to rehearsals in the bowels of the opera house, when one of his prima donnas performed. Shortly after I joined the Studio, he arranged for me to audition for members of the Fisher family. As a result of that audition, I was engaged to sing for the opening of the Fisher Art Center in Marshalltown, Iowa, and then the Opera Guild gala in Dallas. The gala was perhaps the pinnacle of my singing career. My mother came from Tulsa and was placed at a table with the Count and Countess Gotzy and Francis Robinson.

Two years after I joined The Studio, the Musicians' Union called a strike. The big house shut down, I was back "between engagements," a euphemism for unemployment. I was again making the rounds of cattle-call auditions for chorus and bit parts and seeing still-auditioning old-timers I had first seen when I had arrived in New York eight years before.

I asked for the appointment with Gutman when it seemed that the strike would last the whole season. I didn't know if the Studio would renew my contract when the strike ended, or even if there would be a studio. When an expensive gown was needed for an exceptional performance, young prima donnas sometimes ventured to Gutman's office in the singers' holy of holies, but this was a first for me.

"You," Gower Champion said.

"Who, me?"

"How tall are you," he asked.

I was five six. "Five-seven," I said. Another tenor my same height glowered at me.

"On point?" Champion said and laughed. "Oh well, come back for the dance audition."

The interview came at the end of a week in which I had gone to twelve auditions. During a lineup of tenors auditioning for a road company of *Hello Dolly,* Gower Champion pointed to me.

"If I knew there was light at the end of the tunnel," I told John Gutman, who had recruited me for the Studio. "I can keep on living in a coldwater-flat and struggle to make ends meet."

He shook his head. "You still have much to learn." Too many languages, too many roles remained to be learned. The brass ring had swung tantalizingly near. I was forty-two. I had started too late.

"And what," Gutman asked, "constitutes light at the end of your tunnel?"

"The chance to sing great music with first-class musicians, a contract with The Met. I need to know if I will ever be able to live with some security and dignity."

He leaned against the high back of his leather chair, templing his fingers under his chin. "Sometimes it's best not to know."

"But I must know," I persisted. "Everyone is so encouraging, but I sense there is something I am not being told, like the emperor with no clothes." If anyone could predict my chances, Gutman could, and he was the only person I could think of who would tell me the truth.

"There's not much room at the top," he said. "You have a superb instrument, sometimes reminds me of Bergonzi."

Following the interview, as I waited at the Lincoln Center subway platform, I contemplated the third electric rail. How quickly the humiliation could be quenched. The train roared to a stop, and I got on. I climbed the four flights of stairs to my apartment, indifferent to the reek of urine, and filled a pint Mason jar with Chianti, placed an LP of Bjorling arias on the record player, and threw myself down on my cot.

"I don't know how old you actually are," Gutman had said. I had taken off a few years, as everyone did in show business.

He shook his head, bushy brows raised in a look of compassion. "You still need much experience. I don't know exactly what you mean by security and dignity. You will travel all the time and live out of trunks. Regional opera, yes. But the great houses. . . I do not see Corelli stepping aside for you."

Not long after the interview, Eve Queler asked me to sing a comprimario role in her New York Opera production of *The Tales of Hoffmann*. No. If I can't sing the lead, then I won't sing.

～～～～～～～

"Your voice is too far back in your throat," Bill said. "Sing through here." He pointed at the bridge of his nose. To show me how, and showing off for Clifford, he imitated Butterfly McQueen this time: "I'ze sorry Miz Scarlett."

I followed his suggestion, and the next song flowed more easily. Like getting on a bicycle after not having ridden for years, I discovered I could still sing. My voice felt even freer than before. Years too late, Bill had done for me what the New York teachers and coaches couldn't. He had gotten me to sing for him after I came to Key West as the county arts council director.

People had praised my performance of *Ave Maria* in the last Christmas concert. I was encouraged to believe it might be possible for Clifford, with his new digital camera, to record evidence that it had not been a fool's dream.

"You are not there to demonstrate your voice," the great tenor John Vickers told a young singer, "You are the servant, first of the composer, and like the composer, the poet, of the public. You're there to give, not to show-off." To another, he said: "Never make your voice soft. Allow it to be soft. Never make it loud. Let it be loud. Let your voice surrender to the deepest possible meaning of the text. That will allow you to surrender to the emotion. Don't be afraid. Surrender."

I started over a third time. Finally, the music took over. The final cadenza felt as effortless as a feather floating in an updraft, and the high note, a bird set free.

I sang Clifford's favorite, *Ah fuie duc image* from *Mignon*.

"You sound better than ever," Clif said, tears in his eyes. The tears, because he knows it isn't so.

Perhaps because Clifford is fifteen years younger than me, or perhaps because I have appeared younger than my age, I have thought I could defy aging, but lately, I am winded after running only a block. My old voice teacher, Madam Averino once asked me to tell her when it was the time she should stop singing. I promised I would tell her, but, of course, I didn't.

I was still undecided whether to go into the ministry when I enrolled in the group-therapy course during my final semester at Boston University School of Theology.

Across the river at Harvard, Timothy Leary and Richard Alpert (a.k.a. Ram Dass) experimented with lysergic acid, claiming mind-expanding properties for the drug. At Boston Psychopathic Hospital we were told that the drug might induce temporary insanity. The experience would provide useful insight into the psychosis of people we were attempting to help. All but one in our group volunteered to take the drug.

Shortly after taking our dosages we gathered in the office of Dr. Smith, the psychiatrist who was leading our group-therapy study. Already feeling the effects, one of the group slumped over with his arms wrapped around himself and would respond to no one. The following day he reported that he had felt as isolated as if he had been sealed in a coffin. Another started giggling. When I asked him what was funny, he viciously growled for me to get away from him. The following day he too was so sore from laughing, he could hardly move.

Dr. Smith told me that I was resisting the drug, which hurt my feelings. I wanted to be a good player, so, acting silly, I sat on the floor. When I looked back at the chair, it had grown so tall; I had to climb back on it as a baby climbs onto a highchair. Dr. Smith absentmindedly rubbed his temple causing his short reddish hair to spike up. The hair on the other side of his head grew into a matching horn.

"You are doing that on purpose," I shouted.

"What?"

His smile exposed tobacco-stained teeth that had become jagged, and his nose elongated into a hook. A detached part of me observed the whole scene.

"You're deliberately trying to look like a devil."

Later an interviewer asked, what was I feeling?

"Wait a minute," I said. "I need to find the *feeling.*" I closed my eyes and found myself in aquamarine with acid-green ribbons floating about. The ribbons had fuchsia fringe quivering like millipede's legs. I opened my eyes and reentered the room with the interviewer. I could remain coherent if I moved carefully from thought to thought as if pulling a chain, hand over hand, link by link. If I let go of a thought before grabbing hold of the next thought my mind flew apart, like freeing butterflies from a cage. Each time I closed my eyes I flew into new worlds of vibrant color. When I went snorkeling in the Caribbean a few years later, the colors of the coral reef were already familiar.

In one of the final experiments, I was given a lump of clay. I hoped the drug would release the creativity that has always seemed caged inside me. Before, when I tried to create something, the results were pathetic. An oblong form took shape into which I pressed deep grooves. Dr. Smith came into the room and sat next to me. My mind went into the moist darkness of the clay. I began to cry.

"Why are you crying?" he asked.

"There is no art in me. I'm not a singer. I'm not a potter. I'm not a writer." I said.

"Perhaps your art is with people," he said. "The ministry."

I graduated from theology school two months after the Boston Psychopathic lysergic acid experiment, and became a minister of education in a Congregational Church near Boston. There I received ordination. The Congregational Church would become part of the United Church of Christ, the first mainline Protestant church in the U.S. to ordain an openly gay man, but that would be twenty years after my ordination.

I did not present myself as openly gay, though I am confident that most folks who cared to recognized that I was gay. However, a colleague of mine raised a questioned whether a gay man was fit to work with young people. This led to an investigation by the church's conference officer, who spoke with the leadership in the two churches I had served. He reported only approval for me and my work; even so, it was devastating—the specter of humiliation I thought I had left in Oklahoma rose again and haunted me, and my relationship with the man I had met my last semester in theology school was falling apart.

After seven years in the ministry, I quit my position, borrowed money from my lover's family, and on a snowy Easter Sunday, flew out of Boston to St. Thomas. I managed a sleazy bar for the next six weeks. I then headed for Africa. In Rome, I climbed St. Peter's dome. In Ghana I taught for a while in a school located deep in the bush, a part of the West African nation seemingly untouched by Western Civilization.

I drifted on through Nigeria, the Congo, and down to South Africa where I had affairs in Cape Town, Durban and the Kruger Game Preserve. I wandered through Nairobi, Addis Ababa, Khartoum, Luxor, Cairo, Jerusalem, Damascus, and Beirut, arriving in New Delhi for the World Council of Churches Assembly. I was a guest in Bombay in a private Krishnavite temple, then took passage on a freighter east along the coasts of Asia. Eighteen months after I flew out of Boston, the Yasha Shima Maru freighter I had sailed on out of Yokohama, slipped under the Golden Gates.

Two months later, I announced to my family that I would pursue a singing career. I was already thirty-three.

Madam Olga Averino Federovsky

~~~~~~~~~

THE ORIENTAL RUG UNDER THE CURVE OF THE PIANO, WHERE A generation of singers had stood, is worn to its warp. Jagged as lightning, a crack on the wall strikes at a picture of a Venetian canal. The studio had once been the upstairs salon of an old mansion near Harvard Square. Afternoon sun ignited loose strands of her hair into a Faustian halo as—unconcerned with wrong notes—she beat the piano into an orchestra.

Although I followed a professional calling into the Christian ministry, since my teens and through college I had also studied voice. I was the associate minister at the First Congregational Church in Cambridge, my second position after graduating from Boston University. Our music director frequently called on me to sing solos, so I went looking for a voice teacher and found Madam Olga Averino at Longy School of Music—a stone's throw from the church.

I had been serving in the ministry seven years. My love relationship was on the rocks, and I had begun to question my calling, so I took a sabbatical leave, a year and a half of travel. Japan was the last country before I boarded a freighter in Yokohama bound for the States. During the long voyage across the Pacific, I decided to return to Japan as soon as I could find the means. In the meantime, while I worked out a way back to Japan, I returned to Cambridge and resumed voice lessons with Madam Averino. It was then that she introduced me to the big operatic arias. Up to that time, I had sung mainly art songs and oratorio, but the vocal ski jumps that lift the voice to vocal stratosphere of Verdi and Puccini, I had not yet attempted.

Growing up, I had longed to be tall and slender, but fate bequeathed to me a tenor's stature, short and wide-chested with the capacity to reach notes high on the musical scale. Those notes, which thrill, are achieved in a way similar to the pitcher lining up the ball's trajectory or a pole vaulter aligns his body for a jump. Reaching the upper range for the singer is like threading a needle.

I rehearsed and rehearsed "Che geli da manina," the famous tenor aria from Puccini's *La Bohme*, but each time I came to the thrilling high "C," I broke off. Then one afternoon, as I approached the high note, Olga fiercely hammering the old Steinway, stabbed at my groin and screamed, "Breath from where you are a man!" And as dust motes danced in the sun's rays streaming through a torn window shade, my voice soared. As if disconnected from me, it took on a life of its own, like an eagle broken free. In that transporting moment, I experienced the thrill the flute or violin must feel—not the player, the instrument itself! Ego melts. One becomes the servant of the sound, of the song. Only twice have I been granted such a transporting moment—when I stepped out of the way.

When, finally, I let go of the high note, Madam Olga Averino—who had sung before Tsar Nicolas—clapped her hands. "Eddy," she cried, "you are a true tenor. You could have a career!" (I was known as Edward before I took Grant as my stage name.)

She escaped the Bolsheviks by trading a jeweled brooch for passage in a boxcar across Siberia to China. She filled my head with aspiration, as Joseph Campbell urged to follow my bliss. At midnight on New Year's Eve, she once told me, if you place a candle between two mirrors facing each other, you may glimpse the future. She also told me that after her husband Paul died, he came to her.

"Death," she said, "is much like the living side—one lets go slowly, first of the physical world and then gradually of the spirit world until finally, one slips into the netherworld." I attended Zen meetings with the Russian, and who told me; "Darling, if you wish a career as an artist, all else must be second. Yes, Rachmaninoff had a family, but for the entire family and all his friends, his music came first."

When Olga entered a room, the lights bounced brighter. I gave her a topaz ring.

~~~~~~~~~~

That afternoon, not having checked in with my old happy-hour crowd since my return to Cambridge, I went to see if they still gathered late afternoons at the Brattle Bar underneath the Brattle Theater near Harvard Square.

As I came down the stairs, someone at the far end of the bar yelled, "The vagabond returns."

"It's on the house," the bartender said as he plunked a Scotch and soda in front of me.

"Tell us all about it," someone said. "Don't leave out a word."

"Mine is a long and tedious story," I said.

"Then leave a few words out and give us just the high points."

I didn't tell about a hillside overlooking Kobe Harbor, where my friend with a complexion as translucent as the cherry blossom petals that fell about us, said he would surely die if I didn't take him with me.

"I'll buy you," a newcomer to the group interrupted. I didn't know if he was drunk or kidding. "You can do all the traveling you want. Do whatever you want to do."

It turned out that he was not drunk. He owned a spice importing company, and was in need of someone to travel and buy spices. As his spice buyer, I could satisfy my wanderlust and earn a good income. But that evening the thought of doing whatever I wanted to do repeated in my brain over and over, like a chant.

I finally fell asleep, but awakened hours later, my mouth as dry as if I had eaten a green persimmon. I couldn't go back to sleep. The spice merchant's offer, "You can do whatever you want to do," took up where it had left off, and chased Olga's cry, "Eddy, you can have a singing career." By morning, "You can do what you want to do" had caught up to "You can have a career." And my life again veered off course. Rather than return to Japan, I would be a singer.

I called my mother and told her that I was now pursuing a singing career! There was a long pause at her end of the line.

"We love you, darling," she broke the silence. My father had died while I was still in college. My brilliant older brother was shot down over Korea, and now her prodigal is off on another fool's errand. Thank God for my sweet sister.

Thirty-two years old and ten thousand dollars in debt, I took a job as a gardener in exchange for room and board.

Olga's studio and small apartment were shrines where, over cocktails or dinners, she mesmerized her acolytes with stories drawn from her exotic life. The brooch the Bolsheviks passed over thinking it mere costume jewelry bought boxcar passage across Siberia for Olga, her husband, and child.

And she told us, the great Russian bass, Chaliapin, had a neurotic fear that he had foam in his throat.

"Olga, wasn't your mother a princess?"

"One of my father's wives," she says, dismissively. "There were so many Russian princesses it didn't matter."

Before the revolution, her father had been the director of the Moscow Conservatory of Music. After her escape from Russia, she entertained in the Russian community in Harbin, Manchuria, and Peking. Rachmaninoff helped her, her husband, and daughter to immigrate to the United States, where she made her Carnegie Hall debut the day the stock market crashed. Sergei Koussevitzky brought her violinist husband, Paul Federovsky, to the Boston Symphony. When the Philadelphia Symphony performed Alban Berg's opera, *Lulu*, they called on Olga, who was one of the few sopranos capable of singing the atonal music.

Once a great beauty, mixing Russian with French accents, the stories cascaded one after the other. Olga was my benign Svengali, a sorceress—as if by magic, rooms grew brighter when she entered.

Her passion was not simply for the voice itself, as it is among many operatic singers, especially tenors. Her passion was for the voice as an instrument to serve the composer and poet. Familiar with Russian theater director Konstantin Stanislavski, she taught that motivation should spring from inside one's emotions. "Feel! Don't act!" She commanded.

In Schubert's song, *Ir Bild*, the picture of a loved one stirs poignant memories. The song concludes, "Oh, I cannot believe you are lost."

When I had hit every note perfectly, she said, "Singing is not to show your voice. You must experience what the poet is feeling." I sang *Ir Bild*, a second time, I imagined I held a photograph of my dead brother.

"But dear," she said gently when I nearly came to tears, "the experience is not for you. It is for the audience. You must be *in* the moment and at the same time see yourself having the experience. You must become the observer and the observed. Otherwise, your singing is mere self-indulgence." Perhaps it was then I began to see myself from afar.

I can thank Olga for one of my many "roads less taken." Olga arranged for me to give a recital in the home of the writer and opera librettist, Ethan Ayer. Not only was Ethan to become one of my greatest friends, but he also became my patron . Years later he would be a principal character in novels I would write long after my singing career sputtered to an end. A cape usually draped around his six foot three, three hundred pound form, Ethan was an incarnation of Oscar Wilde.

The central hall of Ethan's home served as a venue for recitals by Olga's students. It was a daunting experience to stand in the crook of a nine-foot Steinway, facing as many as ninety guests in Ethan's Cambridge mansion.

Ethan and his family dated their arrival to America back to early New England settlers, their mansions, and horses, and General Patten, his uncle, pulled back the curtain for me to glimpse old-moneyed gentry. I sang in his home. Olga told me his mother inherited twenty million dollars, and it made no difference. I dined at their tables and swam in their pools, but never made the mistake of thinking I was one of them.

In New York, I continued my studies with other teachers. I sang and danced in summer stock and four star-studded Broadway musicals. I sang on the *Ed Sullivan* show the same night Diana Ross and the Supremes appeared. I appeared on national radio and sang at the White House.

Finally, the Metropolitan Opera Studio took me in. But fame wasn't what Olga had in mind for me. She had meant me to be an artist.

～～～～～

Do I regret following roads less traveled? Do I regret that ten-year odyssey caused when I fell under a sorceress' spell? Not now I don't.

How else would I have found myself backstage watching Ethel Merman belt out "There's no business like show business!" How else would I know the ecstasy of singing a Puccini aria? How else would I have learned what it is like to reach for the unreachable?

Ethan

~~~~~~~~

I HAVE SUNG SINCE I CAN REMEMBER. WHEN THE CHURCH CHOIR needed a tenor soloist, they called on me. I was regular entertainment at the Rotary Club and sang for the Women's Temperance Union meetings. My *Road to Mandalay* was a favorite. Longy School of Music, where I took up voice lessons with Olga Federovsky Averino is just down the block from the church I served as an associate minister. The First Church Congregational, now United Church of Christ, shares credit with the First Church Unitarian for the founding of Harvard. When the church split over the Trinity, the Unitarians got the old frame church building and the cemetery. The area clustered around Harvard Yard reeks of history. Paul Revere is reputed to have ridden his horse right past where my church now stands, facing across the Cambridge Commons to Harvard Yard.

Olga took me to have cocktails in Ethan Ayer's home on Brattle Street, a block from the Alfred Lord Tennyson house, where George Washington spent the night. Ethan's thirty-room shingled cottage-style house was designed by the nineteenth-century architect, Henry Hobson Richardson. His Romanesque style influenced many public buildings of that time, and most famously Boston's Trinity Episcopal Church. Only a short distance from the conservatory, Olga's students frequently gave recitals in the central hall, which could seat as many as ninety guests.

Soon after I met Ethan, evening cocktails by the fire in his cozy downstairs library became an evening ritual. His fifty-foot long upstairs library, where he wrote, was reserved for more special occasions, such as New Year's Eve. Ethan once told me, "The difference between old and new money is that people with old money are farther from their crimes."

Carrying a silver-headed walking stick with his mass of white mane, six-foot-three-inch frame, and three hundred pounds, the librettist would say, "I don't just look like Oscar Wilde. I *am* Oscar Wilde." Ethan wrote the libretto for the critically acclaimed opera, *The Wings of the Dove*, composed by Douglas Moore, starring Beverly Sills in the New York City Opera performance.

I was to learn that Ethan, nearing sixty, had never sexually consummated a love relationship. "It is not easy to find someone attracted to this three-hundred-pound, six-foot-three corpus," he complained.

He knew better than I that if I were to go anywhere as a singer, I would have to cut the apron strings tying me to Olga and go to New York. He arranged with his family's office to set up a stipend for me, to cover modest living and voice lessons, and coaching in Italian. Before heading to New York, I spent the summer singing in a summer-stock theater near Boston. Then with Ethan paying my way, I went to New York to try my luck at grabbing the brass ring. I got church and synagogue singing jobs, bit parts in off- and off-off Broadway shows, and did more summer stock. In between shows, I collected unemployment. For six months I lived with a Danish ballet dancer. When Ethan was in town, we would have cocktails in the Algonquin's lobby and dinner at the Waldorf's Bull and Bear.

One of the singers I met in summer stock put me onto an apartment in an old tenement. The fourth-floor walk-up apartment cost forty-five dollars a month. The old Upper Eastside tenement buildings, built for European emigrants in the 1800s were under rent control and manna for struggling singers and dancers who flocked to New York. My bathtub was under the tiny kitchen counter, and my toilet squeezed into a telephone booth-like closet.

~~~~~~~~~~~~

I went to auditions where they line us up like cattle, *cattle calls,* as Broadway gypsies refer to them. There is always a demand for loud tenors. Soon I was on the road learning how to get along, staying in the cheapest possible accommodations, and pocketing the housing allowance the Equity Union required the producers to pay us. I went from show to show, building a small bank account. I couldn't get over what a friend said to me. He said, *I was being kept.* I felt I was a prostitute, though we never had sex together. As I write about Ethan, I shouldn't be proud that I never gave my friend what he so deeply needed.

Wherever Ethan traveled, if someone went with him, *good old Ethan* picked up the check—always paying for dinners, drinks, and taxi fares. I wanted him, for once, to experience *not having to shell out.*

Dean, a former college classmate, owned a bar in St. Thomas, where two years before I had run the place while he was on vacation. That was before I headed on around the world and a whole other story. Dean was going to be off-island for a week and invited me to come, bring a friend, and stay at his place—no bartending this time.

The trip to St. Thomas, my paying my own airfare and providing us a place to stay, was my chance to show Ethan what it feels like to not always have to pick up the check.

The first night after we arrived, we went to Sugarloaf Lodge, overlooking the harbor. Shortly after we were into our first drinks, second drinks, which we had not ordered, arrived at our table. The waiter said the drinks were sent to me by a man standing at the bar. He pointed to a slender black gentleman who greeted me with a smile and beckoned me over. It turned out that Benjamin was a friend of Dean's, whom I had met on a previous visit to the island. I invited Ben to come join Ethan and me, and from then on, for the rest of the evening, I might as well not have been present.

Ben wasn't particularly good-looking, but his smile was irresistible and, whatever he lacked in looks, he made up for in wit and charm. It soon became apparent that Benjamin's interest was in Ethan, not me.

Ethan stunned all his friends when he returned from our vacation to the Virgin Islands with scrawny, black Benjamin in tow.

One afternoon I rushed directly from the unemployment office, where I picked up my check, to meet Ethan at the Algonquin. I jumped off the subway, exited at Forty-Second behind the public library, and ran up Sixth, past Town Hall on Forty-Third, and on up to Forty-Fourth. It had been a hectic week of cattle-call auditions. I had survived New York, which was a lot better than most hopefuls who gravitate to the Big Apple with stars in their eyes. I always felt a thrill when I entered the darkened Algonquin lobby; Dorothy Parker's and Alexander Woollcott's ghosts lingering in its shadows. The lobby is more like the drawing room of an elegant old club than a hotel. Ethan had already claimed his favorite chair in a corner. I hurried across and collapsed into the chair facing his.

"Half the cast from my last show were in the unemployment line," I said, "but not many are having drinks at the Algonquin with the great librettist."

"Pish-tosh," he said. "You'd be surprised how many of the smartly dressed clientele are on the dole."

"Abigail Northrop had phoned the past week. She still wanted me to direct her foundation. I told her I couldn't make up my mind. I need to know if I am ever going to get a real role in a show or opera."

"Sometimes it's best not to know," Ethan said, "like I don't want to know who Ben goes with or when finally he'll not return." He rang a bell affixed to a table next to his chair, signaling a waiter.

"Ben loves you," I said.

"That I don't doubt, but for how long?"

"I need to know," I persisted. "Not that I haven't had the breaks. I'm grateful for all you've done for me, but the life of a Broadway gypsy, living in a cold-water flat, and auditioning over a dozen times just for a part in the chorus, isn't why I struggled through seven years of university."

I can pass for younger, but I know how old I am—already forty years old—not enough time left.

Giorgio Tozzi

TEARS RAN DOWN MY FACE AS I STOOD WATCHING GIORGIO Tozzi and his wife Monte singing, *My heart is so full of you.* I wept because I knew it was true! Monte noticed, and more tears flowed, and then Giorgio, then the director called for a ten-minute break, and I was banned from watching them rehearse. They were playing the lead roles in the St. Louis Muny's production of *Most Happy Fellow.* But they weren't just acting; I know because I had performed their marriage ceremony.

Giorgio would be nominated for a Tony award for his acting, continue as principal bass at the Metropolitan Opera and then go out to Hollywood where he played the role of Dottore opposite Burt Reynolds' Shamus McCoy, in the film *Shamus.*

The famous bass-baritone burst into my life shortly after I signed a contract with the Metropolitan Opera Studio.

My contract included the Met paying for a coach to teach me the music and words and the style of the particular song or role I was studying. I had been paying a *voice teacher,* but those funds had run out. There were a number of coaches on the Studio's roster from whom I could choose. I made a fateful decision in choosing to coach with Max Walmer when I learned that the Met's principal bass-baritone coached with Max. He must be very good, I decided.

Max was a funny guy and a musical savant. He rarely needed a musical score; he simply played from memory. The music was already in his bones. And he was a doorway to an amazing world. He never admitted to his conniving, but I cannot believe it was an accident that he scheduled my rehearsal right before Giorgio was due, and that he had me singing an aria that showed off my *high* notes. Just as I let go of the final B-flat, there came a tapping at the door, and in walked the great bass-baritone! I was flabbergasted!

Giorgio complimented me and asked me to sing the aria again. When I finished, he suggested ways I might better place my voice as I approached the final phrase. *The principal bass of the Metropolitan Opera demonstrated by singing the phrase in my tenor range!*

Giorgio then offered to give me free lessons. Max must have told Giorgio that, short on funds, I had to give up voice lessons. Giorgio turned out to be the best teacher I would ever have.

One thing followed another as if destined. At the time, I was sharing the basement of a tenement with a furnace. The landlord, who charged me a small rent, had allowed me to chop a hole in the sewer line and install my plumbing. The toilet rocked a bit. I've never learned to set a toilet properly. I framed in and then painted a variety of colors the meters for all of the building's apartments, which hang on my living room wall. It was my an attempt to transform them into an art installation, or so I thought.

Seeing I was resourceful, a short time after I began studying with Giorgio he suggested I might be more comfortable living in the half-finished chauffer's quarters above the garage on his Montclair estate, an acre near the top of a New Jersey hill.

Not long after I moved to Montclair, I met Clifford at an opera party in New Rochelle, New York. It was our second meeting at opera parties. This time he came home with me. He must have thought he had struck it rich, as I was staying in the big house, while Giorgio with his new wife was in Hamburg, Germany where he was performing the title role in *Die Meistersinger*.

Giorgio and Monte returned from Germany. Clif continued to come out from Manhattan to visit me and help with my reconstruction of the chauffeur's quarters until Giorgio finally invited Clif to just move in with me. Thus, I, from the edge of the dust bowl in west Oklahoma, and Clif, from the Panhandle of Texas, the other edge of the dust bowl—our twangy accents intact—stumbled into the grandly operatic world of Giorgio Tozzi, a big, gregarious Italian from Chicago.

How amazed the farmer who built the original house would have been to see throne chairs from the Old Met gracing the entry vestibule, and two-story Tiffany windows in the stair tower, the baronial living room with coffered ceiling, formed from molds taken from an English manor, a fireplace out of a castle at one end and a nine-foot Bechstein grand piano filling a bay window looking out over the Hudson River and distant Manhattan skyline.

It was a wild music-filled life we were drawn into. Sunday mornings, he would call up to us, "Bloody-Mary time!" Nearly every Sunday evening there would be a gathering of singers, and muckety-mucks of the singer's world—conductors, managers, agents and the like. Those Sunday evenings Max would be at the Bechstein, vodka in hand.

One memorable moment was a Sunday the New York Times published a rave review of Lili Chookasian's performance of Earth Mother in Wagner's Ring Cycle. "Dark velvety contralto voice," the critic had written; we begged Lili to sing for us. After much pleading, she conceded, but rather than a Wagnerian aria, she sang, "You'll Never Walk Alone" from *Carousel*. These many years later, I can't recall ever again hearing a song sung so heart-breakingly beautiful.

I love telling about a Sunday evening parties. Max, as usual, was at the piano when Monte came in from the kitchen wiping her hands on an apron.

"Sing for us, Monte, sing," we chanted, and Max began playing the opening strains for "Una Voce Poco Fa," from *The Barber of Seville,* one of the most challenging and spectacular arias in the soprano repertoire. "No, no, no, "Monte shook her head.

But Max kept repeating the opening phrase, until finally, amidst our clapping, clowning like a little girl called before the front of the class, Monte made her way to the bow of the piano and flawlessly ripped off a virtuoso performance of the difficult aria. On her last trill, feigning a faint, she threw herself on the floor and supine, finished the aria.

Oh, yes, I sang as well, and folks were always encouraging.

The Studio sent me out with a quartet to take operatic music to places such as Fargo and Minot, North Dakota, and Bemidji, Minnesota. We performed cabaret-style *Vienna* to *Broadway* and *Shakespeare in Opera and Song.* The Studio was created by John Gutman to be a kind of finishing school for winners of the Metropolitan Opera's national auditions. And take music to the hinterland.

Clifford and I lived in the chauffeur's quarters four years, then Clif got a position at the Fashion Institute of Technology, and I went off on tour, as soloist with the Camerata Coral, singing in Carnegie Hall and at the White House, but my singing career was headed down the tubes. The Musician's Union went on strike, which shut down the Met Studio. I was back to *cattle calls*. As promising as a spot on the *Ed Sullivan Show* with Ethel Merman may sound, or the White House gig, and a solo performance on national radio, it wasn't in the cards that I should arrive where so many of the folks at Tozzi's *had* arrived.

Wesley Hotchkiss

THE SEA IS CALM. TWO PELICANS SITTING IN QUIET MEDITATION pay me no attention as I approach the water's edge. The sea grape has grown too since I was last here, and the sea cider is crowding the honeybush. Not wanting to take time from my writing, I've let things go. I promise myself that I'll get some help and knuckle down. But I can't stop my story without including Wesley Hotchkiss.

I had squandered my theological education; my singing career had gone nowhere. I was at a loss as to what to do with the rest of my life. There didn't seem to be much market for a person with a theological education, a defunct singer, a dyslectic who can't spell and barely multiply and divide.

Someone suggested I talk with Wesley Hotchkiss at the United Church Board for Homeland Ministers (a national church office for my denomination, the United Church of Christ).

I didn't know my fortunes were about to change once again when I walked into the old building on Park Avenue South around the corner from Gramercy Park and boarded the elevator.

As I entered Dr. Hotchkiss' office, he stood, laid a book aside, and came around to shake my hand. ""Skip the Dr. Hotchkiss," he said. "Wes will do."

I noticed the book he had been reading was by Arthur Koestler:

Sleepwalker, I believe was the name of the book. I mentioned that I had read Koestler's *The Lotus and the Robot*, about the authors visit to India and Japan seeking to learn whether those countries' cultures and philosophies had anything worthwhile to offer Western culture.

For a few minutes, we chatted about Koestler's books. Wes was particularly interested in the changing vision of the universe that seems to be taking place. Then Wes asked, "What can I do for you?"

I gave him a brief rundown of what I had been doing since I graduated. "I don't know when it began," I told him, "but from early on, I have confused art with religion."

~~~~~~~~~~

Something must have clicked for us. Perhaps, because I had read Koestler's book, he thought I was smarter than I am.

A gaunt, tall man, Wes was the executive of the Division of Higher Education and American Missionary Association. The Congregational branch of the United Church was keen on education, and social and racial justice. Wes' Ph.D. from Chicago University was in geography. He considered himself a scientist, though he had been given many honorary Doctor of Divinity degrees. Bridging between the rational, empirical, and the religious was his passion, and in art, the aesthetic, he sensed that bridge might be found.

I left Wes's office with a six-month contract as an art consultant, to travel around the country and sniff out what was happening with art in communities near colleges and theology schools related to the United Church, from Berkeley to New Orleans. After I returned to New York and presented my report, I was set up with an office and provided a secretary, a Black Muslim.

About the same time, Clifford gained a tenured position at the Fashion Institute of Technology, and with a down-payment loan from the United Church board, we bought a brownstone in a reviving Brooklyn neighborhood. As prostitutes, drugs, and pimps moved out, we started fixing up our own home. I wasn't "out," yet soon after I joined Wes's staff, Clifford was invited to join in when there were gatherings that included spouses. Nothing was said, Clif was simply invited. A few years later a United Church association would ordain a very-out minister.

<p align="center">~~~~~~~~~~</p>

My arts consultant days were was blown when Wes announced his retirement. Never appearing on organizational charts, my work had gone on for ten years under Wes' wing.

Clif and I moved from the Brownstone to Key West, where Clifford worked at the museum, and I became the county arts council director.

Not long after we moved to Key West, Wes and his wife, Mary Ellen, followed us to the Florida Keys. By then, greetings were with a hug. One New Year's party, Clif and I asked Wes to bless our union. I first met Clif on New Year's. Wes' blessing was all the marriage we felt we needed, although years later we did the official thing in Santa Fe, New Mexico.

When they came to our Key West parties in our little cigar-makers house in Key West's Old Town, I'd be chopping or mixing something at the counter, overlooking our splash swimming pool under a gumbo-limbo tree and Wes, leaning over me, would be explaining new information about the Big Bang, the Singularity, or how the Quark may provide empirical evidence of divine intervention in creation. He told me that I was the only one who understood him. I didn't exactly, but I guess the love that had grown between us counts as understanding.

My sight is blurred. I think I'll go down to the water's edge and commune with the pelicans.

Rachmaninoff's Second
Piano Concerto

THEY HAVE SEASON TICKETS TO THE SUNDAY SYMPHONY IN THE grand old Jose Peon Contreras theater, which dates back to the city's palmy days. The newly renovated, Renaissance-style jewel was built when Mérida had more millionaires per capita than any other city in the world, and when Paris and Havana were the Yucatán's wealthy hacienda owners' playgrounds.

They are excellent seats. A little more toward the center we would have preferred, and stage right rather than left, so that we could see the piano keys, still, excellent, seats A and B, front row in box 15 on the first level. At the beginning of the season, I had rushed to obtain the seats a level lower than the positions they had held for the last four seasons.

Five tiers of bowed boxes, faced with freshly restored, cavorting cherubs rose from the orchestra level. Golden swags draping from the front of our boxes bear a fresh sheen. As it must have appeared a hundred years before, thousands of facets glitter in the dimmed light of the theater's great chandelier.

On the orchestra level, a poet friend leans forward, visiting with a gentleman I don't recognize. Her poems about her life in Mérida have been translated into Spanish. A former administrator of the English Library with his husband wave to us as they take their seats a few rows behind the poet. They have both been married to women and have children. In the aisle seat, row F, stage right, their friend, an amateur pianist, sits where he has a good view of the keyboard. He has held that seat for years. Without a good view of the keyboard, he refused to attend performances. That's the way he is. For years, his annual carnival parties were the glue of the expat community. The parties have long ceased as the expat community has grown unwieldy.

For the first years after the orchestra was reformed into the fine ensemble, it now is, I sat with our old friend, Judd. How he loved the symphony! It is now ten years since Judd died. Our seats were the first two seats off the aisle, row E.

Clifford and I moved to seats in an upper-level box, not because of the expense, but because we preferred a fuller view than being off to the side. Clif thinks the acoustics are better at the upper level. He is younger and hears better, so perhaps he is right. I can't tell the difference.

An opened nine-foot Steinway, its golden interior catching the spotlight, dominates center stage. Soon the lights dim and the concertmaster, receiving applause with a toothy grin, strides out. He strikes the "A" key on the piano, and the orchestra begins to squawk like a chicken yard. The concertmaster has failed to touch up the crown of his dark auburn hair. If a guy, especially a performer, wants to dye his hair, he had best invest in a two-way mirror to see the balding moon-like crown of his head.

More applause and the guest conductor strides on stage. He's lithe, tall, lots of hair, well-trimmed goatee, handsome, and gives every evidence that he knows it. As the applause subsides, the soloist enters to fresh waves of clapping. He bows, applause dies, he sits, twists nobs on the side of the piano stool, pulls a handkerchief from his pocket, dabs his brow, places the handkerchief next to the closed music rack, rocks back, pauses, eyes the conductor, then raises his hands, talon-like, and attacks.

An instant before the sound reaches my ears the hackles raise and an ecstatic thrill, like a lover's first caress, shivers through me. I float back the first time Rachmaninoff affected me in this way.

~~~~~~~~~~

The Bulldog Theater smells of popcorn and urine, but I smelled only the rich perfume of heavy-lidded Jane Powell listening to handsome José Iturbi. That afternoon, the beauty and grief of Rachmaninoff's Second Piano Concerto invaded the soul of the snotty-nosed boy, who hadn't a glimmer of who he was, and who needed desperately to go to the bathroom. Warmth spread in my seat as the beautiful music broke my heart, as beauty would wound me over and over again throughout this long life.

When I hear Rachmaninoff's music I think of Madam Olga, her many stories of Russia, the tzar and the Bolsheviks. The glamorous Russian lady's words still haunt me: *"Eddy, you can have a career!"*

I still long for beauty to bloom inside me. Following the heart attack, more aware than ever before of the inexorable seeping of the sands of time, I obsessively yearn to be an instrument through which the essence at the edge may flow. *Princes come/Princes go/ An hour of pomp and show/They know./Princes come/And over the sands of time/They go./Wise men come/Ever promising/The riddle of life to know./Wise Men come/But over the sands/The silent sands of time, they go/Lovers come/Lovers Go/And all that there is to know./ Lovers know./Only Lovers know.* When I still dreamed I'd be a great singer, I sang those words, set to the Russian, Alexander Borodin's music in the Broadway show, *Kismet.*

The pianist had to have begun learning the notes, etching

them into his unconscious, as he learned to speak. The child's hands would not yet have been large enough to span the chords (Rachmaninoff's hands famously could embrace well beyond a full octave) until after his adolescent growth spurt. He played as if he, the Steinway, and the orchestra were a single instrument.

The heartbreakingly beautiful, slow adagio movement transports me to a grassy knoll overlooking my hometown. I sit on a marble bench beneath gnarled cedar trees. Fields stretch for miles, some fallow and others planted. More benches and stones scatter down the hillside to the town

A rabbit hops out of a nearby hay field. It is a cottontail rabbit. Summers plowing, after the wheat harvest, I'd stop, jump down and lift baby rabbits out of the furrow.

The cottontail hops to the bench nearly halfway down the slope. My family's name is incised into the stone. My brother's name is there, though his remains lie scattered somewhere in Korea. I too will lie under the green, green sod, where, after all my striving, I belong. The music swells; I grab Clifford's hand and with him we fly, clutching the bunny, out beyond the glittering chandelier into the stars.

As the final chord decays, the audience sits in stunned silence and then bursts into applause. Many jumped to their feet shouting *bravo, bravo,* and members of the orchestra stomp their feet. Abdiel Vazquez bowing, modestly places his hand over his heart.

Dirt

~~~~~~~~

NOT ABLE TO DECIDE BETWEEN COFFEE AND TEA, AND THEN mumbling the old saying about the sun and the yardarm and feeling slightly guilty, he grabs a beer. (Guilt is a gift from his youth; he wouldn't get anything done without it.)

Before he crawled into bed the night before, as a kind of *Last Supper* for the plants he planned to execute, he had dragged the hose around to the patch where he now sat, and set a sprinkler going, then crawled into bed with a whodunit. He forgot the water until near midnight, as he reached to turn off his reading light. He congratulated himself for remembering—something he seemed to do more and more lately. His father taught the pulling-weeds chore is much easier after a good soaking.

Saturdays were weeding days. If he got his assigned batch of weeds cleared by noon, Saturday afternoons, nickel award clutched in his hand, chewed fingernails still dirt embedded, he'd run to the afternoon double features, *The Mask of Zorro* and *Flash Gordon* at the Bulldog picture show. His father had taught him so many practical things: to change a car's oil and filter, how to clean spark plugs, and mix plaster. At times, it still seems his father's hand guides him. My "Sunshine Joyboy," his father had called him, but his father died before he saw how his son turned out. Perhaps it was just as well.

Amazing how a handful of dirt is like coming across a torn photograph while cleaning out the attic. Hours later you're still sitting on a dusty old trunk lid remembering a licking you got for sassing your first-grade teacher, and when you got home, you got a second licking; or a photo brings back a first kiss and a first broken heart. The crabgrass had been hardly noticeable, but a deeply ingrained instinct required it be eradicated. He was a weed puller almost from birth.

Those summer afternoons out weeding the victory garden of crabgrass must have slipped into his DNA. Every place he traveled he'd come across a sprout or patch, just two or three plants huddled at the edge of a sidewalk in front of Buckingham Palace or under a tree in Paris' Bois de Boulogne. And here he is, in front of a banyan tree, not far from where a Maya pyramid once stood, its stones embedded in the first cathedral built on the American continent. The old man jabs a knife at his nemesis. Crabgrass has stalked him from his family's frying-pan-hot and dry West Oklahoma victory garden, to this foreign land a lifetime later. He has dined in palaces, shaken the hand of presidents, swam coral seas, kneeled in zen gardens, and indulged in carnal pleasures, and yet he feels no greater sense of well-being than when fondling the earth's crust.

The great banyan is a far cry from the catalpa tree dripping beans that he and the neighbor boys smoked behind the Johns' barn, down the alley from the family victory garden. The banyan's branches meld into roots that flow like honey over the remains of an ancient stonewall. A small lawn spreads between the tree and the house, and a tangle of philodendron carpets a miniature jungle growing on the other side of the tree. The sickly philodendron struggling in a milk bottle in his grandmother's kitchen window comes to mind. The doves shamelessly mate just as they did in the catalpa, but there were no bickering parrots where he pulled his first crabgrass—"You never listen to me"—the parrots sound like his parents out for a drive—"You flew left when I asked you to fly right!"

The towel beneath his shorts has grown pleasantly, earthy damp. He smiles, he could stay like this all day.

He reveres life, all life, rescues bees floundering in a pool. He regrets squashing roaches or killing hardworking ants, and won't poison mice, but let him loose on crabgrass, and he is Attila the Hun. His fingers, skilled as a piano prodigy, feel down the stem to the dirt's surface. With sensitivity gained through hours of practice, sensing just the right amount of pressure to exert without breaking the stem, he gently shakes and pulls until the roots, like a charmed snake, slither from the moist dirt. The sensation of roots giving way yields the pleasure of conquest.

The feel of roots giving way is as satisfying as scratching an itch. And when he misjudges the tensile strength, the root snaps off, and the weed has won the bout. The weed will resurface deeper and double in size to taunt another day. The defeat is worse than striking a foul ball or having a fish slip the hook.

How little we appreciate dirt, he thinks. People ooh and ah over trees' autumn colors, chrysanthemums and hollyhocks but not the dirt that feeds them. Folks applaud the surface of things, the singer more than the poet, the painter, not the paint. Where would the painter be without linseed oil and pigment or his acrylics and canvases? We are awestruck by the ancient sequoias, but don't give a thought to the eons-old dirt that sustains the trees. *Getting down in the dirt* is a satisfying thing to do.

He wraps his fingers around stems radiating from a central hub from which the root shoots deep into the ground. Brush-like seeds sprout from stem ends. He carefully places the seeded grass in a pile he will burn. Another day of neglect and the seeds might have spread out of his control.

A compact clump of seedlings comes loose. He leisurely shakes free each sprout, some only a single blade.

He is eleven or twelve again. The war is raging in Europe; it is a blistering hot day. Their victory garden is in a vacant lot on the other side of Johns' horse lot. Even the horses do their part, supplying an abundance of manure fertilizing half the victory gardens in the neighborhood.

Mr. Johns is the town's drayman. When someone needs anything hauled, Mr. Johns is the person they call. His arms are as big as thighs. He and his big draft horses are a good fit. He has half a hog curing in salt on his back porch. Mrs. Johns sings hymns as she goes about her housework, "On a hill far away, stood an old rugged cross," and "I come to the garden alone, while the dew is still on the roses."

Horse manure isn't as good as cow manure. If he started life over again, he muses, maybe he would be a botanist specializing in manure and dirt. He knows the qualities of horse, cow, chicken, and even hog manure, and understands that well-rotted manure of any kind is better than fresh. Still, manure shouldn't rot too fast or too long or it loses its nutrients.

He pictures himself, hunched over toad-like, in front of the banyan tree. Perhaps from the dirt he held in his liver-spotted hands, the Maya grew the corn from which they believed they were created.

He holds the dirt to his nose. It is black and herb-smelling. The fragrance, he thought, of a thousand seasons of banyan leaves, parrot and pigeon and deer droppings. A windmill once stood in the middle of the half-acre extending behind the high-ceilinged, almost two-centuries-old stone house. There would have been outhouses for the owners and servants, a hog lot, and chickens scratching around. The dirt is rich and loamy, like the dirt in east Oklahoma where his grandparents gardened.

When his family visited his grandparents in Muskogee, his father would drive his grandfather out to look at land. They would drive toward Tahlequah near the Arkansas border to look at acreages. His grandad had a strong hankering for land. The first thing his grandfather would do is climb over the fence and kick the dirt. His father would kick the dirt, too, and he'd kick along with them. They would take up a handfuls, squeeze and rub it, and then let it sift through their fingers. Not interested in sheds or fencing, they would head for stands of oaks and cottonwood, signs of moisture. There would be a creek, or a spring bubbles up from under a rock feeding a bed of watercress. They'd gathered watercress, and his grandmother would make a tangy salad or watercress sandwiches.

About as close as his grandad got was a two-acre cow lot. He sold the milk to neighbors, and the cows' manure fertilized his grandmother's beans and foxgloves. His folks had souls of dirt-farmers. Dirt in Eastern Oklahoma was like the dirt sticking to his hand. Not sandy like in the western part of the state. He had to shake and comb the dirt from roots.

In the depth of the depression, his father, unable to find work in the more fertile eastern part of the state, took about the only job offered, selling car supplies—fan belts, motor oil, and tire patches—to small-town hardware stores and roadside filling stations in the parched state's southwestern corner. It was the heart of the 1930s Dust Bowl, west of Oklahoma City where the plains roll like the inland sea that once covered them. Unlike loamy or clay soil, the prairie sand filters off the roots and through fingers like fine sand. The wind blows the sand into tumbleweed-clogged barbed-wire fences and drifts into the scrub, forming sand dunes and hills where none had been before foolish farmers set deep digging plows in the ground.

It is grass country and should have been left the way it was, when, after the Louisiana Purchase, surveyors declared it desert and unfit for cultivation. The government first gave the land to the

Indians they had displaced from the fertile southern and eastern regions. Relocating the Cheyenne and Apache Indians, the government gave the land to what they called the civilized tribes and made Muskogee the capital of the Choctaw, Chickasaw, Seminole, and Creeks, and then soon took it back, and gave it to European farmers accustomed to the deep-black dirt of their forested and well-watered homelands. They scoffed at lazy farmers who merely scratched the surface to plant oats, barley, and wheat. Digging deep was almost a religion for the Lutheran and Calvinist farmers, and they set their moldboard plows to dig deep and turn the soil over on top of itself, leaving the field clean and looking like chocolate cake icing and vulnerable. Their plows, at the end of a long sweaty day, gleamed as proudly as silver wedding gifts, a testimony to the farmers' virtue. But digging deep destroyed the land meant for grazing. Not all religious beliefs are right. The prairie is too soft to be treated the way they did back East or in Europe.

He was just a boy when Roosevelt created an alphabet of remedies for the climatic and economic disaster—C.C.C., W.P.A., T.V.A., etc. They dammed creeks and rivers, dug drainage ditches, taught farmers to terrace the land, not plow too deep, and to plant winter wheat. They hired the unemployed to plant rows of trees along the north side of fields to tame the scouring winds, built post offices, paid artists to paint murals depicting the country's history, and even created W.P.A symphonies. The Japanese bombed Pearl Harbor and victory gardens became patriotic. His country has been at war ever since.

The flutter of doves brought him back to the dirt he shakes from the grass in his hand. It comes from a layer only a half-foot or so before hitting porous calcium stone, once the floor of the sea that covered the Yucatán. The stone is as porous as Swiss cheese. Twenty feet or so down, water gurgles from the forested Puuc Hills, thirty or forty miles further inland toward the gulf. Countless sinkholes, *cenotes*, and undiscovered caverns lay below the surface. He imagines a cavern below where he digs, the roots of the banyan having long ago found their way there. Someday, long after he is gone, and after humans have destroyed themselves, this crust will give way, and the banyan roots will claim its walls.

~~~~~~~~~~~~

The clairvoyant, Edgar Cayce, believed a river runs through each of our lives. If we swim with the current, our lives will go as they are meant to, but if we resist the current, we are never fulfilled. That is the way his life has seemed.

Struggling to come to terms with himself, there hadn't been enough time for him to come to terms with his father. His Aunt Grace, his father's sister, had screamed when she learned his father wished to he be buried in a wooden coffin without a vault to delay his body's return to the earth. He smiles at the dirt crumbling from his fingers.

The underground streams are like the authentic self he feels must lay within the caverns of his mind, and somehow through that authentic self he connects. It is written somewhere, "Our life is a faint tracing on the surface of mystery."

He thinks about being and non-being, about what it is to be fully conscious. A person never needs to leave home, he now understands. Myriad satisfactions exist within our own yards if we merely get our hands down in the dirt.

He sits back on his haunches and looks into the branches of a royal palm, a seedling when he first planted the grass, and now it overshadows even the banyan.

A person could just lie in the grass and examine all the goings on and grow as wise and sophisticated as a world explorer. When he was a boy, he thought the water he poured down cricket holes came out in China, where a Chinese boy sees it bubbling up.

He had been pulling and digging for over an hour. Almost all the sand from the upper chamber has shifted to the lower chamber. He knows more about dirt than about anything. It pleases him to think that soon he will join his father in this nourishing substance that sustains the world.

Yard Broom

~~~~~~~~~~~~

PROPPED UP ON PILLOWS BUNCHED AGAINST THE HEADBOARD, he lays his book aside. Perhaps it is the pair of squabbling blackbirds that draw his attention from the *New York Times* "Editor's Choice" to the leaf-strewn grass beyond the bedroom's window-wall. Japanese Bermuda planted first between tiles in the courtyard and then taken, small sprigs from the courtyard to the bare ground that stretches from the back of the house into shade too dense to sustain growth. He had used a hand-pick to loosen the soil. The grass grew slowly beneath the now-gone sour-orange tree laced with vanilla orchids, which never bloomed. Gone too are the guanabana and scraggly quince, which struggled from the base of the wall near where their thirteen-year-old dogs, Vita and Dulce, sisters, now lay, wrapped in towels and covered with small stones and sifted soil. At the corner where the path turns, a recently planted yellow bamboo sends up a spear-like shoot as thick as a man's wrist. The bamboo grows inches a day. The hard soil is not hospitable to grass. Still, the sprigs gradually establish themselves, spread into cushions, and finally, a thin carpet.

A mowing has left gray pockmarks. A blower can make quick work of the leaves and clippings; yet, the thought of the rude noise in this place, where hands have nurtured, seems a sacrilege, just as in the town of his youth, the sound of a powered mower on Sunday sent heads wagging. Enough reverie!

He bestirs himself, pulls on a pair of shorts, goes out into the morning, and finds a yard broom. He has left this pleasure to others for too long. The swing of his arm, the broom's thongs clicking like soft castanets awakens the memory of summer's Saturday mornings, neighbors leaning on their yard brooms chatting with passersby.

Yard-brooms' tongs were made of metal before everything became made of plastic! In their part of town, a carefully maintained front yard was as important as Sunday morning church. And neighbors help neighbors. If one becomes ill or is just too old to do the work, someone will mow their lawn for them. It is a kindness and maintains orderliness. Neighbors lend clippers and pass around extension ladders. Mowing lawns for enough to buy a ticket to the Saturday picture show is a rite of passage for young boys.

Lawns, well-maintained spirea, and honeysuckle were as American as apple pie, homemade ice cream, and potluck suppers. Good lawns and tasteful Christmas displays make good neighbors. And good caring neighbors are as much the glue of the nation as the Apostles' Creed, the Ten Commandments, and the Pledge of Allegiance.

In wealthy communities, once a week rickety pickups pass through their gates and unload crews of hard-working Mexicans, who make quick work of mowing, trimming the curbs and flower beds, and sweeping lawns. Professionals clean the pools, and at Christmas time, professionals hang the lights.

He rakes the leaves into small mounds, bends—good exercise he tells himself—scoops them into a tub and drags the tub to the high stonewall, where he dumps the leaves. In the tropical heat, the banks of leaves soon decompose. He'll use some of the compost if he gets around to potting a desert rose cutting he's been meaning to tend to. They do well in pots.

The leaves rustle. A lizard pokes its head out, assesses the situation, and then burrows back into his domain. If he were clairvoyant, it would be plants, compost, and soil that speak to him.

Having done not much, but enough, he goes into the house, takes up his electronic book—*electronic*, just imagine—and finds where he left off before he got sidetracked by the leaves and clippings. He dozes off, before the end of the first paragraph. He no longer cares much about *who done it.*

Sandy Road

HE DOESN'T KNOW WHERE HE IS GOING. HE DOESN'T KNOW IF HE is running away or if he will keep on going when he reaches the section line up ahead. Sometimes he gets that far before he turns back.

Sand dunes spill into the road, down which the boy walks away from his home. On the other side of the road, beyond a barbed-wire fence stretches a pasture. The grass is short and burned, only a scattering of green remains. It is at the end of a long hot summer. A jackrabbit pops up and hops lickety-split across the pasture toward a stand of cottonwood trees growing near a pond, gone to mud. Cottonwoods are the biggest trees here about. Folks saw them up for barn siding, but it isn't much good because it buckles so bad. He heard a farmer complain, "Come next season, the inside of the barn is what was the outside a year before." The farmer was most likely joking. He's not always sure.

They moved out to the house on a knoll a year before when he was entering the fourth grade. Behind the house stands a milkhouse, windmill, and water tank, and behind that, their small barn. The windmill draws water from a well more than a hundred feet down, cool enough to chill the milk.

There are chickens, three cows, and a litter of pigs. One of the pigs drowned in the slop. His father had sunk the slop barrel in the ground so the pigs wouldn't knock it over, but the pig rooted off the lid and fell in. The boy and his brother buried the pig, so their folks wouldn't be mad. They had a lot of pigs. When the old sow got real fat, his father took her to be slaughtered. They also killed his pet bull calf. Everything on the farm got killed.

The road he travels is a section line. Up ahead it joins another, which marks off the top of the section. The land was marked off into mile square sections before the rush when white folks on horseback and in wagons raced in to claim what they could. Some folks got a full section of land, six hundred and forty acres. They are rich farmers. His family's farm is only forty acres. Mostly sand, it used to be sharecropped. He and his dad planted watermelons. Watermelons love sandy soil, but terrapins like sand and melons, too. They live all over the place and gnaw holes in the melons. His dad sometimes cuts off the part the terrapins haven't touched and cools it in the milk house. There's enough left for the whole family, but you can't sell a watermelon with a hole in it.

They separated milk, put the cream in big cans his dad placed down by the mailbox, where someone comes and takes the cans away and gives his folks some money. Saving back some milk for themselves, they slop the hogs with the rest. He's not a good milker, but his big brother milks real fast and sometimes squirts him in the neck, or at a chicken passing the shed door.

His aunt visited last week and hugged and hugged him to her breast. Her breast isn't as big as his mother's because she never had kids, but that's all right. His mother has given up hugging so much, except when he has a fever or something. She says he is a big boy now. When his aunt visits, the hurting inside goes away a little bit. The hurting is like before supper when all he's had is a sandwich for lunch, but food doesn't fill the emptiness. The feeling comes mostly when he is in bed, the lamp shut off, and he hears a coyote call, and he understands just how the poor fellow feels. His dog understands and sometimes howls along with the coyote or a train whistle. The feeling sometimes comes in school, the teacher at the blackboard explaining something, his mind on the fan pattern of light streaming through slats let down from the blind's rotted cord; a sparrow alights on the sill, and he imagines flying away with the little bird.

Clouds have turned gold. It is near milking time. His mother will stand out on the back porch, wiping her hands on her apron. She'll think he has gone off to skip rocks over the pond at the back of the property and bangs the bell tied to the milkhouse. She hasn't started to worry yet.

His feet sink deep into the sand as he runs back. He is crying by the time he pushes through the gate. He finds his mother where he expected, and flings his arms around her sobbing, "I will never, never leave you!"

But she left, Mother, Dad, and Aunt and Brother, and lovers. Only sister, the last lover, and the unassuageable hunger remain.

Cap Rock

〜〜〜〜〜

HE TAKES HIS COFFEE INTO THE LIVING ROOM, SLIDES BACK THE glass panel, and steps onto the balcony. A moment ago an impertinent crow had stood seeming to converse with the fake owl he had placed on the rail to discourage birds from pooping there. As a child he had dreamed he was a crow with a human head, jockeying for position with fellow crows on a telephone line. The apartment is on the eighth floor. He can see beyond the edge of the High Plains city to where arroyos spill down the face of the Cap Rock, and further where he spent his youth, youth that seems so near and yet so far as to not have been him at all.

His mind takes flight, like a hawk heading north beyond the city, low across the crumbling fields of gypsum, supporting nothing much but sage, tumbleweeds, creosote, and dried up gulches, a lonely farmhouse, a barn, a windmill, a horse tank and a hog lot, all scrunched together, as if hunkered against the harsh weather spilling down off the Rockies. Up near the north Texas border, he comes to his town, church steeples poking up, the Main Street with the picture show, the feedlot, and the Mint Lounge, where his father hung out after a long day hauling cattle, sometimes with his mother. They'd take him along if his older sisters were out on a date and wouldn't look after him. He'd play the electric shuffleboard and then sleep in the pickup until his folks had enough and took him on home.

He flies low over the locust grove near the house he grew up in. It collapsed long ago—not worth saving. The only thing left from back then is a rusted out hay bailer. At times, not knowing what was going on inside him, he'd go out and climb up in one of those locust trees and refuse to come in, even for supper. His sister would bring him something to eat. He'd stay out until a rustling, a hoot owl, or a coyote's call scared him and sent him running inside to bury his head under a pillow.

What happened to him? Boot camp, Da Nang, New York, Venice, Rome, Buenos Aires. Could it have been him dressed in a tuxedo at the opera ball in the Hamptons, sharing a joint with a movie star? Is he that Buddy Holly-looking kid, who was denied his high school diploma because he painted a nude woman? Was it him who stood at a window of the World Trade Center?

He shakes his head, goes inside and pulls the door closed.

Frigate Bird

This morning,
as a frigate bird glides above
weeping coconut palms,
I look out beyond the silvery honeybush
and green cedar
to a slate gray sea.

I imagined my mate sleepy-eyed,
in the ancient city of To'c.
He gazes into royal palm plumes
uplifted in gospel hallelujah
as doves descend and ascend
from the lawn into the high ramon tree,
as if on the breath of gods.
They chortle, "mu-cuy, tzut-zuy,"

Far to the back of his jungle garden,
beyond the high wall,
the sun's rays pierce stone archways
igniting gold
within spent fronds,
hung in humble confession.

And somewhere on a golden cloud
Jessy Norman sings—
"My God what a morning!"
And God, pleased with Her art,
rests on Her laurels
before She takes on the chores
of the oncoming lemon-hot day.

Clifford

~~~~~~~~~~

IN A BLACK-AND-WHITE PHOTOGRAPH, A BOY, NINE OR TEN, STANDS squinting at the camera. His hair is slicked. He wears freshly pressed clothes. The bare dirt on which he stands goes right up to the wall of the house. Scattered about the yard are the rusted head of an engine, some tires, car cylinders, an axle and a driveshaft.

The boy's father built the house, as he was able to salvage plywood. He laid the floor on bare ground and covered it with linoleum. Still, winter freezes reached under and buckled the floor so that all the furniture rocked. By the time the picture was taken, the father had managed to replace the canvas roof with plywood and tar-paper.

Perhaps the photograph was taken on the birthday the boy had given his friends at school hand-painted birthday invitations to come to his house for a party. None came.

His partner knows all this because the two of them have now lived together for over forty years.

Clifford's partner, Pops, carried a Diet Coke for Clifford and a beer for himself into the swimming pool. Clifford stopped drinking alcohol twenty years before. He pulled Pops to him. Both are paunchy now, but the spark still glows. "Pops," Clifford said, "we've got to be grateful."

"As I tell your story, you're an ignorant kid," Pops said.

"Ignorant?!"

"OK, naïve. I see you, walking away from that farm where you had quarreled with the farmer."

"Yeah, tell about its being a hundred in the shade," Clifford breaks in, "and all I did was take five minutes for a smoke and a drink of water."

"You shouldn't have been smoking."

"Tell about . . . "

"Hey! It's my story!"

"But it's about me!"

"I'm just imagining! OK, the farmer was a bastard, and you were the cutest guy who ever wore overalls."

"*Levis*!" Clifford scolded, as he climbed out of the pool. "Time for my show. When can I read it?"

"What?"

"My story."

"It's *my* story about you. Besides, you don't read anything anyway. Take the dogs in with you."

"I read *Brokeback Mountain*," Clifford called back. He disappeared into the house, the dogs, Dolce and Vita, following.

How have two people so opposite made it so long, Pops wondered. He leaned his head back against the edge—*pecho de paloma* (dove's breast) the builders had called the pool's rounded perimeter. When they met, he had expected Clifford would move on to a fresh interest within a week. He was, after all, only twenty-four and charming; Pops, an aging yet still aspiring tenor might have seemed glamorous to the young Texan. They met at a glittering black-tie affair to welcome the new 1972. Pops had knocked a few years off his resume and blackened telltale graying in his mustache, yet he knew his salad had slipped away.

Lights came on in the house spilling out from the parlor's

wrought-iron chandelier across the grassy terrace to the far end of the pool. They had left the hundred-and-fifty-year-old house, with its twenty-foot-high beamed ceilings, much as when they bought it. A banyan tree, its roots trickling like honey over an ancient stonewall, had dominated a trash heap. Where the trash was once piled, now mamey, choch, royal and beetle palms, and bamboo reign over a jungle undergrown by heliconia and rampaging philodendron. The waya palm, already ancient when they bought the place, had dotted its great fan-leafed children throughout the garden. Imagine, all this is only an eight-minute walk from the first cathedral built in the Americas from stones of ancient Maya pyramids.

They had started with almost no money. Pops should have stuck with oratorios and church choirs, and gotten a real job, but vanity had forced him to waste his youth in a foolish grab for the brass ring, fame, and glamour, which swung tantalizingly beyond his grasp. Clifford had gone through his savings within months after he got out of Vietnam. Still, somehow they scraped enough together to buy at just the right time and fixed up a brownstone in Brooklyn, sold it, made some money, bought houses in Key West at just the right time, sold them, and bought the house in Mérida, Mexico, just ahead of the crowd. They weren't smart; they were dumb lucky.

~~~~~~~~~~~~

"You're not paid to sit around, boy! Get those bales of hay up in the loft, and go grease up the tractor."

"My name is not 'boy'! My name is Clifford, Mr. Barker, and I don't accept being yelled at every time I take a break." Clifford turns and heads for the gate. "You just yelled at me the last time," he calls over his shoulder.

"Listen to me, boy . . . young man, what the hell, Clifford! You can't just walk off in the middle of the day!"

"Watch me, Mr. Barker."

"Well, I'll be god damn! You little son-of-a-bitch snot-nosed, mother . . . "

Clifford swings around with clenched fists. "Don't you dare say anything about my mother!"

Barker stands there turning purple, as the stiff-necked boy continues out of the barnyard. It is a sorry part of the country, where scratching out a living made folks short-tempered.

The high noon sun fries mesquite and sage fumes from the silvery scrub. Telephone poles, dancing along the roadside in wobbly procession, offer no relief. Nor does the tumbleweed-clogged barbed-wire fence offer shelter. "Dry as a popcorn fart," his father would say. Clifford has left his hat behind. The sun scorches through his short brush-cut hair. His scalp burns as he blames Barker, the overbearing farmer. His dad got him the job in the first place. They were more to blame, never himself. He was just an unlucky victim of sons-a-bitches always lording it over him. A truck rattles up beside him.

An old man leans over and opens the door. "Where're you headed, son?"

"I don't know." Clifford is too proud to go home. There are few jobs for a sixteen-year-old. He had quit the one job his father was able to land him.

"Riddle's the name," the old man tells Clifford and takes the boy home, where his wife feeds him. Clifford feels more comfortable with the Riddles than in his own home. Mrs. Riddle was round and motherly, her hair, more white than gray, loosely piled on top her head and a fresh apron cinched beneath her ample bosom—Clifford figured Mrs. Riddle religiously changed her apron at least three times a day—and a sunny disposition. Mr. Riddle invites Clifford to stay for a while and help with the chores. "Nowadays, our sons got their own farms and chores aplenty to attend to."

Clifford called his folks and told them not to worry; he'd be home before school starts.

"Got a license?" Mr. Riddle asks a few days later.

"I've been driving trucks and tractors all my life," Clifford says. "Got my license when I was fourteen."

"Well, wheat's ripenin'. Guess you'll learn to drive a combine."

Mr. Riddle hired on another hand, a fellow named Thad. They took turns driving the combine and hauling the wheat into the grain elevators. Clifford enjoyed guiding the mammoth machine as the mower blade sliced off perfectly uniform rows of wheat.

After Mr. Riddle's fields, they harvested other farms in the neighborhood, then crossed over into the Oklahoma Panhandle, and then, following the ripening wheat, continued across Kansas. Mr. Riddle followed the *Farmers' Almanac* as a guide to the ripening wheat. They harvest mostly for small farms, big outfits they wouldn't touch, some any more than forty acres. The grain heads grew longer and heavier as they traveled farther north.

Days the wheat was too wet to harvest, Clifford would find a town swimming pool, a gift from Roosevelt's New Deal. He showed off in front of the town kids, who would greet his one-and-a-half twists with "Wow, how'd you do that?" Thad went off in his own car, while Clifford and Mr. Riddle ate supper together.

One night, when they were staying in a motel on the edge of Salinas, Kansas, Mr. Riddle invited Clifford to go with him to a lounge across the street. It was a nice place, had a shuffleboard machine like the machine in the Cactus Bar in Dalhart, where, when Clifford was a kid, he'd sleep in a booth while his folks drank at the bar. The Cactus wasn't as clean as the Salinas lounge. Mr. Riddle listened and sometimes nodded while Clifford got to telling about back then and about his dreams.

"Hold on a minute, son," Mr. Riddle said. He ordered another round, and then did something that swelled the deepest feelings of trust that Clifford had ever known: Mr. Riddle took a hanky from his pocket, bent over and spit out his teeth. "Here," he wrapped them and handed them to Clifford. "Take care of them, so's I don't choke, if'n I get drunk." Clifford put the teeth in his pocket and returned the teeth the next morning. They followed the ritual on nights when they went drinking until Clifford left the crew.

~~~~~~~~~

By the time Clifford came along, his father was pretty tired and had taken to drinking quite a lot. Clifford was the last of twelve children his father had raised: his father's younger brothers and sisters, Clifford's mother's first brood, and his mother and father's three daughters and finally Clifford.

His father was proudest of Clifford's marksmanship and later on, his Vietnam service. His father made money betting Clifford could shoot a quarter out of the air with his BB gun, but he was disappointed that Clifford preferred pretty things, like his Mama, to squirrel hunting.

~~~~~~~~~

Clifford even told Mr. Riddle the story of when he was about twelve; his father came in from hauling a load of cattle and found him in the middle of a Tupperware party his sister had organized. Clifford had taught himself how to crochet and was teaching the women how to make doilies and doll dresses, the kind with which they could decorate their beds. His father just turned around and went down to the Cactus. That story got a good laugh out of Mr. Riddle.

~~~~~~~~~

They crossed Nebraska. Mr. Riddle and his small crew made it all the way to the Canadian border and, as a matter of pride and adventure crossed over and harvested a few fields, the first time any of them had been out of the country. As fall approached, they worked their way back down the high plateau. Weather slowed them down near Lafayette Colorado, where Clifford met Laura when he hauled a load of wheat into the granary. She was helping her daddy with paperwork and humming along with Bobby Vinton singing, "Roses are Red (My Love)." Clifford told her he liked the tune. They went to drive-in-movies and, almost every night, the A&W drive-in.

When it came time for school to start, Mr. Riddle handed Clifford a big bonus and said, "Don't be a stranger, son. Come out when you get a chance, and have some grub with the missus and me." The Riddles had no children of their own. Laura drove Clifford down to Denver. "Roses are Red" came on the pickup's radio as they drove. "Guess that's our song," Clifford said. "Yeah, I guess," Laura said. She was crying. They kissed at the bus station. For miles, pressed against the Greyhound window and gazing out at fields yet to be harvested, Clifford fought back the tears.

~~~~~~~~~

Clifford's high school diploma was denied because he painted a nude of a woman, frontal, and was caught showing it to classmates. His folks didn't much care about education. "Book learnin' makes a fellow uppity," his father consoled. "The school of hard knocks is the best education," his father liked to say.

High school over, Clifford answered an advertisement he found inside a matchbook. *Draw this, and you may be eligible for a scholarship to an art school in Denver.* His portrait of a cowboy had already won first prize at every art contest in the Panhandle.

The "art school" didn't turn out to be what Clifford had expected. He got a job in a meat-packing plant. One Sunday the church he attended had a special guest, an inspirational artist. The artist stood before a chalkboard and drew as he recounted a parable. At first, the drawing made no sense to his audience. As he continued, a face began to form. Then, as he reached "the moral of the story is!" the face of Jesus suddenly emerged. Some gasped as if they had witnessed a miracle; someone called, "Praise the Lord." The woman next to Clifford simply said, "Well, I declare!" Clifford went up to the artist after the class and told him that he knew the trick. The artist, whose business was mail-order portraits, invited Clifford to show him. When he saw Clifford's talent, he offered Clifford to become his apprentice and to live in a basement room in his home. While the artist was out doing an inspirational drawing one night, the wife brought Clifford a plate of sandwiches. She nearly forgot her panties and bra when they heard the artist's car pull into the drive.

〰〰〰〰〰〰

Standing tiptoe at the end of the board, his wide back to the pool, Clifford sprang. His arms beat like a raptor taking flight. In a smooth backward somersault, arms outstretched now, he pierced the water leaving scarcely a splash.

Almost six feet tall, he is thin and muscled, so thin that his mother burst into tears when he returned home after his first tour of duty in Vietnam. A finicky eater, he hadn't gained any weight during his second tour.

He climbed up to the three-meter board. Attempting a double twist, he landed with a belly flop. A sympathetic "aww" came from the only other swimmer. It could have hurt worse. The Y was bathing suits optional, but Clifford had opted to wear one. His success on his second try was greeted with applause. It was early afternoon, and they had the pool to themselves. He returned to the one-meter board and redeemed himself with a jackknife followed by a half-twist.

As Clif stripped for the shower, the other swimmer entered. "Thanks for the show," he called. "Got nice legs."

"About all that is left from boot camp." Clifford judged the man to be in his fifties, a bit of a gut, silver-streaked blond hair.

They were about four lockers apart as they toweled off. The man reached out his hand. "Henry Butler."

"Clifford Ames." He took Henry's hand.

"Boot camp? I took you to be Navy."

The officer at the recruitment station had told Clifford they would send him to school if he volunteered to be a Seabee. Instead, they sent him to boot camp with the Marines.

"I'm stationed at Quonset Point, waiting for my discharge. Can't be too soon!" He'd been screwed, glued and tattooed. When he volunteered for overseas duty, he had thought Europe or at least Gitmo. Sure, he had it pretty easy the first time over. He earned ribbons for marksmanship and rode shotgun on trips into Danang. During one of those trips, a captain put his hand on Clifford's knee and suggested they go on R&R to Tokyo. Clifford, knowing it is the enlisted man who gets the dishonorable discharge when he's caught with an officer, took his R&R with a prostitute in Okinawa.

When they told him he had to go back a second time, he put up a fight. "First time," they said, "you volunteered; now we are sending you! So, get your shit together and get your ass on that plane, unless you want to spend the rest of your duty wipin' out latrines."

They offered all kinds of incentives for him to reenlist, but "no thanks!" He was mustering out of the Seabees, out of his relationship with his French-Canadian Catholic lover and out of his engagement to the sweet Irish Catholic girl he had also been sleeping with.

"Don't they have a pool out at Quonset?"

"Yeah, but the boards here are better," says Clifford.

"Going back to Texas?"

"How did you know?" he said, pulling on whites tailored to fit his slim frame. He had lost little of his Texas Panhandle accent.

"Clairvoyant," Henry replied.

With his cap cocked on his forehead, his heavy, black plastic Buddy Holly glasses failed to rob his face of impish good looks. Holly had been his high school idol.

"Got time to join me for a drink?" Henry asked.

"Gosh, I'd like to sir, but I've got to be back at the base in an hour."

"A quick beer then, and don't make me feel ancient. It's Henry." He clapped Clifford on the shoulder.

Henry came up to Providence from New York two days a week to teach an acting course and to work on the libretto for the opera, *Mourning Becomes Electra*, with composer Marvin David Levy. In New York, Henry stage directed at the Metropolitan Opera. He also played distinguished uncles or other bit roles in TV soaps.

After their YMCA meeting, every chance he had, Clifford took the train down to New York. He told Henry right off that he wasn't ready for a commitment.

"Of course you aren't. No strings." Henry's Irving Place apartment was a garret with a Pullman kitchen and tiny bathroom plastered with playbills. It was located two blocks down from Gramercy Park and the Players Club, where they often dined, and diagonally across from where O'Henry wrote *The Gift of the Magi*.

They went to Broadway shows, plays, opera, dinner at Sardi's and regularly ended up at Joe Allen's. Unimpressed when he was told that the lady he had just met was one of the most famous singers in the world. "She's sure got a big mouth," Clif observed.

The opera crowd found him refreshing. While Henry directed backstage, Clifford watched from the Met's general manager's private box. Henry took Clif to Thanksgiving dinner with Joan Sutherland, and she taught Clifford to needlepoint. Proud of his find, Henry took Clifford to parties in the Hamptons and Fire Island. Tall, slender, hazel eyes, military crew cut grown out to a mop caught between brown and auburn, he had an open, honest face and a beguiling gap-toothed grin.

When a famous fashion designer invited Clifford to lunch at the Russian Tea Room, Henry said go! The designer gently suggested that Clif not run his knife through the tongs of his fork, and commissioned him to do a painting. The painting, a four by six-foot hard-edged graphic was a sensation at the party celebrating the designer's newly redecorated brownstone. Clifford painted obsessively for a while and was seen about town with the designer.

He was offered a gallery at Bonwit Tellers, where he was to create images to match various decors. He struggled to produce paintings for the market. The harder he tried, the more depressed he became. "My paintings are *my* colors, not someone else's," he cried when he could scarcely put paintbrush to canvas. He took Valium and went to bed.

~~~~~~~~~~

Henry's Guggenheim grant came through, and he invited Clifford to travel with him to Italy. Clifford took the remainder of his small savings left from his Seabee stint and signed on.

He likes to tell about his "*Hey, look at me now, moment*:

He and Henry are waiting at Venice's Harry's Bar when a long white launch pulls to the dock, and a white-liveried boatman announces; "Senores Butler and Ames. The Count and Countess Gozzi's launch is here for you." Henry starts for the boat, but Clifford grabs his arm. "Wait! Make him say it again."

The launch whisks them out across Venice Bay to a private island where sheathed in a tightly pleated Fortuny and holding a brace of wolfhounds, the Countess Gozzi stands at the top of the stairs leading down to the boat landing.

"About time you came to see me stuck out here on this deserted little island," she said. "Get your sweet little asses up here."

"You'll have to excuse La Contessa," Henry said. "You can take the girl out of Kansas, but you cannot take Kansas out of the girl." Both she and Henry grew up in Wichita.

"Pay no attention to him, honey." She held out her hand to Clifford. "Directing those grand operas goes to his head. We've got lunch ready, but first, let's have us a drink. The Count's restin'; he'll be down shortly."

Drink they did. A footman standing behind each chair kept their wine glasses full. The old Count eventually joined them. They were served Kansas steak and french fries.

In a Ferrari convertible, he and Henry cut across the Italian boot and down the Amalfi Coast to Port Hercules. They stayed in a castle with pianist John Browning, and one afternoon while swimming in the bay, as Clifford rested on a dock, a distinguished-looking gentleman with a large nose came down and invited him up to rest in a chair.

"That was Leonard Bernstein," Browning told Clifford when he got back.

In Rome, they visited the Sistine Chapel and in Florence, admired *David*.

Back in New York, Clifford got a job in the display department at Lord & Taylor. He was loaned to the Fashion Institute of Technology—a branch of New York State University—to help with one of their displays. The director of the school's newly formed museum/archives observed Clifford's talent with lace and fabric. Clifford could instinctively analyze and explain, as he had to the ladies at his older sister's Tupperware party, how the most complex stitching or lace was done.

The director at FIT wrote up Clifford's resume and submitted it to the personnel office. Suddenly Clifford was on the staff of the Fashion Institute of Technology as an archivist. The boy, whose high school diploma had been denied, was employed at master's degree level, and with tenure in New York State University!

~~~~~~~~~~

Dulce licked Pops' ear and whimpered. She is a breed with a three-thousand-year history of begging from the Maya before the Spanish arrived.

"You want some of my beer, don't you?" He pours what is left in his bottle on the pool ledge.

~~~~~~~~~~

Oh, the fights, the jealousy, possessiveness, the hurts, the drinking and praying and codependence and the constancy. Not tonight. Not this story. This is about a boy named Clifford who lived a life he could never have dreamed.

"You still out there," Clifford calls.

"What about your TV shows," Pops asks.

"They're all reruns. I'll bring you another beer."

Clifford slips into the pool next to his partner. "I was thinking; you could end my story with me walking into the Sistine Chapel and saying, 'Oh, my God,' and Henry saying, 'Exactly!' That'd be a good ending, don't you think?"

Pops put his arm around his lover. "This is the way I end *my* story about *my* lover: I tell him to look around right now! Here, where we are, this very moment, look up into the royal palms towering above us fronds spread in a hallelujah, the banyan tree roots dripping over the ancient stonewall, and the flaming purple bougainvillea spilling off the tile roof of the porch! Then you gasp, 'Oh my God!' "

"I kiss you and I say, 'Exactly!'"

Dark

~~~~~~~~~

IT WAS DARKER THAN CLIF HAD EVER KNOWN, DARKER THAN the Vietnam jungle—the kind of dark that eats the light, that eats all joy, darker than the moonless nights when the frigate, laying off Da Nang beach, zinged cannon shells so low overhead it felt as if he jumped up, he'd get his head blown off.

Darkness numbs, but it doesn't take away the agonizing fear of losing his lover. For five days and nights, he had watched over Ed, tubes running out of the old guy's chest and pecker. The fifth night the old guy lifted his head and ordered, "Go on home," just the way Clif, a lifetime before, had scolded his dog, Tippy, who always followed him to school. He had felt like Tippy, slinking off with his tail curled between his legs.

But in the middle of his first night back in their condo, alone, Clif is seized by a terrible urgency to be with his mate. Throwing on clothes, he races from the apartment. He furiously jabs the elevator button, which seems to taunt deliberately. The guard in the lobby, hunched over a magazine in a pool of light, looking up, saying nothing, merely nods as Clif runs into the garage. They had splurged on the Buick. The garage door opens, and Clif eases into the dark. Not a car in sight.

It's a family town; anyone out this late is up to no good or on night duty. He reaches the interstate. As he steers under the interstate, an eighteen-wheeler grumbles overhead. The trucks dimming rear lights glow like bats' eyes in the back of a cave. Daytime, and well into the evening, cars and trucks play games of chicken on the coast-to-coast highway, but this late, most travelers have packed it in for the night. Only a single pair of lights dance in the rearview—a trucker on the night shift, pushing from Nashville to Albuquerque or maybe on to Phoenix.

~~~~~~~~~~~

After Clif got out of the service and met a guy back East, he discovered he was more attracted to the guy, an opera director, than the girl he was about to marry. At operas and plays, he attended with his friend, he sometimes felt like a horse attracting flies. He liked folks older and educated. He knew right off after they met, he'd hang on to this one if he could. It was an opera party, imagine, and him a kid from the Texas Panhandle. Ed didn't seem that much older; he took care of himself and he was from the same neck of the woods, Oklahoma, but he'd gotten citified.

Clif kind of likes being a head taller than Ed, and, in the service, he had buffed up a bit. You couldn't pinch the fat on him. Old Ed was cute—his hair that lay so limp and grayish white against the pillow had been wavy black, shaggy in the fashion of theater folks back when he and Ed met. He still sees them the way they were when they met—Ed's dimples and the gap in his own teeth before he had the gap filled in. Happy, oh so happy!

They'd both strayed, him making no secret of it, and Ed not letting on, but Clif's sure he was not the saint he pretended to be. Still they never split. Perhaps they should have; it is too late for "perhaps." There's not all that life left for either of them. Sometimes he feels he could just strangle Ed, and sometimes understands he is choking the life out of the old fellow. Ed was a singer when they met and then decided to be a writer. He is always ambitious, never satisfied with what they've got and that is a lot.

Could this dread be what Ed went through the night Clif nearly killed himself? Ed told him later it was the worst thing that had ever happened to him, even worse than seeing his father die. Now Clif knew how Ed felt, seeing him unconscious from taking too many pills. They'd both been drinking when something snapped, the way it sometimes did with him—he just went crazy. Almost all Clif knows about that night is what Ed told him: Ed, in the middle of the night, finding Clif naked, sprawled out on the ground scarcely breathing. The paramedics wouldn't let Ed ride in the ambulance; he had to drive himself to the hospital. Not knowing if Clif would live, Ed later told Clif of hours sitting alone in the emergency room, television turned to a late-night show. "It was close to hell," Ed said to him, like the way Clif now feels, returning to the hospital, afraid of what he will find.

Clif knows he has a problem with depression—maybe he developed it in Vietnam, or maybe it just was the way he is. His father once tried to kill himself or threatened to. That's why Clif took the pills—to stop the demons. He hasn't drunk liquor in twenty-five years. Ed says it's the best thing he has done for both of them. Ed still drinks. He doesn't go mean. He just gets sleepy. Even now, liquor isn't what Clif considers. If Ed lives, he's got to take care of himself, so he can look after the old guy.

~~~~~~~~~~

Clif lets down the car windows. A sweet, clean smell washes through—mesquite, sage, and creosote. Lying out on Da Nang beach, cannon lighting up the sand and smelling rotting seaweed and overflowed latrines, he had longed for just one more breath of the sweet High Plains air before one of those shells exploded his life.

He and old Ed had talked about the big party they would give for the fiftieth anniversary of their meeting at that fancy party in New York—both had been in tuxedos that night.

If Ed doesn't make it, he won't kill himself, but life will just stop, because living won't be worth a thing.

The silent hospital stands in a pool of yellow light. He grew up fifty miles north. The road in front of the hospital continues on up over the Caprock. It's his country, what they told him he went to war for. Beyond the Caprock are cattle pastures, and hay and wheat fields—once buffalo country. The last animal shot to decorate rich men's cabins, as rugs in front of fireplaces, and the bulls' noble heads stuck above the mantel. The animal's magnificence, or its prior claim to the land, doesn't stop the hunter.

Clif swings the car under the portico and into the open space between two other night watchers. Folks at the desk nod as he passes. He knows his way down the long Lysol-smelling corridors, past waiting half-asleep people, slumped over magazines and electronic devices. An old woman retrieves a magazine slipped to the floor at the feet of the snoring fellow next to her.

Premonition swelling, Clif rushes to the bank of elevators. Everything seems deliberately trying to keep him from Ed. The door finally slides open. He jumps in and pounds Ed's floor number. Again the machine taunts, binging leisurely past each floor. When he reaches Ed's floor, Clif flies between the half-opened elevator doors. A nurse calls his name as he races past her station. Someone runs after him, calling, but he won't stop. He doesn't stop until he falls across his lover's empty bed—gone! And Clif not even there to say goodbye!

An orderly pulls Clif to his feet. "It's alright," he tells Clif. "We've moved your friend back to ICU. I'll take you down."

"I thought he was dead." Clif falls into the orderly's arms. "We had to move him back." The orderly puts his arm around Clif's shoulder and guides him back to the elevator. "It was a close call. His heart stopped only a few seconds."

"I know," Clif says. "I felt it when it happened. I thought he died then."

"No, it started back on its own. We don't think there's any damage." The orderly stays with Clif until they reached ICU.

They are all kind, knowing Clif from the days and nights he slept in a chair by his lover's bed. Yes, they all understood.

"What are you doing here?" Ed pushes aside the tube running through his nostril and puckers for a kiss. "Give me some ice to chew on. They won't let me have anything else, and I am as dry as a popcorn fart," Ed says, quoting one of Clif's father's famous lines.

One of the nurses brings Clif coffee. She confides to Clif that she has been a surrogate mother for two gay men. "Gave them twins. My church threw me out."

Ed is finally released with a pacemaker installed. He still lies about his age, claims he is ninety, but he's only eighty-seven. Clif celebrates his seventy-second birthday with his family and Ed. The following day the two drive to Santa Fe, New Mexico, where the law allows them to be married.

"Though I speak with the tongues of men and angels and have not love, I am nothing," the young woman pastor reads from the Apostle Paul's Letter to the Corinthians.

Feliz

〰〰〰〰〰〰

I'M NOT A DOG, NOT IN THE ORDINARY SENSE. I KNOW, "IF IT quacks like a duck, it's a duck," ha, ha. What I mean to say, for the time being, I'm channeling on a more anthropomorphic level. So you humans can understand, I am channeling human words. We, who walk on four legs, long ago chose not to adopt the strident mode of communication you humans call speech. Ours is a far superior method of communicating. We still rely on our God-given instinct.

Oh, I know, ever since you found you could chatter, humans have been trying to override instinct, or at least Homo sapiens think they have, but just look at how far that has gotten you—the world overpopulated, and your best minds turned to war and world destruction. I rest my case.

OK, you are wondering what this is all about.

First, a little background:

About fourteen thousand years ago, before you took up this language thing, we, mostly gray wolves at the time, seeing your developing hunter-gatherer skills, realized there was potentially a symbiotic relationship in the making. We had no idea just how destructive you would become to yourselves, other creatures, and good old planet Earth. Well anyway, the dye was cast, so to speak—in for a penny, in for a pound—get my drift; you needed us, and yep, we needed you. The rest is history.

Oh, one more thing regarding background. Back fourteen thousand years and long before that, your world was full of spirits; it still is, for that matter, although nowadays you are mostly unaware of them around you. Matter of fact, you are simply unaware of a lot that matters. Your species back then was in constant contact with all sorts of spirits flying back and forth between you and God, but gradually, as you developed more and more high-and-mighty ways, you cut yourselves off from the spirit world. I'll bet you are not even aware of the *fantasma* living in your front bedroom—old fellow who died there before you bought the place hasn't vacated. Nor did you realize when you let that Ceiba tree grow up near your back wall you were inviting Ixtsbay, a murderous witch that hides behind the tree and *disappears* drunk men. Memo, your houseman knows. He's still in touch with his Maya ancestors. He probably hasn't told you about the *aluxes* in the laundry room.

How do I know all this? Well, you see, my instincts are as sharp and clear as my ancestors were fourteen thousand, even twenty thousand years ago. I can still dip into that deep pool, while, quite frankly, you humans are all screwed up. For example, you can't tell the difference between love and lust, greed and hunger, courage, and brutality—don't get me started. Truth be told, you expend so much energy trying to put mind over matter, you don't take the time to smell the roses.

Once you thought you had a grasp on reality, you began to consider folks who hear voices to be crazy or a religious fanatic. OK, so some are. You denigrated the spirit world, ghosts and the like. You relegate Zeus, and trees that speak, to ancient superstitions. I know, some of you still accept the Holy Spirit and a few angels, seraphim and cherubims and the like.

OK, OK, I'm getting to the point.

What I am trying to prepare you for is that you are not hallucinating; the weed hasn't left any permanent damage. What is happening is what I told you before I started the background, I am channeling what the credulous among you believe to be an angel. *Your* angel, who, so to speak, saw you bumbling around in the desert, to use a metaphor. I'm still just your sweet, lovable dog. Your angel is merely using me as her mouthpiece; she speaks *through* me. Well, I do editorialize a bit. Come to think of it, maybe I am your lost soul. I'll have to work on that idea—perhaps a catchy metaphor is called for.

What I am saying, to use the words of your Aunt Tillie, is *I was sent to you.*

The sweet folks I took up with on the beach, who knew I needed some TLC and a little surgery if I was to keep my svelte figure, had no idea they were preparing me for my major mission in life. The bottom line is that I was destined to give up my foolish ways and to take over the training of two old lovers who don't seem to have enough sense to come in out of the rain.

There I was out on that beautiful beach, not a care in the world. With my looks I didn't have to beg for scraps; folks practically threw to me more prime beef than I could handle. The truth is, I much prefer fresh ceviche, not too much lime. As I say, I was trotting along, happy as a clam, when your angel tracks me down. Why she chose that lazy summer afternoon, or me of all the dogs available on the beach that day, beats me. Maybe she couldn't stand one more cocktail party's conversations, like the one you all were having, devoted to that north-of-the-border fool, President Trump. I don't know, but when the spirit calls, who am I to question?

You all were gathered on a porch facing the sea, like a smarmy advertisement for fine wine or Reeboks.

I took up my position in the shade of a sea grape. Framed by the large bluish leaves, which set off nicely my blond coat, and with the sea pounding in the background, I was a heartbreaker. It doesn't take much time before I catch Junior's eye. From there on it is right out of a bedroom scene in *Modern Romance*. He is such a softy; my skills were wasted on him. I didn't let up until he scooped me into his arms.

~~~~~~~~~

A month later, it all became clear, when your older dog begins to breathe heavily. Dulce, you had named her, and you named her right. Of course, I understood what is going on, but I had no way of warning you. The older fellow laid down next to her and put his arm around her. That is when she knew she could go. She understood as only dogs can, the boys now had me—imagine an octogenarian and septuagenarian calling themselves "boys!"

"The Lord moves in mysterious ways" is giving an awful lot of credit to the Lord. Still, here I am, taking over where Dulce left off. They named me Feliz, "happy," and I try, Lord knows I try!

Quite frankly, this channeling is depressing. Words are too approximate, too inadequate to communicate love, pain, beauty, happiness, and contentment. Words build machines and keep teeth clean. It's with our eyes, touch, embrace and an occasional lick we arc directly into the heart and soul, should there be such a thing as a soul. The angel's got me where she seems to want me to be, so if it is OK, I'll leave speech to humans. I'm pretty much in charge now, so angel, if you wouldn't mind, you can just bug out.

Wheat

~~~~~~

RIGHT ON SCHEDULE, CLYDE PULLED INTO THE SELMA CROSSING truck stop. He began stopping there a month or so after Ruth passed. Thought he'd go crazy with the solitude, and the town was too far for driving after sundown and wasn't much account anyway. Once the thruway went in, folks sped right on into the city to do their shopping at Kroger's, eat a Big Boy hamburger or enjoy a Dairy Queen. Even the old picture show folded, not that Clyde was much for that sort of entertainment. An RC Cola and a game or two of checkers with Marvin, the Crossing's owner, suited him, and Marvin welcomed the company now that business was so slow. Nowadays the only folks who stop at the Crossing are local farmers—gas, a loaf of bread, but mostly fried okra. Marvin had got himself a deep fryer; dump in a batch of frozen okra and three minutes later out of the boiling grease comes fried okra better'n your grandmother could make. It was okra that kept the Crossing alive. The Crossing and wheat farms occupied by old folks are the only signs of humans for twenty miles in either direction—just old folks. The children have gone off to school and then off to cities or the military, to return only once or twice a year to look in on their parents and grandparents. Wheat country, not much need for people—plow the land with the twelve-foot-wide disk plows they've got now, sow the grain, and then take off to Florida or the Rio Grande Valley while the wheat grows all winter—come summer, a big crew comes through, harvests the wheat and hauls it off to granaries—crew heads on north, clear into Canada, farmer heads on back to one of those double-wide prefabs in The Valley, or RV park near Tampa or Sarasota, or Harlingen, Texas.

The problem was, Clyde didn't want to go anywhere. He could still feel Ruth's presence about the place. He'd let the cows go, but he kept the barn, because evenings when he'd been rattling around, looking for an old lanyard or something as he'd approach the back porch some evenings, he'd swear Ruth would be standing there wiping her hands on her apron, waiting for him to come in with the milk.

Life changed for Clyde late one afternoon. He finds Marvin's butt sticking out from under the hood of Fern's old Packard, a straight eight-cylinder job. Melvin had all the old black beauty's spark plugs laid out for cleaning. Clyde hadn't seen Fern since he and Ruth last went to church. He had heard Fern's sister, Jolene had died, but word got to him too long after for him to say or do anything. He had had a crush on Fern before Ruth's family moved to town. After that, he gave up on Fern, and there wasn't anyone else but Ruth for Clyde.

Fern and her sister Jolene went off to college. Then about the time Clyde and Ruth got around to tying the knot, the sisters' folks' car slid on a patch of ice and slammed into a bridge abutment; killed them both. The sisters came home and took over the largest spread in the county—hell, it was nearly as big as the county. They never married—ran the fifteen hundred acres as good as any man. Talk was, they traveled with a Colt 45 in the seat beside them. That's as far as the gossip went.

Fern was inside sitting at the table where Clyde and Melvin generally play checkers, her boots up on a crate. Hair pulled back tight and no makeup on her leathery tanned skin, she was still what you might call a handsome woman, no extra flesh.

"Clyde," she called, "how're they hangin'?"

Once Marvin got all the spark plugs back in the Packard, he came in, offered Fern an RC and took out a monopoly board. Clyde still liked Fern; he really did.

They had been meeting for monopoly nearly a year when Fern talked Clyde into joining his spread to hers and moving in.

They still come by the Crossing a couple of times a week, get an order of fried okra and take turns beating Marvin at checkers.

Alfalfa Field

THE WRITER CHECKED THE TIME. IT WOULD BE HOURS BEFORE the kid gets home from school. The kid has to do his chores—slop the hog and feed the chickens—before his folks let him, "*go over and pester that old man.*" The kid's folks had often apologized for their son's visits, "and you, a writer, have more important things to do." He assured them their boy was no bother. A bit after six the boy will come biking down the path. Adam is the boy's name, but he likes the writers calling him *Kid*.

The writer glances down at hands pecking the keys—dark spots, shriveling skin, and blood vessels roping over lever-like tendons, hands that had scooped wheat and steered his uncle's John Deere tractor around miles and miles of dirt for six summers before he went north to University. When not plowing or scooping, shirtless and wearing cutoffs, he hoed weeds. Come fall he was proud to be near the color of his Indian friend and proud of his white butt when he stripped to shower.

Hound grumbles but scarcely moves as the writer eases his foot from under the dog's muzzle. He then stands up from his work—trying to spin yarns that someone would pay attention to. He told his old friend, "If I don't write, I'll become a loquacious old fool." Writing didn't cure him. Folks at church socials give him about three minutes before they have to *go take up something with the pastor* or *check to see if the casseroles are ready.* Before he even gets to the point of his story, guys at the Elks Club have to *take off for the head.* Understandable. Lately, he spent half his time peeing. And it amazes him how folks stand around laughing at the pastor's jokes that weren't funny at all or patiently listened to the banker's long-winded goings-on. That was before *Reader's Digest* took his story about a pet hog and he came to fancy himself a writer. But these days he doesn't get much writing done. His mind meanders.

The kid reminds him of himself at that age. For stories, he often digs back to times growing up, but he doesn't wish to live that life all over again—oh, some of the times maybe. Like evenings when his family gathered around the piano, his mother is playing and his sister, brother and him singing, his Dad whistling off-tune. Yes, that was a taste of Heaven, but later that same night, he would lay awake wondering who he was and would feel utterly alone in the whole world. Living is too hard work to do over again. Still, the past is scattered with jewels.

He looks back at his long days, after the wheat harvest, plowing under stubble. He'd conjure himself into an eagle, and from the vantage of a cloud bank, with eagle's eyes he'd looked down on a lone boy, and sees himself on a tractor in the middle of a vast field. Or sometimes, those hot afternoons, his imagination flew to movie places where on the back of a horse beside Buffalo Bill he'd gaze down from the crest of a red rock canyon onto Indian powwows. He'd leave the blistering heat out of his story, or throw it in if it takes his imagination further. He would even throw in hail or sleet, anything to fill the recollections of those long days.

Work was the ethic back then. A fellow could be a son-of-a-bitch, but if he was a hard worker, all was forgiven. If a guy says something bigoted about a colored or a Mexican, someone else, maybe the foreman, will cut him off; "Yeah, but he's as hard a worker as any white man," and other guys nod their heads, and the bigoted guy shuts up.

And finish what you start, practically scripture was bred into his bones. He wasn't particularly grateful when they added headlights to tractors. Come sundown, you don't stop until the assigned section is plowed under, and before supper, no matter how late, he had to pull the tractor into the barn lot, grease up and fuel up ready to be back in the field come sunup. Still, he was glad he had been taught to finish things, not that he was particularly good at much, but by golly, he got it done—milking cows, university (not high grades), hitchhiking coast to coast, and all debts paid. Fights too—if he started a fight, he was honor bound to finish it. The fact was, even if the other guy picked the fight, he was still honor bound to finish it—often him with his nose bloodied, but often enough he pinned the other guy to the ground until he cried "calf rope."

He gets up from his computer—*computer, imagine him working at a computer*—stretches and then twists the stem of his watch. At least two more hours before the kid will come kicking up dust behind his bicycle.

The writer stands out on his porch and gazes over his domain, a field of alfalfa spreading an entire quarter of a mile all the way to the humming interstate. A light breeze brings a lavender-like hay fragrance. The acreage is a dream come true. He was twenty-one years old, hitchhiking from Oklahoma City to Amarillo to see a girlfriend. The trucker who had given him a ride dropped him at an intersection outside Sherman, Texas. Across the road and down a ways stood this ramshackle house set back against a stand of oaks and facing a sea of alfalfa in delicate blue bloom. In spite of the heat, the scene had a cooling effect on his mind. It was about the prettiest thing he had ever seen. That blistering day, he waited almost an hour, mostly gazing at the alfalfa place, and, maybe even then, dreaming of owning such a place, before a fellow in a Model-A gave him a lift to Amarillo.

Thirty years later, after his writing gained him a little more than he needed for food and booze, he returned, hunted down the owner and bought the place. The farmer, who had planted the alfalfa, and who, the writer believes, had the soul of an artist, had died ten years before, and his heirs, having let the shack fall into ruin and the field go to weeds, were happy to be rid of the place.

He restored the shack, brought in electricity and indoor plumbing, but left its weathered clapboard siding unpainted and the rest as unchanged as possible. He replanted the alfalfa and installed irrigation, and the alfalfa rewarded him with a vast plush lavender-blue carpet right up to his doorstep.

Wife number one found no joy in the place. She'd had enough of farm life growing up and preferred the modern apartment they maintained in town. After she passed, wife number two found neither the apartment nor the house in a field of alfalfa to her liking. She did find to her particular liking a lanky cowboy and took off with him to Arizona. The writer didn't contest, nor did he try wedded life again. Hound, a hobo mongrel, who drifted in between number one and number two, stayed loyal, though he had long since given up almost everything, but eating and sleeping, most of the time, his muzzle on the writer's foot.

The writer's past supplies him sufficient material for writing about crazy love and heartbreak, but he doesn't hanker to dig into that stuff; besides, it had been done better by others. He thinks of Tolstoy, Alice Munro, kooky Joy Williams, and younger writers with a hipper vision. He sooner sticks with hay. When he goes, he figures he may leave the place to the kid.

It's a ritual; as soon as the kid finishes his chores, he comes riding on his rattling bicycle. He grabs a piece of pizza from the writer's fridge, nukes it, grabs a Dr Pepper, and, smelling raunchy, gangly arms and legs sticking out of his sleeves and jeans, leans against a pole on the porch, slides down to sitting, and then fixes his story-teller with expectant, unblinking gray-green eyes, portals to infinity. Through some alchemy the writer had never before experienced, stories flow like music through a flute, and the two drift off to Neverland. The kid is the celebrant of those sacred evenings.

Near dark, half a pizza devoured, two spent Dr Peppers sitting at the porch's edge, the kid climbs on his bike, a bent fender rubbing its wobbly rear wheel. At the gate, twilight transformed, his voice, like music, calls, "Goodnight Mr. Snow" and the boy vanishes into the dark.

Lately, the writer thinks about *going*. He gets annoyed when people say he looks much younger when he tells them his age. They mean it to be a compliment! Of course, they're lying. As if being *old* isn't something to be proud of. Yet, he is disappointed, when no one says he looks younger than he is.

He's no fool. Even though he feels pretty good, watches his alcohol so as not to damage his liver too much, he's aware that before long he will be leaving, yet, there seem to be so many loose ends. He must finish what he has started; still, taking care of the loose ends can't be why he exists. Some pious folks say God created everyone for a purpose. What purpose? If he has a purpose, God never made it clear. Still, he hangs onto God. He gave up on the devil a long time ago, so now God gets all the blame. Death, that's what he is thinking about—not dreading it, but not looking forward with any particular pleasure. He likes what the Presbyterian minister he once knew called death, "the big surprise." Must he, as Dylan Thomas would have him, "not go gentle into that good night. Rage, rage against the dying of the light." Times, when he's alone on the porch, looking out over the alfalfa, Thomas' tremulous voice reading those lines comes floating out of nowhere. He bought the recording when he was thirteen, and Thomas' recorded voice has hung around all these years, "rage, rage." No, he doesn't rage at his own going.

~~~~~~~~~~~~~

Hundred-degree temperatures have let off a bit. Out on the interstate, an eighteen-wheeler hums past going above the seventy-mile-a-hour speed limit. As if on cue, a jackrabbit's floppy ears poke out of the hay, and, gazelle-like, leaps to the neighboring field. Hound doesn't lift his head these days — too hot! Hound loves the kid. Lays with his head on the kid's lap as they sit and listen to the writer ruminate. He'll come biking down the path, and Hound will rouse himself, tail wagging, and meet the kid at the gate.

There's pizza to warm in the oven and Dr Pepper. Soon the kid will sit on the edge of the porch and lean back against the post. They'll be like a Norman Rockwell *Saturday Evening Post* cover, the wide-eyed kid's head full of stories of an old man searching for and finding his place on earth.

The sun, sinking in the west, nears the top of the kid's family's silo. Scarce clouds seem like an artist has wiped the last of white out of his paintbrush. Dust lifts from the road the kid bikes down. It's a dust devil, not the kid.

Tears stream down the writer's face. It's over a year since the pastor turned in off the highway and drove down the road running along the writer's alfalfa field. Not many folks come to see the writer; he's made it clear that he needs solitude.

"The boy's parents would have come," the pastor told him, "but they're so caught up in their own grief, they asked me to come. Boys out quail hunting. It was an accident. His folks told me, the pastor said, their son was very fond of you—loved to hear your stories.

Three Old Men

JIMMY WAS LEAVING MÉRIDA. SEVERAL YEARS AGO HE HAD DIS-tributed cans to stores and hotels throughout the city to collect contributions for an AIDS hospice and on his own regularly gathered the centavos and pesos, delivering the money to Hospice San José. He was leaving the city, so he asked Fred to help him find someone to take over his rounds. As I own a car, Fred turned to me. I told Fred I no longer take on obligations that extend over indefinite periods of time, and thus fell into a trap. Fred said I only needed to do the collecting until Bill, temporarily immobilized by a broken hip, could take over; furthermore, Fred would collect from locations near the *Zocalo*, the main square.

The following Tuesday we set out for my orientation. The temperature had reached a hundred by the time I picked up Jimmy and Fred. I turned the air on full blast as they crumpled into my small Chevy. Unusually gracious for Fred, he said, "No, no. I'm fine," when Jimmy offers to pull his seat forward, a virtual impossibility with his knees pressed against the dashboard.

Jimmy, a big man, wears loose-fitting pants and a faded shirt. His hair, starting halfway back on his head, sticks up like Jiggs of the Maggie and Jiggs cartoons. His eyes are a pale indeterminate color. Mostly he peers above the rim of his glasses.

The huge glasses Fred wears gives his China-blue eyes an owlish look. His goatee is neatly trimmed. In his usual costume—white shoes, white knee socks, white guayabera, and a cane—Fred looks as if he may be on his way for an afternoon Pimm's cup at his Bombay Club. He once confided to me, "I was never handsome, but I have always had a persona."

I was in my usual shorts and sandals. I prefer to be described as stout or husky rather than chubby or just plain fat. Folks used to comment on my gray eyes, but haven't for some years now. Lately, since I caught a reflection of the back of my head, I have begun combing my white hair more carefully.

~~~~~~~~~~

In the central part of the city many expats have renovated ancient houses into architectural gems; however, Fred and Jimmy have chosen to live more modestly in rentals and, as many Méridanos do, for whom Mérida's parks serve as meeting places and living rooms, Jimmy spends much of his time in the Zocolo chatting with locals. He seems more comfortable among Mexicans than he is among most fellow foreigners. I think I understand, but that is another story.

You also may find Fred at early evening under an umbrella in front of the Gran Hotel sipping red wine, then later at the restaurant under the portico in front of the Municipal Palace, nibbling a sandwich, and finally at Café Habana sipping dark-roast coffee before he takes a taxi home.

As for me, most evenings find me by the pool in our home we were able to acquire when prices were still affordable, sipping a beer or gin and tonic.

~~~~~~~~~~

Our first stop was the Montejo Palace Hotel. I left the motor running and the air conditioning pumping for Fred, while Jimmy and I went in for me to be introduced as the new collector. The man at the desk greeted Jimmy warmly. When Jimmy explained the reason for our visit and my new role, the clerk seemed genuinely saddened that Jimmy was leaving.

The collection cans are Jimmy's design made from four-inch plastic pipes with a cap secured by a small lock. Glued to the side is a red ribbon and photographs of children from the AIDS hospice with an explanation of what the money goes for. Some residents of the hospice are parents accompanied by their children. My opinion about the human race notched up as I felt the weight of the can. While there have been many glamorous benefits held in Mérida to raise funds to assist HIV-positive victims, Jimmy has year after year unobtrusively raised thousands of pesos with these cans.

Jimmy took a ring with a dozen or more keys from his pocket and, to find the one that fits, began to try each key on the lock. Each can he has distributed over the city has a separate lock and key. His fingers are thick and stubby, and his eyesight is poor.

"Here, you try," he says, and I go through the collection two more times. None fit. We decided to take the can with us. I will return it to the hotel after we open it.

The next stop is across from Santa Ana market, a small internet café. There, the can is chained to the desk. I am introduced. We find the right key this time.

We passed a *tlapaleria* (hardware store), which opens onto the street and bought a new lock. "Can the store owner help us open the offending lock?" He has nothing that will cut the steel loop, so he sets about sawing through the lock's brass body. Twenty minutes later we are back in the Chevy.

It was time for lunch. Fred had planned the day. We were to go to VIP's up on Paseo Montejo, where with the senior citizen card we would receive a ten percent discount. I found a parking place in front of the restaurant. We slowly extracted ourselves from the car and made our way up the steps. As we passed a window I glimpsed three old men, bent and heads thrust forward—Fred leaning heavily on his cane, Jimmy recently having had both knees replaced balancing with his hand on my shoulder, and me with my belly hanging over my belt. I sucked my stomach in and threw my shoulders back. Too late! The image is indelible.

After ordering our meals, we unwrapped the new locks. Their keys were on a metal ring. We have difficulty freeing the keys from the ring. We pass the bunch around until finally I wedge a knife into the ring and bent it open. The keys don't fit the locks! Tomorrow I will return to the *tlapaleria* and seek to correct the problem.

Following lunch we deliver Fred to his house—he hasn't been feeling too chipper lately—and Jimmy and I head on to complete our rounds. At Grand Plaza the Cookie Store owner asked to exchange bills for the change collected in the container, so Jimmy and I took the money to the food court and dumped a pile of low denomination coins on a table. We make stacks of ten and twenty centavos, and one, two, five and ten pesos, but we lose track of how many are in each stack. We had no paper or pencil. As long as I have lived in Mexico, the currency still seems like play money to me. I usually leave counting to my younger partner, Clifford. Finally, a kind waiter loaned us pencil and paper.

Next, we stopped at a pharmacy where Jimmy had a not quite legal arrangement to buy, at half the retail price, drugs he needed. The pharmacist brought the drugs in a black bag from the back of the store. They were samples the manufacturer *gave* the pharmacy.

We had collected all the money. Now we were to go to the money exchange to trade our bag of coins for bills.

"Where are you going?" Jimmy asked as I sped down Avenida

Itzaez.

"Where you told me," I said. "Plaza de Las Americas to change the money."

"But Grant, I said Fiesta Americana." Mérida has Parque de Las Americas, Plaza de las Americas, and Fiesta Americana. How's a poor guy keep them straight?

The money exchange was not open. Jimmy stepped into a shop to tell one of his friends goodbye. The exchange opened. Should we wait for them to count the money? It was getting late. I'd pick up the money the next day after checking on keys for the locks.

Jimmy has sold most of his things. What is left will go to the AIDS hospice. He will stay until Saturday for a friend's birthday. He will have taken care of all his loose ends in the city he has lived in for six years. He will board a bus early Sunday morning. His senior citizen card got him a ticket at half price. He will start a new life in Queretaro, the fourth or fifth Mexican city in which he will have lived. He lost his Mexican lover to AIDS in one of those cities.

Now and then Fred and I will collect money for the hospice. We will meet at a sidewalk café in the *Zocolo*. Fred will sip red wine and I a beer and we will wonder how Jimmy is doing. Fred will annoy me with his cynicism and I him with my naive optimism.

Bar

~~~~~~~~~

HE PUSHES THROUGH THE SALOON DOORS, SHAKES THE RAIN off his slicker and makes for the bar. Four men caught in a pool of light bent over a red and black checkerboard thumb the brim of their hats, tan, and gray Stetsons and two straws. Further back, on green felt shimmering in another pool of light, his suspenders scarcely adequate to their task, Cecil possessively cracks balls.

Del takes a seat, a stool away from the other old fellow leaning on the bar. The guy looks over, nods slightly and then returns to studying the bottom of his glass. With two fingers to his eyebrow, Del returned the greeting, and with the same two fingers in an economy of motion, signals the bartender. The bartender tosses a cube of ice into a whisky glass, pulls down an amber bottle, splashes in two jiggers of booze, and plunks it in front of Del. The bartender leans back into his pool of light, and the room returns to the soft clicking of snooker balls, an occasional snap of a triumphant checker, and the clinking of ice.

"Got thirty bushels an acre off the quarter section north of town," Del says to no one in particular. "Good bottom land, had it in alfalfa a couple of years. Farm Bureau guys say alfalfa adds nitrogen to the soil. Guess they's smarter than they look."

Not meaning to interrupt the checker players, and knowing the snooker player, Leroy, was a no account for conversation, Del turns to the fellow a stool away. Not saying a word, the old guy's face turns red, and he burst into tears.

Del jumps up, goes over, and pats the man's shoulder. "I could just kick myself for being so braggidy. Hell, I know about hard times. I only got ten bushels an acre on my quarter section of oats, not even enough to pay off my loan."

The bartender breaks in. "You ain't helping, Delbert. He's crying because after he bought a hundred lottery tickets, sure he was a going to hit the jackpot, he bought that gal he's been seeing over in Hobert an Escalade. Then, when she found he'd lost the lottery, she took off to California with his cowhand."

"Aww, gee," Del said. "Least I can buy you a drink. Name's Del, Delbert Slack." He held out his hand.

"Claude Overton," the old fellow said, wiping snot onto a bandana. "It ain't all that bad." He chuckled. "The good side's, my wife also took off."

That's how it started. Claude went home with Del that night and stayed. They joined their spreads and, together, bought ten tickets. They hit the jackpot two years in a row. They now own a whole square mile of some of the best land in the county. Plant half in alfalfa and half in wheat and every four years switch fields—regularly harvest over thirty bushels an acre. Not wanting to test God's patience, they never bet after that. Wheat brings in more than the lottery.

When Del's and Claude's names come up, folks just scratch their heads and chuckle.

Cecil and Patrick

~~~~~~~~~~~~~~~

HE HAD GOTTEN UP TO PEE FIVE TIMES. THE LAST TIME HE WENT out and peed off the edge of the porch, the reddening sky forecasting another scorching day. A place in the city and a place on the beach, and Glen, who has stood by him these many years, he should be grateful. A lot of old men would give their right arm to have what he has, but, damn it, he wants something more before he shuffles off and it isn't another cruise, more parties, more tickets to the theater, or more time sitting in front of the TV.

He started out to be a writer; stayed at it for a year after graduation—living on peanut butter sandwiches, in an apartment without hot water—toilet at the end of the hall. He wrote in the glow of candles dripping over Chianti bottles. Those noble days abruptly ended with a note attached to his father's final check—a model of brevity, his father had written: "THE END!" And now, since the heart attack and surgery, Cecil has been seized with an insatiable need, more than ever before, to give voice to the creature within that has lain dormant these many years since his bohemian days.

He goes inside and heats up a cup of instant coffee. While waiting for the water to boil, he studies one of the yellowing pages he had brought to the beach with him. He had come across the writing while searching for a book on grammar among the stuff his sister had sent after closing the family home.

"After humans invented time." Cecil had written. "Humans fretted at how short the time was between birth and death; then humans invented souls, so they could live for eternity." *Smartass*, he thought. He had written it for his philosophy class, hoping to annoy his professor, who also taught religion. It was a Methodist college.

He puts the paperback with a stack of other nonsense scattered on the desk beside his laptop, dumps the rest of his coffee in the sink—he hates instant, why had he bothered? Why had he bothered to leave his partner in the city? They could play a game of chess as they had so often in the early days, as passion deepened into profound caring.

He returns to the porch, slips his feet into sandals and heads across an expanse of sand and weeds to the beach. The sun is already nearing its zenith. The boys he had hired to clean up the place had gotten as far as chopping away, but not carrying off the *miel*, honeybushes growing along the embankment leading down to the water. The bushes protect the sandy embankment, yet, if they are not cut back, he will lose his porch view of the Gulf. He breathes in the honeyed scent as he makes his way to the water's edge. The day he hired them, for some reason, must not have been fit for fishing—perhaps their outboard was in the shop. Today, the boys are likely in one of those white chips moving along the horizon. May is the end of the dry season, "vestibule to hell," locals call it, before June's rains mitigate afternoon heat and turn evenings to bliss. May is also good fishing.

Far down the beach, a figure ghosts in and out of view within the stone remains of a house afloat in quicksilver. Seeming unwilling to release the figure, a shimmering mirage clings, trailing, halo-like, before it shrinks back to its rocky lair. As it nears, the shape transforms into the old fellow who had shuffled past Cecil's place several mornings ago. They had nodded, but they hadn't spoken. Cecil is surprised the old guy is out in the heat and without a hat. He has the fair complexion that doesn't belong under the midday sun.

The locals can stand it, their lovely browns and tans, cinnamon and café olé complexions merely deepen to even more agreeable shades. Part Maya, the locals are descended from a great civilization—astronomers, builders of pyramids, and creators of their own written language. They discovered the zero, which allowed them to count far back and forward in time, which they believed may soon end. Though seeming unconscious of their great heritage, Cecil believes their legacy, at some deeper level, sustains them—that the thousand years their civilization climbed to the peak of all civilizations in the Americas is encoded in their DNA. Perhaps the outsiders clambering over the remains of the Maya royal edifices are searching for the wisdom they have given up on finding in their own heritage. Was it all make-believe, he wonders? Lately, Cecil feels the membrane separating the visible and the invisible—past, present, future, and even eternity—has become permeable.

As the fellow comes closer, it is clear that something is wrong with him. His face is beet red.

Cecil calls, "You alright?"

"Guess I'm not, everything has turned wiggly and sparkly."

"You'd better get out of the heat. Come on up to my place; cool off." Cecil is almost glad for the fellow's condition—giving him an excuse for not writing. He helps the fellow up the embankment. They are both puffing hard by the time they settle into camp chairs on the porch.

"Cecil's my name," he finally gets enough breath to say.

"Patrick, and thanks. Don't know what hit me."

"Let me get us something to drink."

Cecil hurries into the house and returns with rattling glasses of water.

"Thanks!" Patrick takes a gulp. "Appreciate your rescue. Not many folks here this time of year."

"Are you living here or a snowbird?" Cecil asks, taking the empty glass from Patrick's hand.

"First few winters we were, snowbirds, but after she took sick, the trip back and forth was too much for her, so we stopped heading north every spring, and gave our home up north to our son, who'd fallen on hard times. I went up once after she died. Our son had let the place rundown so bad, it would have broken my wife's heart. I sure couldn't stand to stay there. Listen to me rattle on! You? You a snowbird?"

"Like yourself used to be, but no more. I tell folks that I come out here to write, but I think I come here to find myself."

Patrick snickers. "That's pretty good." Flesh around the old man's light blue eyes crinkles as he smiles and, for a moment, Cecil glimpses the man he must have been before his wife's death took his life with her. "I mean, you come to the beach to find yourself," Patrick explains, "and I say I come here to collect myself."

Bouncing a little, as if the chairs they sit in are old sprung-metal porch chairs, they fall into comfortable silence. Gulls swirl near shore and pelicans clumsily nosedive, as if, through all the millennia, they never learned how. Farther out boats, small flecks of white on corrugated slate, spool white thread-like wakes as their occupants search for fish or octopus.

Cecil tells his partner, who remains in the city, he must have this time alone to write, to channel his muse. True, some of his stuff has been published, but the writing is a ruse to tap into a self within himself. He has been too busy making a living, creating a home, and partying to have time to commune with the ineffable essence, approachable only in solitude. Maybe he searches for the soul he so cavalierly dismissed in his callow days.

"Never needed to know who I was," Patrick says. "Ellie took care of that department. She's still with me. Kind of in my head, you know."

"I think that might be wonderful," Cecil says. "I never had a wife. And my partner, I keep trying to tell him who I am. After all these years, he's still trying to figure me out." Since his heart attack, Cecil had given up the charade of pretending to be straight. If folks have a problem with his being gay, it was *their* problem. "That's probably why I write," he says. "I'm searching for a voice like your Ellie's."

"Wife and kids, don't leave much time for looking inside. About the only times I look inside me is when I lose my temper, and wonder, where in the hell did that come from. Lately, I almost start blubbering, and I don't know why."

"I was taught to listen in Sunday school," Cecil says, "that God or Jesus would tell me what was right and the devil was behind all the bad things folks did. Maybe I was such a chatterbox, is why I never could hear anything but myself."

"You're funny, you know, Cecil."

They go on like that for hours—exchanging a few thoughts and then falling into silence. Finally, Patrick gets up to go.

"Much obliged for the water. I think I can make it now and leave you to your search. You find him, let me know. Meanwhile, maybe I'll collect pieces of me along with those shiny little shells folks collect around here." He heads across the sand, comes to the honeybush at the embankment, turns and waves. "See you around sometime," Cecil hears over the surf's murmur. Patrick's head bobs as he makes his way down the embankment to the water's edge, then disappears behind the honeybushes.

"Old fool," Cecil says to himself, brushing back tears.

Lately, little confetti-like recollections seemed to flutter in and out of his consciousness—there it goes, *consciousness!* "I think, therefore I am." Now, where did that come from? *I know, Rene Descartes!*

Cecil goes into the kitchen, takes a goblet from the shelf, and smiling to himself pours the remains of yesterday's wine. So many years ago his sophisticated friend had taught him the thinner the crystal, the better the wine tastes. Those days it was cheap Chianti.

He ambles back out onto the porch. Beneath towering cumulous clouds, boats are scudding for safe harbor.

Once human beings began to think, they developed self-consciousness. Then they realized that someday they would die, and their selves would no longer be. Scholars say we weren't even conscious of *self* until about five thousand years ago. Wouldn't that have been nice. if we didn't have to worry about death, and be like a dog living in Dhama, not *conscious* we are alive! Cecil imagines Clifford back in the city, sitting in front of their television, their dog beside him, supremely content with the crumbs she steals from Clif's sandwich. The dog doesn't worry about not existing. "Angst" some call the fear of nonexistence.

If he had not read the book of the philosopher, who he so admired, could Cecil have escaped anxiety, the throbbing sense that not far in the future he will no longer exist? Is that why he is obsessed with capturing the stories that play hide-and-seek.

He senses Glen's dismay at his disappearing into himself, scrambling to give voice to whispers, bring to light half-formed images. Is it merely an egotistical need to astound his reader?

Half-formed thoughts taunt as a song heard from far away, the melody lost, only the soprano's weeping is heard. Is the *balm in Gilead?* Only for those he leaves behind when he no longer exists? It is not angst Cecil feels. He has never been more alive, more curious, and more eager to know and understand. He is a freshman again, eager to tell all he knows, and give voice to the music that sounds in his head, sounds which flow from the edges of time. He does not fear death, not yet anyway. There is so much thinking he has yet to think. Death remains a fascinating enigma, at least as viewed from this side of the door. He'll keep going until he smashes into the final door, and trust the surprise that waits beyond. Perhaps he will blunder into Gilead. Maybe he'll meet himself.

It's early yet. He'll drive into the city, pick up Glen, some beer and, figuring Patrick may prefer wine, he'll bring more wine.

Fathers

~~~~~~~~~

ON OUR FIRST DATE, CLIF HELPED ME HANG SHEETROCK. WE ARE about as different as two people can be, yet our relationship is lasting the balance of our lives. We met at a New York opera party. I can still see him standing there, guilelessly unpretentious, like a newly minted coin among those of us, clawing our way to fame.

We both come from the High Plains, me West Oklahoma and Clif, Texas Panhandle, and neither family was well-off. Until Clif took off with a harvest crew and then Vietnam and me for university, we were never far from the breast that suckled us, but our fathers, much of the time, were away from home—Clif's father, hauling cattle or timber from East Oklahoma; my father, traveling southwest Oklahoma selling auto supplies to filling stations at junctions of country roads and to small-town supply stores. It was men's role, to be off somewhere—office, store, out in the field.

I knew Clif's dad and admired him.

I stood helplessly weeping at the foot of my father's bed as no drug or prayer could revive his blood-starved heart. Clif's father played the harmonica and mine whistled like a bird—*literally, like a bird!*

I've lived with a nagging sense of guilt, not that I was disobedient and not that I didn't try to please him, but that my father doesn't come to mind as my mother often does. I credit her with my thirst for reading, and I credit her with whatever intelligence I may have. I credit Clifford's mother for his love of beautiful objects and his keen aesthetic sensibilities. Both our mothers outlived our fathers. I feel guilty that my father's death brought a sense of relief, that he would be spared the scandal, should my obscene secret be exposed and his masculinity wounded. I found comfort in the thought that my father passed into a realm of greater understanding—but is there such a realm? If not, his immortality is dependent on my *remembering*?

Then! Then last week I found him right there beside me, placing his hands on top of mine as he guided me—reminding me to saw with long strokes—like a lullaby he whispered, "Let the saw do the cutting." It gushed back, his showing me to grab a weed close to the ground so as to get the root, return the pliers and screwdriver to their proper place, how to clean a spark plug and distributor, and how to adjust the timing.

Our fathers have been there all the time, not in our heads, but in our hands—part of my viscera. I tell Clifford, and *this* Clif understands, because as profoundly different as we are, and as profoundly different Clifford is from his father, and I am from mine, we are of the same substance—folk who value work and hands-on. Clif's father, Clyde, expertly guides Clifford's trawling plaster, as my father, Wilber, admonishes, "dig deep." I'm willing to try my hand at about anything and usually succeed, but not very well. Clif, on the contrary, is an expert at most everything he tries.

Over our forty-seven years together we did most of the renovations on our houses in Brooklyn and Key West, and still, we putter on our Mérida home and Clif on our Amarillo condo. Whether we were aware or not, all along our fathers guide us.

Brother

~~~~~~

I TURN DOWN THE COAST ROAD EAGERLY, EXPECTING, HOPING, that you are here. I have been terribly frustrated the past three weeks unable to come to the beach, and all along I felt you waiting.

Over the years, I have glimpsed you in the crowd—from a speeding bus or stepping off an escalator as I'm getting on—hurrying down Fifth Avenue or Broadway, half a block ahead.

How could I not recognize you from the back, the shape of your head and your shoulders broader than mine? We slept together for years before our family moved to a larger house and we each had our own rooms. You would be laying with your back to me, reading, and tell me to stop chattering and go to sleep. I'd study your rich chestnut brown straight hair, so unlike my unruly black mop. The last time we were together, your hair was clipped in a severe military manner. I thought your head was shaped different from mine, bigger and more oval to accommodate your vast intelligence. You knew the meaning of every word, learned Spanish and French, played the piano. You would shush me as you sat Saturdays with your ear glued to our Motorola listening to the Metropolitan Opera broadcasts.

Those summers I'd be out plowing in the middle of a hundred acres of wheat stubble and imitate the caterwauling sopranos you introduced me to. Twenty years later found me vocalizing in the

Metropolitan Opera Studio.

I once thought I saw you crossing the street near Bloomingdale's. I ran and called to you. I received annoyed glances, but you don't turn around, and moments later you disappear down subway steps. I've caught up with strangers, thinking they were you, and have been rewarded with dirty looks.

How offensive my birth must have been. For three years you had occupied center stage, and then I, cute and pudgy, stole the limelight. I resorted to being cute and clowning because you were stronger and smarter in every way. While you were good at everything, I was a bumbling mess. Even milking cows, you could raise a two-inch head of foam in your bucket. I only got a few bubbles. You could squirt milk ten feet and send a chicken flapping and clucking. I only managed to hit my foot. Then I'd feel a wet streaming down my neck and run bawling to Mother and tattle on you. I don't blame you for picking on me; I was a snotty-nosed, whining brat. But you weren't always mean to me.

I often relive our times in that little farmhouse on a knoll about three miles from town. It nestles at the edge of a locust grove. Summer evenings, the family gathers on the front porch. Our sister is born by the time we move to the farm. Mother mixes a batch of Kool-Aid. You or I have popped popcorn. Dad has his arm around Mom. We sat gazing across the rutted sandy road running past the house to the neighbor's hay field where Prince, our shaggy collie, chases the taunting jackrabbit he never catches. We can see forever, it seemed—the neighboring town's granaries nine miles away and towering cumulous clouds pink in the sunset's afterglow.

Remember when we had to help Dad give an enema to the cow that foundered on isogram cane? You climbed on the cow shed roof, and poured soapy water down a hose stuck up the cow's rear-end, and when she let go! OK, OK.

One of the best memories is the time driving home from the city along old Route 66. You, our little sister Martha Nell, and I are in the back of our new maroon Ford V8, the first model after the war. We have just come over the escarpment above the Canadian River. The plains rolled ahead like the primordial sea that once covered our land. You start to sing, or maybe it is Mother, and then we all join in, Mom, sis and me singing, and Dad whistling off-key; *you are my sunshine, my only sunshine*, and you said, "We must be the happiest family in the world." Heaven can't be better than that afternoon.

And your graduation from Annapolis, Mother, her hair almost snow-white by then and Martha Nell, grown to be a beautiful young woman. You there among the midshipmen throwing hats in the air. Your friend Alex (you said his full name was Alexander Graham Bell Grosvenor Junior) taking us sailing on a yacht the Fords had given Annapolis. That was one of the happiest, and the saddest times because Dad wasn't there. He would have been so proud of you; he'd have busted all his buttons.

The last time you were home, before graduation—it seems, sometimes that a power intervenes—you and Dad reconciled. He had been so furious with you when you joined the Catholic Church; Dad, a 33-degree Mason. He thought you had done it just to spite him. There was always a tug-of-war between you, maybe because you were the oldest. You were stubborn while I was a sycophant.

The time came for me to register for the draft. Suspecting something, Mother asked me how I filled my military service registration? I told her, as a conscientious objector. She said that it would kill Dad. I got my card back and scribbled out that declaration. See how I was not standing up for my beliefs.

You graduated from the Academy at the top of your class, as you always had, and joined the Air Force. You already could fly a plane; you had started on Piper Cubs at that little airport near our farm.

How old were you then? Fourteen? Sixteen? You wrote about flying your jet across the desert only a foot off the ground. Your letters about flying were poetry. Flying was transcendent for you.

And you wrote me letters—folks wrote letters then. The last letter you wrote to me—Oh brother dear, so beautiful. No, beautiful is too banal—golden? Those words, those jewel-like findings of our bond continue to sustain, ever with me all these years.

The telegram was waiting for me when I came in from a day of making concrete blocks, helping rebuild Krefeld, Germany, an industrial city on the Rhine River. Ten years before our bombers had spared Colon Cathedral, a few miles upriver, but almost obliterated Krefeld. I was studying theology by then and taking the summer off to volunteer with a Quaker group. We hoped that by joining our sweat, maybe we would stop killing each other. We lived in a hostel a short distance from the river.

The message reached me a month after your plane disappeared into the clouds over North Korea. There has been no sighting of you since, I mean in the ordinary sense. I felt you watch me that night, hurting and confused, as I walked out on the bridge over the river. I welcomed the cold drizzling rain, which soaked my clothes and hair and ran down my face lending me tears. Totally unaware of the bewildered American huddled above, a coal-laden barge ghosted through the inky water below. The stern red light glimmered suspended in darkness long after night had swallowed the craft.

<hr />

Another northern came through last night. This time of year storms roll like bowling balls hurled from the Louisiana coast, across the Gulf, right at our little stack of concrete blocks situated between two small fishing villages. I heated a cup of coffee, went back to bed and watched the waves churn against our beach. Fine, wind-sifted sand reaches our seaside doors. On warm days, I push back the doors, so that nothing blocks my view of the water, the diving gulls, and pelicans, and fishing boats skimming the horizon. We planned it so we could look out to sea while comfortably sitting up in bed. Our sugar cube-like house sits behind a low dune. Nearer to the surf's edge, silvery, salt-tolerant bushes shroud the remains of a house destroyed by a hurricane.

I wanted to meet you out here by the Gulf to show off my partner's and my little square of sand. You suspected I was gay, didn't you? Another way I embarrassed you.

Remember our sandbox out under our pear tree? We'd build sand villages and then flood them away. I am back in that sandbox every time I scoop sand into my hand and build sand castles on our beach, and you are always there with me. When we moved to the farm, we left the sandbox and the piece of granite salvaged from the stonecutter, marking the grave for our pet chicken. You preached the funeral for that little hen-pecked chicken we had rescued. Remember, she had been so picked upon, she walked upright like a penguin. The neighbor dog killed her.

Those days, I loved attention—still do. I have written about your finding me singing and dancing at the medicine show. I was just supposed to buy Mother the liniment and hurry right home, but it was amateur night. You practically dragged me home, berating me for embarrassing the whole family. I became a good singer, you know. That was you, sitting in the mezzanine at the premiere performance of *Kismet*. Did you notice my name in the program? It lists me as the first Muezzin. One of the few times I got billing.

My voice teacher once told me that the song was not for me to show off my voice. I must let myself be in the moment. I was singing Shubert's setting of Heine's poem, *Ir Bild*, the picture. The poet is gazing upon the image of a person he loved. The last line goes, "but oh, I cannot believe I have lost you."

When I sang the song again, it was your face in the picture. You quietly entered the studio. Tears blinded, I sang, "and oh, I cannot believe I have lost you."

I failed to become a great singer. But hope you were there, the few times when I was able to step out of the way and let the song flow through me.

Most of my life I have been afraid to be alone. To be alone has seemed to be not loved and unlovable. Perhaps it's why I tried to steal the limelight from you. Confident my partner will always be there when I return, the beach has become a hermitage in which I finally meet the person that has hidden from me all these years. Perhaps not hidden, rather, he has been there in plain sight. While I've been so intent aggrandizing myself, I have failed to stop talking long enough to hear the one that I am, rather than the one I paste together.

Soon, I must go back to the city. Will you be here when I return? Perhaps I'll see you in a box at the Symphony across from ours, or sipping wine under the umbrellas in front of the Gran Hotel. I used that setting in two of my novels. I included our sister in my last novel. *Imagine, me a writer now.* It was almost biographical, but I didn't include you. I'm not sure why; perhaps I feared I would embarrass you, even though I changed all the names, even of our town. I think the real reason I didn't include you was because you and I are a saga beyond my capacity to fathom or explain.

I was always embarrassing you. The family understood, without putting it into words, that day you were leaving home for good. You had said all the goodbyes, hugged Dad, Sis and hugged Mother a dozen times. Against your protestations, I carried your bag the two blocks to the corner where our street intersects Highway 66, our town's Main Street. You were to hitchhike to The City and from there catch the train east. At a loss for words, I stand there, choking back tears until you order, "Go home! I'll never get a ride with you standing there."

I left in a trot, holding back until the floodgates burst. I slammed into the house and into our room, then only my room, and my world came to an end.

Still, out here at the beach along about dusk, I see you disappear around the rubble of a hurricane-destroyed house. I don't cry out or run after you. I know you have been looking after me. Always you will be as near as breath. I have but to look in a mirror.

Dry Tortugas

~~~~~~~~~~

AS SOON AS THE FAST CATAMARAN CLEARS KEY WEST HARBOR, Clifford goes out onto the forward deck, while Bill, waving me to join Clif, stays seated in the cabin.

Bill is my former lover, come down from Gainesville where he lives in a retirement complex on the edge of the university campus. His family is part of Florida's history. All his life he has explored her sinkholes, springs, rivers, and hummocks. Bill has a soft drawl, like his mother. He and his family were a window to Southern gentility. As a boy he swam in the Gulf's phosphorescent water off the pier at the family camp, and sloshed through the Everglades, but he had never gotten to the Dry Tortugas, and is determined to visit the coral islands, poised like the stinger at the tip of a scorpion's tail off the southern end of Florida. Neither have Clifford nor I, although we have lived in Key West nearly twenty years.

On a full plane under a cotton-ball sky, the catamaran skims above the midnight-blue waters of the Boca Grande Channel, a narrow shortcut, through which the Gulf Stream squeezes into the Atlantic. I imagined we are gliding above a coral-encrusted galleon burdened with Montezuma's gold destined for Spain.

I stand near the bow next to Clifford watching the porpoises pacing our fast boat, as we skirt a dozen uninhabited mangrove and buttonwood forested keys. The sun ignites gold and copper strands in Clifford's chestnut brown, windblown hair, lately flecked with silver. He has grown heavy, yet I still see him as the slender young man I met New Year's Eve thirty-one years ago. As we approach the pier, our boat's twin hulls slice through bands of sapphire, cobalt, and aquamarine water.

We swing into the lee of Tortuga island and tie up at the end of a wooden pier. Passengers scramble ashore as if the boat were about to sink. We rejoin Bill at the cabin door and take our time. Still, the effort sends Bill wheezing.

"Go on ahead," he urges, "find us a place to settle. I'll catch up." So Cliff and I hurry on to stake our claim to a table about a city block away, near the water's edge. I help drag the table into the speckled shade of a buttonwood tree. We call to Bill, walking head down. He looks up, confused. Then recognition clicks in, and he shamble over.

He wears suspenders over a dress shirt yellowed with age. His baggy trousers look to be from an old suit. I'm shocked by his deterioration in just a year since I last saw him. As soon as he reaches us, he collapses onto one of the benches connected to the table. He fishes around in his pocket and pulls out a plastic mouthpiece, inserts an aluminum canister, draws upon the mouthpiece, and then grunts, hog-like. I hate seeing my old lover's grizzled eyebrows untrimmed. Deep crags score the face that had been so handsome. On good days, he says, he can still snorkel, and he is planning a trip to the South Pacific. I admire his tenacity.

I don't recall his smoking much the eight years we lived together— only at parties. But maybe, knowing I objected, he only smoked when I wasn't around. That had been his way—gentle, considerate, never confronting, yet secretly going his own way. We never really argued. Still, it was my jealousy at his meandering that parted us. I had thought, after we split up, that I would never again allow myself to be so vulnerable. And it was ten years before I met Clifford.

A few yards down the beach a toast-brown young man sensually massages oil onto the glowing back of the young woman snuggled against him. Cliff and I head off to explore the island, leaving Bill, his attention fixed on the sunbathers. *Death in Venice*, I think.

~~~~~~~~~~

Clif and I walk along the top of a wall separating the sea from the moat surrounding the fort. At the leeward side, the water is so clear it seems the psychedelic fish cavorting among sea fans might just as well join the white-throated frigate birds hovering over the fort's battlements, scarcely moving their long blade-like wings.

In 1513, while searching for the Fountain of Youth, Ponce de León discovered the low-lying coral islands between Cuba and the North American Keys, abounding with turtles, thus the island's name. During the Civil War, the Union built massive Fort Jefferson on the island.

On our first vacation together, Bill and I flew to the Caribbean island, St. Lucia, caught a freighter on down to St. Vincent and then sailed across to Beque, one of the Grenadines Islands sprinkled between St. Vincent and Grenada. It was a honeymoon. A coral reef lay practically at the front door of our small guesthouse. That trip was the beginning of Bill's infusing in this child of the hot, dry high plains, his love of under-the-sea life.

Beyond a spit of land connected to a guano-spattered rookery congested with dysfunctional families of birds, Cliff and I cross the moat into the fort's vaulted galleries.

~~~~~~~~~~

The fort is the country's largest masonry structure. Its mass of brick brings a palpable sense of the brute cost in human labor, suffering, and of colossal jingoistic waste. It never came under fire, nor was it completed. It became our country's Devil's Island; its most famous prisoner, Dr. Samuel A. Mudd, held seven years in a dank dungeon for setting John Wilkes Booth's leg, broken as Booth fled after shooting Lincoln.

The Dry Tortugas was the first US land reached by causalities rescued after the battleship *Maine* exploded in Havana Harbor. Dr. Mudd saved many of the sailors' lives.

I was as unfaithful as Bill, and I might have tired of him if he hadn't tired of me first. There always seems to be the one who loves and the one who is loved. After all these years, I still hurt from his rejection. He says he was amazed, not only that I still sing, but that I sing better than forty years before when I sang with his choir. I show off, imagining he sees me effortlessly jump from stone to stone across the moat, as we return to the table. I want him to wish he hadn't let me go, to envy me. All day, in fact, ever since he arrived, I have searched for feelings of affection and compassion, to counteract the fury I harbor at his growing old.

~~~~~~~~~

We met at Boston's Symphony Hall. A friend had given us tickets to an organ recital by the French organist Marcel Dupré.

Tweed jacket, suede patches on the elbows, slender, I thought he might be a prep-school teacher, perhaps a soccer coach, given his lithe build.

Marshal leaned across me. "Bill, this is Ed . . ." The introduction was interrupted by the first chord of Bach's Fantasy and Fugue in G minor. When Marshal gave me my ticket, he had deputized me to learn all I could about his other guest, who had wandered into Trinity Church the day before while Marshal was practicing. Bill had asked if Marshal minded him listening. "Not at all!" Thinking Bill unusually handsome, Marshal offered him a ticket to Dupree's concert. "President of Boston's chapter of the American Guild of Organists should have its privileges," Marshal said.

"Well, what do you think?" Marshal pulled me aside at intermission. "Is he?"

"I'm not a mind reader," I said.

The second-half of the program was dominated by French composers, for which I had little appetite. *A prep school teacher, maybe coaches soccer?*

Frere Jacques, Frere Jacques. The melody pulled me back. Dupré had begun the improvisation portion of his program. The tune floated like a toy boat through a storm of dissonance, with every pipe in the organ sounding. Any moment, it felt like the plaster of the hall might give way. The music paused, then, as the last reverberation decayed, trumpets blared the theme again. Finally, the storm passed, and the child's song grew softer and softer, and as if from a great distance, came the sound, like a shower of crystal, tinkling bells. The palms of my hands were tingling when Marshal pulled at me. "Let's get out ahead of the crowd."

After mustering out from the Navy as a junior naval officer, Bill had taken a year's Fulbright to study music in Germany. Two or three inches taller than me, he had the build of a swimmer or gymnast. Long lashes curled back from dark blue eyes had the effect of a child just awakened. He had a killer smile.

He wasn't a preschool teacher. He had just become the organist-choirmaster of a church near Boston and invited me to dinner the following Friday at the venerable Copley Plaza. We met in the gilded lobby. Champagne waited in a chilled bucket of ice in the room he had reserved. We didn't make it to dinner.

I was in my last semester at Boston University School of Theology. I ditched my plans to return to Oklahoma and become a social worker. I got a job as a youth minister in a church near Boston. Those were idyllic days.

Eight years later my possessiveness and anger crushed both of us. He loved me enough to hate hurting me. And I loved him enough to realize what I was doing to both of us—amphetamines in the morning and midnights when he still had not come home; blessed oblivion came from gulps of barbiturates.

It was time for me to give us both a break. I attended the World Council of Churches in New Delhi, knocked around the world, ran a sleazy bar and perhaps somewhere along the way hoped I would find myself or the Grail. The irony is that his kind father made it all possible—providing me with a Lloyd's of London letter of credit. He understood! I paid it back, but they never expected me to.

~~~~~~~

We never stopped loving. He wrote me beautiful letters.

I came across this letter telling me about a return to Beque years after we *discovered* the island:

Beque is yacht heaven now, his letter read. *For every sloop or sailing yacht in the bay in '57 there are 50 now–stretching even into the horizon with pennants and flags of many nations flapping in the breeze–even Ireland and Greece. The island is beautiful as ever (the unbuilt parts). The tree frogs still squeak in the night, and there are still mosquitoes, and when you get under the mosquito net it is clammy, and you think it'd be better outside of the net and just slap. The more things change, the more they are the same. It is not as hot, even so, as it was the summer of '57.*

Even after all these years, he writes me wonderful letters.

I attended St. Mary's this morning, remembering when we attended in '57. Remember the vicar (as he was being fanned in splendor by his attractive teenaged acolyte of a Saturday afternoon) explained that non-Anglicans were "not permitted" to receive the Eucharist... I being Episcopalian was permitted, but not you, a Congregationalist. I went up anyway, deserting friend in the pew whose soul was clearer than mine. It even occurred to me this morning NOT to go up to the altar, punishment for abandoning you those many years ago, but that does not wash with the Almighty either? I can remember crossing a picket line once, too (something you would never do), before I knew anything about those things and you had it right (again) and stuck with a friend instead of an ideal. You taught me a lot.

<hr>

When we returned to our picnic table, Cliff and I found Bill asleep in the sand, curled into a fetal position, his hat pulled over his ears. I wanted to kneel and cradle him in my arms, and I wanted to kick him. How dare he be so old and tired?

It occurred to me then that the reason he never had another lover is because of *me*; he too never again wanted to become so vulnerable.

His brother sent me a letter he had addressed to me before he died. His last words to me were, "Don't worry. We got the laundry in before the rain."

Barber Shop

~~~~~~~~

SHAKING HIS HEAD, HE TURNS OFF THE NEWS. THERE HAD BEEN a time when he thought the world was moving toward tolerance. He is near the end of his journey, he tells himself. He had once believed that he could make a difference—be somebody significant, even a hero. The dogs nose his hand. *Malishes* the locals call them, Mayan for mongrel. He and Clifford saved them from of a village street where females are especially abused. He scratches their muzzles, leaves his coffee cup by the chair's arm, and takes the dogs outside. More and more of late he leaves things around—the bed unmade and clothes strewn on the floor.

Pollen clouds the swimming pool. As warm as the water gets this time of year, the filter must run all day or algae will bloom. Clif swims all seasons, but the old partner only goes in the pool when the water reaches bathtub temperature. He makes his way around to the filter at the far side of the pool. Glancing back to be sure he is following, the dogs take the lead, noses to the ground, as if on a hunt. It has been weeks since he inspected the back garden, where he has nursed philodendron to cover the ground behind the great, ancient banyan tree; roots like spilled honey trickling over the remains of a stonewall. Only the dogs' tails poke above the philodendron. The lush field of green brings to mind the yellowing vine on his grandmother's windowsill.

Nattering parrots sway in the tops of bamboo, towering above the small jungle. When they bought the house twenty years ago, except for the banyan and a mahogany tree, the place was all weeds and refuse. They did much of the work themselves. He and his Clif had chopped and dug with pickaxes and machetes. In the tropical heat and with abundant water, everything they planted flourished beyond their imagination. Nowadays he is fortunate if he accomplishes a single project. He had washed the dogs the day before, something he had been planning for over a week. He feels unanchored. He slips outside himself and sees himself from a distance as if the person in his body is a stranger. He watches that stranger, lost in reverie, walk among his plants. Soon, his Clif will return from The States, and then, perhaps, he will return to himself.

He kicks aside drifts of purple and white bougainvillea blossoms as he makes his way to the front of the house. He must remember to turn on the sprinklers when he returns. He'll likely remember tomorrow. Their old well, dug by hand two hundred years ago when the house was built, still supplies limitless water. He crosses the courtyard to the *sala*, where a huge painting, great splashes of reds and purples, dominates the wall above the sofa at one end of the high-ceilinged room. He and his partner adored the strappingly handsome painter, one of the terribly many friends who died of AIDS.

The front door's handle is hot, and heat smacks him as the door swings open, and he steps onto the narrow sidewalk. He flattens himself against the wall of the house as a bus whooshes past.

Only a ribbon of shade remains. The old guy has been foolish to dally till the morning is half gone. He used to arise early, as the natives do, so as to accomplish things before the stifling heat.

Ahead is a house painted chartreuse and a few doors beyond an Art Deco facade sparkles bright blue and farther along a façade is barn red, and beyond that, purple. Down the street as far as he can see, brilliant colors relieve the monotony of crumbling masonry. Tasteless, he judges, but delightful.

"*Buenos dias*," he steps into the street to let an approaching woman pass. *Buenos dias, senora*, he replies, as folks their ages do. She walks slightly bent over. Pulling back his shoulders and sucking in his stomach, he picks up his pace. The week before, he glimpsed himself with a friend his age walking past a store window. They were both shuffling with their heads thrust forward, and stomachs were overhanging their belts. Not yet, he vowed!

The cantina at the corner is silent, but come five o'clock troubadours' music will spill into the street. A block and a half farther is Santiago Park, laid out as the conquistadors designed, a church, open plaza, and a market. The statue of the Black Christ dwells in the Santiago church.

Across from the open meat market, the metal front of the barbershop is rolled up. Roberto busily cuts the thick black hair of a customer sitting in a barber's chair out of another century. The customer faces a clouded mirror over a dusty counter cluttered with barber paraphernalia. Plastered above the mirror are fading posters of sleepy-eyed matinee idols — senoritas with lace flowing from tall mantillas and mustachioed *muchachos*.

Four other men slouch on a wooden sofa pushed against the wall, cushions covered with black plastic bags. Two of the men look like the characters in the Saturday movies of his youth. He chooses a rusting chair webbed with frayed plastic tubing, and grabs a dog-eared comic book lying beside *Por Esto*, a periodical featuring photos of traffic accidents' mangled bodies lying in roadside weeds, and corpses of decapitated narcos. The book's cover displays a pulchritudinous, raven-haired woman in the steamy embrace of an equally pulchritudinous blond-haired man. A *bandido*, thumbs stuck in his gun belt, scowls at the lovers. The black mustache of a waiting customer is a copy of the mustache that brackets the gunslinger's cruel mouth.

Roberto shakes the proceeding customer's hair from the apron and motions him to the barber's chair, wraps a ribbon of toilet paper around his new client's neck, then fastens the apron. The barber of Santiago is a small, neat man with a well-trimmed graying mustache. He speaks little. Scarcely moving his upper body in tiny dance-like steps he minces around his customer, his scissors snipping like castanets.

Sunlight spilling in from the street highlights half the old man's sagging face, gouging deep furrows. He neither likes nor wants the face glowering back at him from the filmy mirror. He tightens the muscles around his mouth into a smile. Better. He pulls in his lower lip. He despises the sight of sagging lower lips he sees on other old men, cupping stained teeth swimming in spit. He grins more broadly. His dimples disappear into wrinkles and pouches push up under his eyes. He purses his lips in an exaggerated kiss. Poncho Villa, slouched on the sofa, stares back. "The old guy must be off his medication," he reads Villa's mind.

Roberto carefully parts and combs, taking pains to the back of the head, swirling the silver hair. Triumphantly, he holds up a mirror for the client's inspection. Silver hair artfully hides the balding. The barber clips offending hairs from his client's ears. The client pays three dollars for the best haircut he has ever had. The cost of a haircut in New York is as much as many Mexicans earn in a week.

A trumpet blares to the beat of a drum. "Diez pesos," he tells the senorita. When she grabs the large bunch of cilantro, he realizes he said ten when he meant *cinco*, five. He makes these mistakes more often it seems, or is he simply more conscious of them, as friends assure him? He correctly tells the lady at the *tortillaria*, *cinco*. The tortillas are hot and fragrant. Not even a ribbon of shade remains. Mad dogs and Englishmen he mutters, but it isn't funny. He leans against a tattered poster advertising a bullfight. His house seems miles away. After a moment, he pulls himself erect.

When finally he arrives home, he hands the dogs cookies, and slips a hot tortilla from the middle of the stack, slathers it with butter, and takes a beer to the porch. The dogs lick his hand. They don't care how he looks. It's his smell that they adore.

Grateful

～～～～～～～

NO PHOTO, OR WORDS, CAN COME CLOSE TO EXPRESSING MY gratitude for and astonishment at the *Journey*. I think of those who taught me to walk, those who helped me stand, those who walked beside me, those whose paths have joined mine—those who, when we came to a fork in the road, bid me farewell; grandparents and parents, aunts and uncles, sister, brother-in-law, nieces and nephew, the friend who stood with me under cherry blossoms overlooking Kolby Bay, the old woman on the Greyhound bus who shared her fried chicken, the truck driver who pulled over as it began to sleet and gave me a lift; the friends in the work camp, rebuilding a town in Germany; the voice teacher who said I could be a star—she didn't say *star*, but star is what I heard—the fellow singer/dancers who encouraged me, and the director, who, as kindly as possible, advised me that becoming a great singer did not lay in my future. I am grateful to the believers and nonbelievers, the lesbian friends, the gay friends, the straight friends, the friends who don't approve yet remain kindly, and friends who are just *friends*. And still I have failed to mention a legion more, but I must not neglect to speak my gratitude for Clifford, my partner of forty-eight years! And just imagine what is yet to come.

Is Anybody Listening

"HELLO, HELLO, HELLO! I KNOW SOMEONE IS THERE, I HEARD A pickup and a whooshing air sound. Pardon me, but I have been trying to reach you, literally for ages. I usually give up and leave a message. One would think, given the advances in smart phones—so smart, it takes a graduate degree to figure out the damn things, that one should have no trouble getting through to the Almighty! Oops, don't cut me off, if you happen to be there and still listening. It's just that I get so darn mad trying to get through to anybody these days. Everybody's noses are always stuck in cell phones, computer screens or Netflix.

Are you getting all this, Miss or Mr. Air-whoosh?

"Hold on a moment."

"Oh, my God! You were listening all the time! I thought you were just an open circuit."

"This is an automated answering service; the Boss is either not receiving calls at the moment or dealing with far more important matters. If you will just be patient, you will be patched through to an assistant."

"No, I don't want to talk to an assistant. I want the Boss. I'll call back, maybe around midnight."

"Very well then, we'll put you on a callback list."

As he reaches for a second or is it a third Demerol, he notices it is already half past midnight. Was it a dream or had he actually gotten through? He had been calling since he was three years old, usually in a time of crisis, such as when the neighbor shot his dog for stealing chickens. It took twenty years for the neighbor to be killed in a hunting accident.

"Just *believe!*" he had been taught. "Faith can move mountains." Where was the help when he was bullied, or when the love of his life didn't even seem to know he existed, or the dozens of times he wished he had never been born?

The call came through sometime after the third or fourth time he had gotten up to pee. "So what is it this time that it is so important that one of my assistants can't handle it? Holy Week is coming up, and I'm already driven to distraction with supplications."

"Is it really you? I mean, after all these years? Am I dying? Or am I already dead? Is that why I finally got through to you? Are you tuning in just to let me know you're not going to let me through the Pearly Gates, just because of what we boys did behind the barn? Good Lord—excuse me—we were only twelve—or because I passed that beggar every day and didn't give him a cent? I paid my pledge to the church... Oh, not enough huh, not a full ten percent. But you never let me earn enough to be generous."

"First of all, let me point out that it is I who got through to you. I didn't open channels to hear your petty sniveling. For heaven's sake, you need to buck up. Think what I go through morning, noon and night. You think you have problems? It's you humans who give me migraines. I hoped that when I opened a channel to Buddha, Zoroaster, Leutze, Moses, Mohammed, a slew of Jews, including Jesus, I'd get some rest. But, no, you twist my teachings into excuses to hate and kill each other. I know, I know, you've got problems. So I don't always take your side in the arguments you have with your mate, but don't think I don't pay attention. And I saved you from scarlet fever and a nearly burst appendix. I staved off a head-on collision. Your whole family would have been wiped out. The tires had been repaired once too often. A truck was speeding down the hill toward you when the tire was about to blow. I let out a slow leak, enough for your father to feel a shimmy and know he had to pull over to the side of the road. The tire blew just as the truck whooshed past, remember?"

"Golly! Thanks! And I do remember, we were coming home after a visit with my grandparents—on that hill, right before you reach the Canadian river."

"I even overstepped," God kept on. Boy, when he gets going he doesn't let up. Talk about injustice collection. "When I took care of the neighbor who shot your dog. Yes, that was me. I hate animal cruelty as much as you do. Vengeance is mine. Still, I shouldn't have taken it out on the old guy. After all, your dog was stealing his chickens. The Devil made me do it. Ha, ha, a joke. Did you get it; the *Devil*? Never mind; it's an in-joke."

I stifle a yawn. I hadn't expected God to yadda, yadda on like this. Of course, we wouldn't have had the Bible and all those sayings. The truth is, I'm about to doze off when he gets to quoting himself.

"*Come unto me, all you who are burdened and heavy-laden and I will give you rest.* I said it and meant it, but I tell you, I get over-whelmed. Just remember, while I'm shouldering your burden, I have all the rest of creation to look after. Sometimes keeping an eye on sparrows flitting about, and getting into all sorts of trouble is more than a body can stand. Sometimes, I think back to the good old days, in the beginning, when I was The Word, and Wisdom was my bride, and the only substance around was a tiny singularity. Five billion years ago—just a blink of an eye to me—I wasn't really thinking much about creating time and partials, and all that would lead to when I set off the fireworks. I simply wanted to pretty up the universe for Wisdom's sake, you know, spangle the sky. Who had any idea what lay in store when I popped that little singularity; it was such a tiny, innocent-appearing bit, not yet even matter."

"Oh my God! Now you're getting into quantum physics!"

"Maybe I overdid it, but what came after the Big Bang was so awesome, Wisdom and I wanted to share our amazement. That is why we created you. I'm sorry to lay all this on you, but I need to give Wisdom a break; she's heard me complain so often, she sometimes takes off to the netherworld, and I don't see here for eons, not that I blame her!

"Creation, you might say, sort of spun out of our control. I don't go along with that Swiss theologian, John Calvin, his predestination theory. I may be the Alpha, the beginning of creation, but Omega is beyond the stars. Omega, the end, maybe more humans' doing than mine.

"Can you really blame us for creating you? Do you have any idea how much patience it took? It was Wisdom's idea to begin with chimpanzees. We needed someone to appreciate us—what we had created. We, the God you know, can't even exist unless you invoke us.

"I see it is getting late, or early depending on your point of view, and I've got miles and miles to go before sunset. Now, if you don't mind, we'll get around to whatever it was you wanted to talk to me about, maybe tomorrow night. It was nice you let me do the talking for a change. If you'll take my advice, which you rarely do, cut back on the Demerol and gin; they don't work well together. Now go back to sleep. Sweet dreams. See you around the base, Ace!"

Shafts of sunlight pierce arches that rise above the garden's east wall. Its rays turn palm branches golden. Orioles, returning from Guatemala, flit through high branches, and sometime during the night, a purple water lily burst open in the koi pond at the base of a giant ramon tree.

He crawls out of bed, steps outside, clasps his hands under his chin and bows to the morning, then playfully waves and blows a kiss.

Death

~~~~~~~~~

I SIT ROCKING GENTLY AT THE FOOT OF HIS BED. IT HAD BEEN A long, exhausting night—a long week. I have grown to love him in spite of the risks he has taken. Was that why I have let him go on bumbling from one crisis to the next. Sometimes I don't know myself. First, there was the scarlet fever; he was only four. If he lived there would be some brain damage, but then again, these days, few reach adulthood with undamaged brains—if not drugs and alcohol, there is football, bronco-busting, and riding bikes without a helmet. Is "brains" the most important reason to live? About the time he entered the first grade, I nearly had to let him go, when the pain in his groin hit, but they got him to the hospital minutes before the appendix burst. There were the times he experimented with a controlled substance, and another time he passed that truck on a hill. Why didn't I let him go then? He is no rocket scientist. Maybe we'd all be better off with fewer rocket scientists or nuclear physicists.

Ever since I let Alexander Fleming live, I have regretted it. Penicillin has made my work so much more difficult.

I probably shouldn't have let Hitler or Dillinger live, but who am I to judge? I'm just death, not God. Why am I so hated? I bring great comfort. The Apostle Paul said, "Death has lost its sting, but in me, there is no sting!"

So many live such worthless lives, skimming on the surface, watching TV, reading modern romances, spending two-thirds of their time making money so they can indulge in escapist recreation—Disney World or Las Vegas or Carnival Cruises, shooting deer or shooting each other, when all around them is an abundance—Tristan, Tolstoy, Toscanini, Puccini, or Proust. How about just walking in the woods, sitting quietly by the sea or in one's backyard and yes, smelling the roses.

I hate taking babies and some old folks, who don't harm anyone. I'd like for them to live to be a hundred—sweet old things, but if I ruled from my heart, we'd be overpopulated in a generation. My most successful times seem to be over—bubonic plague, smallpox, and Spanish flu. Antibiotics have made my work more difficult, but just when the human population gets out of control, along comes atom bombs, wipes out more in an instant than pestilence, earthquakes, or tsunamis—obliterated two cities, just like that. What if I had taken out Oppenheimer? The smart ones seem always to start out sickly.

"Are you awake? I let your last clot pass, this time. You'll drool a little, but you'll finish that book you've been working on."

I stop at the door. I ask myself, should I tell him, this reprieve is just long enough to get the book done? "I'll be seeing you soon." I softly close the door behind me. No one sees me slip out of the hospital.

Next time will be goodbye, no warning pain between the shoulder blades or shooting up and down the arm. It's the least I can do. We've been through a lot together and a lot of close calls. Just lights out, next time.

Expat

～～～～～～

"EXCUSE US, DO YOU LIVE HERE?" THE YOUNG COUPLE APPROACHED the white-haired gentleman drinking a beer in a restaurant courtyard.

"Oh my, yes—ages. Lost track of how many years. Time just flies by, don't you think? Not for you two, being so young."

"We wanted to ask directions to Santa Ana Park?"

"Oh, yes, Santa Ana. Lovely, lovely part of the city. Live near there myself—sit, sit, have a beer with me, or something else if you like, a margarita, yes that is what you should have a margarita, that is unless you are Baptists, ha, ha, meaning no disrespect."

"We don't want to bother you."

"Bother, bother, no bother; sit, I insist! One doesn't bother in this city. North of the Rio Grande time is money but here, my young friends, time is for living! Yes, living. *Joven,* bring this lovely young couple whatever they want. Much too hot to be wandering around the city—it's only for mad dogs and Englishmen, Englishmen, ha, ha, yes Englishmen."

"Aldridge Pennypacker," he stood, pulled out a chair and indicated for them to sit.

"Carol and June Stewart," the young man extended his hand.

"June, June, lovely, and you do resemble the lovely June Allyson, but you are much too young to remember the Hollywood star, lovely creature as you are my dear. Ah, yes the forties were the golden days of films; not the dreadful violence we have today—and ridiculous sci-fi time travel! Listen to me go on."

The waiter took their order for three beers.

"What is your interest in Santa Ana, the Virgin of the Candles perhaps?"

"The owners at the B and B where we are staying told us he has a friend selling his house near the park."

"Yes, yes, it seems everyone is scurrying around buying, fixing up, and selling. Popular neighborhood—mostly young men, you know. Ah, well, they are rejuvenating the historic district. Murder there some time ago, nasty business, crime of passion, ten years or so ago. As I said: time flies. Sweet people, the Méridanos, but passionate, oh yes they can be passionate. Mostly dancing and music, but don't get them riled; passion, you know, easily turns to violence.

"Violence! Oh, my they could be violent. During the Cast Wars, the 1840s if memory serves me right—memory's not what it used to be. Used to know the capitals of all the states, but no more. Sometimes I forget where I put my glasses—search all over the house, then I find them pushed up on the top of my head. The Maya came close to wiping out Mérida, as they did Valladolid—terrible, terrible massacre it was of the *hasiandados* living there. The planting time came, and the Maya all went home to plant their corn in their *milpas* (their patches of land). Slash and burn was their method. Each year they'd move to a different spot of scrub, cut it down and burn it and then plant their corn, beans, and squash. Government tries to stop it now, but comes the dry season, and one sees columns of smoke rising from the countryside—stubborn folk, sweet as can be, but stubborn! They had their reasons, the Maya did, for revolting. The Spanish treated them dreadfully. Cut apostate's hands off if they pretended to be Catholic and then went back to their pagan ways. Apostates they called the backward-sliders. Listen to me, backward-sliders, and I'm not even a Baptist. Christmas and Easter Episcopalian actually. Came from corn, the Maya believed. I say that is better than the clay our Bible tells us we come from. Still, Mérida is safer than most cities in the US."

"Do many foreigners live around here?" Carol asked.

"Expats, we're called. Yes, yes. The locals prefer the modern north part of the city, but the expats are mad for antiquity. Some of us have been here for a number of years, but now Mérida has been discovered. Used to be one happy family, the foreigners. Now the old gang is dying off or splitting up more every day. You got to be careful who you get mixed up with. Downright vicious at times. There's the rich and pretend to be rich, the famous and pretend to be famous. Lots of border promotion, as my friends call it. Oh, my, the gossip, *chisme* the locals call it. And be careful of the real estate agents, seems like half the expats are salespeople. Just listen to me! I'm as bad as the rest. 'Don't start him talking,' my wife used to say, God rest her soul. 'Or he'll tell you more than you ever wanted to know.'

"Are you sure you won't have another one? No, no it's on me! About chewed your ears off. Keep on heading down that way; you'll come to Santa Ana about five blocks. You children best stop in one of the shops and get yourselves straw hats. Sunset you'll find me at the umbrellas in front of the Gran Hotel" . . . Well, *hasta la vista*, then!"

The Hat

~~~~~~~~~

A BLUE AND YELLOW BOAT LIES UPSIDE-DOWN AT THE WATER'S edge, and a few yards offshore men tinker over an outboard motor. An old man stands on his porch looking at the goings-on. The gulf, flat this morning, is green as limeade. The wind will pick up as the temperature climbs to frying-pan hot by mid-morning. It is *pulpo* (octopus) season in Chelem, Mexico. Far out on the gulf, boats with bamboo poles as long as the boats themselves, jutting from bows and sterns, are already mere chips homing in as if by instinct on the *pulpo* treasure beyond the blue where water meets sky.

Vacation over, the city folks' houses stand unoccupied, but locals take advantage of hot days that will last until the Day of the Dead, the end of October. They camp in the shade of green, orange, blue and purple houses, now closed for a winter that seems never to come.

He finishes his coffee, goes back in, rinses his cup, and places it upside down on the drainboard. He takes his morning pills, putting the last tiny one beneath his tongue. He pauses, considering the long day that lay ahead. Letting him enjoy the solitude—solitude in which lately he has found companionship—his partner has stayed in the city to attend the parties the old man no longer enjoys. The expat community has gone sour.

From a collection of straw hats left by previous visitors, he selects one with a wide flat brim. *Madeleine Albright*, he muses as he glances in a mirror.

He pulls the screen to, as he steps back onto the porch and then makes his way down to the beach. The heady fragrance of honey hangs in the air where bushes, named for their sweet smell, shroud the embankment. A recent storm has piled deltas of shells and a band of dung-colored seaweed along the water's edge. He follows imprints of bare feet along the firm, moist sand above the detritus.

He passes a group of glistening café au lait, cinnamon, honey and mahogany-complexioned youth standing waist-deep in the water. He had turned as dark as those youth summers when he worked in the fields of his family's farm. These boys have broad, heavy chests and shoulders, characteristic of the Maya, and the girls, thick black locks of hair.

A single gimlet-eyed pelican glides a few feet above the bathers. Its ancestors long since have accommodated the upright creatures who invaded a millennium or so ago. The birds' claim to this margin of land and sea reaches back to prehistory. Perhaps the straw hat atop the creature, pale as a dead fish, nudges a neuron in the pelican's brain.

The longer the old man lives in this land of color and passion, the more his hold on reason slips; the past penetrates the present, and this world mingles with the netherworld.

He passes a woman, her broad hips sunk comfortably into the sand. Her hair is pulled into a topknot. Perhaps she is already a grandmother, *Abuelita,* her grandchildren would call her. She wears a white sack-like dress, a *huipil*, embroidered with bright flowers at the hem and around the neck. "*Buenos dias*," she murmurs as is the custom. "*Buenos dias*," he responds. His sister is a grandmother and how she basks in the affection of husband, children, and grandchildren. He understands her grief when she learned the way he is—that he would not know such joy.

Further down the beach, a half-dozen boys and a girl yell and scream as they kick a soccer ball, skidding, falling and sending up fountains of sand.

Beyond the players, where the surf has bitten into the bank, a family has erected a green umbrella. This is their land, the old man muses, where the Virgin appears to Juan Diego and where the spirits of their dead relatives return year after year. They know that they belong and yet, long after the soccer players carry their ball back to the village, and the family has folded its umbrella, long after the last blush of sunset has faded, a youth will sit at the water's edge, gaze out past the lights of *pulpo* fishermen into the magical darkness that waits beyond and he will wonder if somewhere there is a place for him or her.

A few minutes beyond the family, he comes to a stone building from which the doors and windows are gone, and further, a pink house stands abandoned on a point jutting into the surf.

A breeze across his sweat-soaked shirt sends a chill. He walks out into the surf and pauses at a mound of shells searching for an unbroken *caracol*. How could he tell his sister of the afternoon lying on the hill overlooking Kobe Bay—of the youth's cheek, as flawless as the petals of the cherry blossoms that showered down around them, or of the Danish dancer, or the constancy, the fidelity, and infidelity of his partner of fifty years?

A quarter of a mile or so beyond the pink house he arrives at a low bluff on which sits crumbling walls where once stood a hacienda. He has gone further than he expected, yet he lingers, wading in rivulets hissing through boulders once part of the hacienda. He crawls through the roots of a tree fallen into the water's edge. Its branches claw into the sand as if to save itself from being swept out to sea. The sun has reached its zenith; the only shade is a thatched *palapa* hut tilting on the embankment too steep to climb. Surely the *palapa* is occupied by vermin.

Dunes of sand roll on as far as he can see. Unable to resist, he takes off running across the sand. After a few yards, he doubles over, gasping. He was for a moment the melancholy eleven-year-old running headlong across dunes at the edge of his family's farm. It was the time of the Dust Bowl. A recent sandstorm blowing down across the High Plains had deposited the sand in tumbleweed-clogged fences. He was so full of longing.

As his breath returns, he finds he is staring into the startled eye of a fish washed ashore, its mouth puckered in a kiss.

A thread of pain shoots down his left arm. It is past time for him to turn back. Shimmering silver floats across the way he has come. In it a shape ghosts in and out of focus; it disappears and then gains substance, disappears into the silver again and reappears, again and again until finally a head and shoulders emerge, and then the full shape of a man strides out. He sways from side to side as the old man does, but even the young locals walk in a similar side-to-side gait.

As they near each other, the old man wonders if the approaching stranger is as curious to see the features beneath the wide straw brim of his hat as he is to make out the features beneath the bill of the stranger's cap.

They draw parallel, and without breaking stride, the stranger murmurs "*buenas tardes,*" for it is well past noon. He has a wide mouth, perfect teeth, and a movie star mustache, almost invisible against his weathered fisherman's complexion.

"*Buenas tardes,*" the old man responds.

The old man continues. His footprints and those of the stranger become entwined as if they had been companions on their walk. Surges of the incoming tide obliterate all traces that either has passed this way. The pain grows. He fumbles in his pocket for the box of tiny pills left sitting on the kitchen counter.

Later, they find his hat lying next to an outstretched hand, and the words "it is enough" scratched into the sand.

Orioles

Would that I could capture the sight of a
    pair of masked-bandit orioles.
accosting their reflected images in the window
above the kitchen sink.
Nay, not capture the bird,
but capture the joy they bring this solitary afternoon,
of a summer storm swept out to sea,
the fragile magic light,
a lone cormorant gliding homeward
through silvered sky above silvered sea.
A rainbow appears in the
dark-blue sky.
My oriole flits home.
I am a homing bird.

Post-Script Beach

~~~~~~~~~~~

"HE WENT EXACTLY AS HE WOULD HAVE LIKED," MY NEPHEW John says, "in the middle of a story."

"The way we would all like to go," my niece Mary breaks in. "One minute, he's telling about his escaping Burma, and the next minute, gone before he ever got around to telling about his adventures the rest of the way around the world."

Family and friends have gathered on the porch of Clif's and my Chelem Beach place around a table filled with dishes of dips, chips, ceviche, a large pitcher of sangria and wine goblets. The Costa Azul, my favorite beach restaurant, has sent the shrimp ceviche, heavily laced with cilantro, the way I like it. The dogs are pressed under Clif's chair. He had to bring them—they haven't left his side since I left.

The gathering is like so many that have taken place here or in Clifford's and my Mérida home. Often our parties start out in our courtyard as the sun's rays climb the great banyan tree at the far side of the swimming pool, or on our beachside porch, as the fiery orb plunges into the gulf waters, striking the sky with blazing hallelujahs. This is one of Clif's and my favorite times. I wanted laughing and joking.

My sister tells everyone, "Bud never let the truth get in the way of a good story." I was Bud and Buddy to my family; then when I entered school, I took my mother's father's name, Edward. Then, when I became a singer and thereafter I took my paternal grandfather's name and have been Grant ever since.

"I love his story about Ethel Merman," Margaret, a singer herself gushes. "He was with the cast of *Annie Get Your Gun*, on the *Ed Sullivan Show* the same night as The Supremes. Just imagine how thrilling that must have been, singing with Ethel Merman belting out "There's No Business Like Show Business!"

"I heard several versions," brother-in-law John says. "I never knew anyone else who could drop so many names. He even had Eleanor Roosevelt to dinner."

"OK," a neighbor said. "I read as far as Burma. Then what?"

"He was 88 when he finished his last book. I guess he got tired of writing or just couldn't remember well enough, so after Burma, he broke off writing about his travels. But when he returned to the States and was heading back to Boston, he stopped off to see us and pretty much filled us in between all the letters he had sent to Martha Nell.

"From Burma he flew to Bangkok. We still have, somewhere a letter he sent from there. That was a short flight. He told us an artist, Baskerville, who he had met in Ceylon, had given him an introduction to Jim Thompson, a guy who made Thai silk famous. But Jim had gone over to Malaysia and was never seen again. Some think a tiger got him. Bud loved throwing in those quirky details. Anyway, Jim's assistant puts him up in an inexpensive little hotel.

"As best I remember, in Bangkok your uncle somehow made friends with his taxi driver who turns out to be a Thai boxer, except he was Chinese, so your uncle spends most of his time in Bangkok's China Town. Anyway, after a few days, he boards a freighter that takes him to Yokohama, Japan, with a stop in Hong Kong. He told me he finally saw that blue movie the Presbyterian Seminar president said he should see. All he remembered about it was the women wore black stockings and garter belts.

"He struck up a friendship with the ship's British first mate. Bud was in the closet, *had to be back then!* I knew, but didn't say anything to your mother. I figured she would work it out if she needed to. After he had got comfortable with me, he told me the story about the freighter's first mate having promised this gay Japanese student if he would stop picking up sailors, he'd find the young man a *proper American.* The Englishman couldn't stand the language the student was picking up from the sailors, so your Uncle Ed turned out to be the *proper American,* which led your uncle to spend nearly a month in a Japanese inn in Kyoto. He and the student traveled across the island to the shrine where the student's parents worshiped. They also visited Hiroshima.

"After about a month, your uncle took another freighter from Yokohama to the States. He planned to return to Japan, but changes his mind. Next thing we know, he announced that he was going to be an opera singer, goes to New York and became a Broadway gypsy. He appeared in a lot of summer stock, four Broadway shows, soloed on a national radio broadcast, and sang at the White House. Finally, he got close to his dream, a contract with the Metropolitan Opera Studio.

"But that's not enough. You know, he was a minister before he took it into his head to run his friend's bar down in St. Thomas, and then head off around the world. After that is when he became a singer!

"Damned if he doesn't meet this guy from the Panhandle of Texas, of all places. They're at some fancy-dancy New York opera party." Brother-in-law John reaches over and pats Clifford holding back tears.

"Then, what do you know, his church, the United Church, hires your uncle to be its art consultant, sets him up in an office in their national headquarters on Park Avenue South. He brought together artist and church folks all around the country, from Berkeley to a little baptismal hole in Pisgah, North Carolina.

"Your uncle starts out in a hick town in Oklahoma and Clif here, his partner, a hick town in the Texas Panhandle. They bought and fixed up a beautiful brownstone like they were real New Yorkers, but Bud was still not finished. The two of them move to Key West, fixed up a couple of Cuban cigar-maker houses and an old post-and-beam fisherman's shack floated over from the Bahamas. He took over as Arts Council Director for a while and then, in spite of the fact he couldn't spell worth a damn, decides he's a writer."

"John!" my sister cut in. "You don't have to swear."

"He decides to be a writer. The day before he conked out, he sent the manuscript for his fifth book. He left instructions to spread his ashes at the beach here, where he wrote most of his stuff.

Flies buzzed in the empty sangria pitcher. As guests begin to leave, a shadow races across the sands in front of the porch. The shadow is made by a huge white-bodied bird. It circles and then, its great wings lifted like a Greek god, descended to the rock jetty reaching out into the Gulf. "Did you see that?" nephew Johnny whispered, "For a second, I thought it was an angel."

"It is an albatross," one of my friends, a birder, said, "a bit north of his usual habitat."

It is my Al, of course. Come to take me home.

"Don't cry for me. It has been an amazing ride. I have loved, and been loved, and had experiences I could never have dreamed possible." Put this on my marker, I wrote, always wanting the last word.

Acknowledgments

As one severely impaired by dyslexia, I have always needed more help than most people. For many years my friend James Milton Buell reordered my syntax and corrected my spelling. His ashes now lie on a hill in Massachusetts and in a crypt in Mérida, Mexico. With Jay no longer correcting me, I doubt that I would have dared continue writing, were I not confident that Lorna Gail Dallin would come to my aid. And my most enduring friend Raymond Watson Branham, who has put up with me longer than any other Mérida friend, and who saves me from my errors. Such friends cause me to believe in angels.

I have had the good fortune to take part in Joy Williams' writers' workshops, where I gained support and rigorous criticism from Joy, Kate Nance Day, Kenneth French, Mary Ann Suehle, Betty Hill, Tone Eccles, and Max Sandusky.

The Mérida writers' group provides an invaluable inspiration and sounding board. Thank you, Marietta Ackerman, Dave Dodge, David Heath, Rudolph Ortega, and Chris Strickland. Thank you Chris, for taking precious time from your own writing to read this manuscript and lending your professional advice. And Lee Steele, who founded Hamaca Press, is like a lighthouse beckoning on. How fortunate for the writer to know that a publisher awaits.

As with all my endeavors, I am sustained by the love and encouragement of my partner, now going on to 49 years, Clifford A. Ames.

About the Author

Grant Spradling, born at the beginning of the Great Depression, grew up in the middle of the Oklahoma Dust Bowl. He graduated from Oklahoma City University and Boston University School of Theology.

For a while, Spradling ran the Foc'sle a bar in St. Thomas and then vagabonded around the world for a year and a half. Always a singer, he has appeared as tenor soloist in countless orators, summer-stock productions, four Broadway shows, on national radio, the *Ed Sullivan Show* and at the White House.

Spradling served as minister of education in two Congregational churches (now United Church of Christ) near Boston, as an arts consultant to the United Church Board for Homeland Ministries, and the Amistad Research Center. He was the founding executive director for Monroe County Fine Arts Council (the Florida Keys and Key West). He and his partner are publishers of works by the noted African American artist, Jacob Lawrence.

About thirty years ago, Spradling rented a room near Santiago, in Mérida, Mexico and took up writing. He has since completed five books and co-created two volumes of *Imaging the Word*, published by the United Church Press.

Spradling and his partner of 49 years, Clifford A. Ames, married in Santa Fe, New Mexico. They now make their home with two rescued Maya dogs in Mérida, Mexico; and Amarillo, Texas.